# PERSONNEL MANAGEMENT
## *for*
## SPORTDIRECTORS

Timothy E. Flannery
National Federation
of State High School Associations

Michael L. Swank
Bay High School
Bay Village, Ohio

Human Kinetics

Library of Congress Cataloging-in-Publication Data

Flannery, Tim, 1946-
   Personnel management for sportdirectors / Tim Flannery, Mike
Swank.
     p.    cm.
   Includes index.
   ISBN 0-88011-757-5
   1. Sports--Management.  2. Personnel management.  3. Sports
administration.  I. Swank, Mike, 1957-  .  II. Title.
GV713.F52   1999
796'.06'93--dc21
                                     98-37669
                                        CIP

ISBN: 0-88011-757-5

**Acquisitions Editors:** Tom Hanlon and Jim Kestner; **Developmental Editor and Copyeditor:** Anne Heiles; **Assistant Editors:** John Wentworth and Kim Thoren; **Proofreader:** Jim Burns; **Indexer:** Diana Witt; **Graphic Designer and Cover Designer:** Stuart Cartwright; **Graphic Artist:** Denise Lowry; **Illustrator:** Patrick Griffin; **Printer:** United Graphics

Printed in the United States of America     10   9   8   7   6   5   4   3   2   1

**Human Kinetics**
Web site: http://www.humankinetics.com/

*United States:* Human Kinetics, P.O. Box 5076, Champaign, IL 61825-5076
1-800-747-4457
e-mail: humank@hkusa.com

*Canada:* Human Kinetics, 475 Devonshire Road Unit 100, Windsor, ON  N8Y 2L5
1-800-465-7301 (in Canada only)
e-mail: humank@hkcanada.com

*Europe:* Human Kinetics, P.O. Box IW14, Leeds LS16 6TR, United Kingdom
(44) 1132 781708
e-mail: humank@hkeurope.com

*Australia:* Human Kinetics, 57A Price Avenue, Lower Mitcham, South Australia 5062
(088) 277 1555
e-mail: humank@hkaustralia.com

*New Zealand:* Human Kinetics, P.O. Box 105-231, Auckland 1
(09) 523 3462
e-mail: humank@hknewz.com

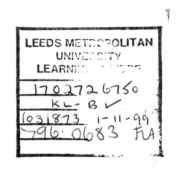

# Contents

Acknowledgments iv

Series Preface v

## PART I:  LEADERSHIP SKILLS

**Chapter 1:  Understanding Your Role as Personnel Manager** 3

**Chapter 2:  Defining Goals and Policies** 13

**Chapter 3:  Developing a Personnel Management Plan** 25

## PART II:  PEOPLE SKILLS

**Chapter 4:  Mentoring and Educating Personnel** 41

**Chapter 5:  Communicating and Resolving Conflicts** 49

**Chapter 6:  Selecting Staff and Evaluating People** 59

## PART III:  MANAGEMENT SKILLS

**Chapter 7:  Setting the Tone for Sport Participants** 79

**Chapter 8:  Mentoring Coaches** 91

**Chapter 9:  Involving Parents** 115

**Chapter 10:  Supervising Officials and Support Staff** 133

Appendix A: Directory of National Sport Organizations and National
Governing Bodies 153

Appendix B: Resources for Sport Directors 157

Appendix C: Coach's Guidelines 159

Index 163

About the Authors 169

# Acknowledgments

I want to begin by thanking Karen Partlow for being a great mentor because she saw something in me that I had not seen in myself. Without her this book would not have become a reality. Jim Kestner got Mike and I off to a great start with his patience and ideas. Anne Heiles came in to save us and helped Mike and I create a more meaningful tool for sport directors. Her questions and suggestions helped us get to the final draft. John Wentworth, Stuart Cartwright, Denise Lowry, and the rest of the Human Kinetics staff brought us home. Thank you all for your creativity and insight and sharing your talents in this project.

There were many who contributed greatly to the contents of this book. Mike Swank for his ability to clarify and identify those things that are important for sport directors to know. Dr. John Olson for his material on communications and his willingness to share. My fellow athletic administrators in the Southwestern Conference, the coaches, parents, and athletes, who helped me learn so much while I was at North Olmsted High School. I also appreciate your willingness to let me serve you for so long.

To the NIAAA for giving me the opportunity to lead and learn. Above all, I want to thank my family: my beautiful wife Fran, my son Ryan, my daughter Bridget, and my son-in-law Jeremy. Thank you for your support and understanding when time became short. I love you all.

Tim Flannery

*Personnel Management for SportDirectors* is the completion of countless hours of effort to bring together ideas and practices that assist you in your professional growth and development. I want to thank the people from Human Kinetics for their guidance and encouragement. I have a special thanks to Tim Flannery for his encouragement, professionalism, and patience. The opportunity to work with Tim on this project was one of my career highlights as Athletic Administrator. I would like to thank the communities and school districts of Bay Village and Sidney for providing me the opportunity to grow professionally and to share what I have learned with others. Finally, I would like to thank my family: my wonderful wife Maita, daughter Richelle, and sons Aaron and Adam. Your support and love is the most essential piece in being able to grow professionally and personally.

Mike Swank

# Series Preface

The SportDirector Series is a revolutionary approach to the craft of managing athletic programs. Underlying the resources in this series is a set of principles drawn from a careful examination of the day-to-day responsibilities sport directors face. These principles have been framed as a sequence of tests, which each series resource has been designed to pass:

- Is the resource practical?
- Is it affordable?
- Does it save time?
- Is it easy to use?
- Is it up-to-date?
- Is it flexible enough to meet different programs' needs?
- Does using one resource from the series make it easier to use others?

To ensure that every resource passes these tests, we have worked closely with an editorial advisory board of prominent, experienced athletic directors from across the nation. With the board's assistance, we have developed the series to enable you to benefit from the latest thinking in directing sport programs. Each resource leads you carefully through three steps: planning, implementing, and evaluating.

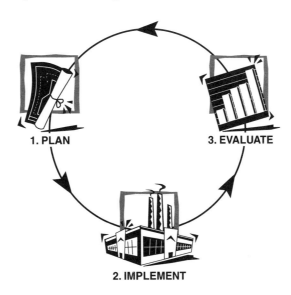

What's so new about the approach? Nothing—until you actually apply it. That's where the series really breaks the mold. Besides telling you how important it is to plan for success in directing your programs, each resource will lead you step-by-step through that planning process. Forms and exercises will help you explore your role and philosophy within the organization, examine your particular needs, and then develop an effective plan of action. In each SportDirector resource these steps are applied specifically to the task at hand. For example, it is essential to assess your needs carefully as you carry out each of your program responsibilities: How you assess promotional needs, however, will differ significantly from how you assess personnel management needs. The series follows the same practical approach to lead you through the implementation and evaluation of your plan.

This approach is possible only because the series authors are experts not only in sport management but also in the specific areas they write about. With the help of the editorial advisory board, these authors translate their knowledge into practical, easy-to-follow recommendations, ready-to-use forms and checklists, and countless practical tips and examples so that you will come away with better ideas for directing your program. The authors also help you take advantage of the latest technology.

New and experienced interscholastic athletic directors alike will find that these resources take into account their widespread responsibilities and limited staff and funding assistance. Directors of Olympic national governing body club sport programs and other national and state sport directors will find valuable tools to enhance their efficiency and increase their effectiveness. Students of sport administration will find these resources valuable companions for understanding how to step into the field with confidence to succeed. And all sport directors will find that these tools help them to help the athletes, coaches, parents, and others in their organizational community.

Even more than a leader, you are the architect of your organization's athletic community. As you design and oversee the construction and maintenance of that community, you are in a unique position to ensure that the program achieves a common purpose. The SportDirector Series is conceived not only to help you attend to your everyday duties but also to coalesce your efforts to carry out your program's mission—to make your athletic community the best it can be.

*—Jim Kestner*

# Part I
## Leadership Skills

# Chapter 1

# *Understanding Your Role as Personnel Manager*

To work successfully in the arena of personnel management, you must thoroughly understand the roles an athletic director plays in the total organization. As personnel manager how you function to direct the people in your athletic department and program grows out of the philosophy that you and your school district hold to. The young athletes, the coaches, other athletic department personnel and individuals who support your athletic program, including officials, custodians, bus drivers, and parents, all depend on you for direction.

You work with and for people every day as their leader. Personnel are people, and personnel management is using good people skills in organized ways. You are instrumental in determining the directions that people pursue in the athletic program. For example, you perform these major tasks:

1. You determine the objectives you and the leaders of your organization strive to achieve.

2. You establish principles to guide you and your staff in managing your program.

3. You form a set of coherent policies to ensure that department principles are adhered to.

In this chapter you will learn about these topics:

1. The qualities of a good personnel manager.

2. Various roles the sport director plays as a manager of people.

3. What responsibilities an athletic director has as a personnel manager.

4. Who you will be interacting with in the normal operation of your program.

5. What responsibilities you will have toward those individuals.

# QUALITIES OF A PERSONNEL MANAGER

To interact effectively with people a sport director needs certain personal traits and must be knowledgeable in the field of athletic administration. You must be fair-minded, practice patience under pressure, know how to interact with different types and personalities of people, know when to keep something confidential, and understand how your leadership style relates to the stakeholders you will be dealing with every day. It is important for you to be organized, to like working with adults and young people, and to strive to be a lifelong learner in the field of athletic administration.

You should gain some background in law. Don't panic—you really do not have to know as much as a lawyer does. Still, it will help you tremendously in your personnel roles if you have some knowledge of state and local labor laws, as well as how Title IX of the Civil Rights Act of 1972 affects the operation of your athletic department and whom you hire. The Americans with Disabilities Act has great implications for athletic departments today. It addresses your encouraging youth with mental and physical disabilities to play if the proper accommodations can be made to enable them to compete on an even playing field.

# THE SPORT DIRECTOR IN THE SCHOOL DISTRICT

The sport director plays an important role in any athletic program with regard to personnel decisions. Before looking more specifically at the responsibilities, first consider the overall organization of a school district and where the sport director fits into it. Look at figure 1.1, which is a typical line and staff chart for a school district. As you can see, the sport director is responsible *to* certain people: the principal, superintendent, and a board of education. The sport director is also responsible *for* other people: athletes, coaches, athletic department supervisors, officials, parents, booster club(s), custodians, bus drivers, contest support staff, and maintenance staff.

The school board determines global policies, which are implemented by the superintendent, principal, and sport director. In most states the board of education is an elected group of individuals that has the authority to make policy, hire teachers and coaches, and select and hire the superintendent of the school district. The sport director is usually responsible to the building principal, who is responsible to the superintendent of schools. The superintendent of schools is directly responsible to the elected members of the board of education.

In a typical hiring of a coach, personnel procedures might proceed along these lines. The sport director would interview the coach. The recommendation to hire the coach would first go to the building principal, who could recommend the coach to the superintendent of schools. The superintendent of schools would recommend the coach to the board of education, which has the ultimate authority to give a contract to that coach. Anywhere along the line the recommendation could be denied or delayed by the person next in authority. You can begin to see how important communication is from a sport director to other tiers of administrators to allow the process to go smoothly.

# Athletic Department Organizational Chart

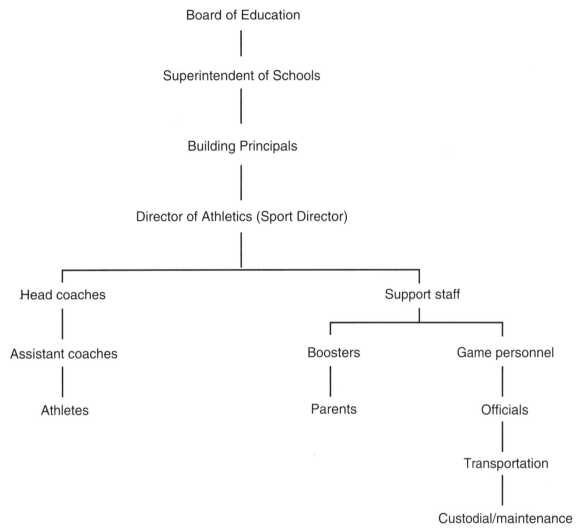

Board of Education

Superintendent of Schools

Building Principals

Director of Athletics (Sport Director)

Head coaches

Assistant coaches

Athletes

Support staff

Boosters

Parents

Game personnel

Officials

Transportation

Custodial/maintenance

**Figure 1.1**  Typical line and staff chart for a school district.

The sport director is a middleman in the personnel management system. The sport director manages, leads, recruits, evaluates, and selects coaches, student athletes, parent boosters, officials, and other support staff. In turn the sport director is evaluated by the building principal in most cases (by the superintendent of schools if the sport director is responsible for more than one school). Furthermore, the sport director is a peer to many other administrators, such as the transportation director or human resource director, and is a colleague to many certified professionals in the school district, such as counselors and teachers.

# THE SPORT DIRECTOR IN PERSONNEL MANAGEMENT

The sport director wears many hats in personnel management, which requires the person's having good management and people skills. For starts, in an effective athletic department the sport director is a leader, a manager, a mentor, an evaluator, a supervisor, and an educator.

A way to appreciate the many roles you play as sport director is to list some of the action verbs that describe your responsibilities: recruiting, interviewing, evaluating, mentoring, supervising, empowering, improving, confronting, problem solving, listening, marketing, promoting, and administrating. The list could go on and on. The point is that a sport director must have special skills and a willingness to improve personally and on the job. More than half of a sport director's time is spent on personnel matters. The better a personnel manager you become, the more you will enjoy this important area of athletics.

## As Leader

Make no mistake about it: you must be a leader in many areas of your athletic department to ensure that the goals and objectives of the program are fulfilled. You must be a leader in such financial matters as budgeting and fund-raising, in educating parents about the philosophy and policies of the department, in recognizing and helping motivate coaches and support staff, and in initiating programs that help student athletes reach their mission.

The mission in the North Olmsted (Ohio) Athletic Department is "to provide an athletic experience that will enable our student athletes to become better citizens." As the person responsible for so many personnel you must be able to lead everyone from support staff to parents toward the achievement of your athletic department's particular mission. A true leader will never lose sight of the mission.

## As Manager

The sport director must manage people and programs. Planning, organizing, delegating, supervising, coordinating, and scheduling are a few attributes of an effective manager. Study this list, which cites an example for each of these attributes you will need to manage effectively.

*Planning.* You determine how many support staff personnel are needed for home football games. How many ticket takers and sellers will you need? How many police?

*Organizing.* You organize many contest details for any particular sport. You must schedule contests that do not conflict with other school events or with the use of the facilities.

*Delegating.* You may be fortunate to have an assistant athletic director or other individual to secure game officials for contests. If you do have help, you're wise to delegate these types of duties to an assistant to free the time for you to take care of other matters.

*Supervising.* Many nights are spent supervising home athletic contests. You must oversee every facet of a contest, from greeting the visiting team to setting up the scoreboard.

*Coordinating.* Perhaps you hold both boys' and girls' basketball games at the same site on the same night. Among other things, you will have to coordinate the use of locker rooms, find officials to referee the games, and assure the safety and routing of fans.

*Scheduling.* If your program is like most athletic programs, you have more teams than you have facilities for athletes to practice and play games in. Designing a facilities usage schedule for coaches, athletes, and parents in which no conflicts exist is one of your important functions.

## As Mentor

In today's athletic department an effective sport director must be a mentor to coaches. A mentor is an individual who cares and shares knowledge and skills to help others to improve. Mentoring is an attitude that permits growth to occur. As a mentor to coaches, you must allow them the opportunity to find out what they each need to be a better coach, and you must be there for them when they need help.

The skills an effective mentor has are mostly listening, giving feedback, and confronting critical situations when appropriate. Mentoring goes beyond what is expected and what you are paid to do. It is an attitude that enables coaches to grow and be the

A few years ago a coach came into my office. She was very upset and concerned because her players had informed her that they wanted to go to the homecoming dance rather than to compete in the district finals that Saturday night. The coach, taken aback by the girls' ultimatum, had come to me for advice. I remember how difficult it was to refrain from giving this coach any advice. I recall asking her several questions: What are your expectations of the athletes? What would like to see the girls do? What could you do to get the girls to understand their commitment to the team and each other? How might you make this a learning situation for them? Rather than my solving the problem, the coach solved her own problem. She held a meeting with the players and reminded them of the commitment they had made at the beginning of the season. She also told them that life is not always fair, that we sometimes have to give up one thing to do another. She ended the meeting by telling her players they had to make their own decision about attending the dance or the game. She explained the consequences for each decision. She emphasized it was their decision to make. All the girls decided to attend the game because they did not want to forfeit awards they had worked so hard to earn. As it turned out, they played the game and were only an hour late to the dance.

best they can be. Mentoring transcends teaching, counseling, and coaching.

## As Evaluator

As an evaluator you must design an evaluation plan aimed at improving the work that people do in the athletic program. Your attitude will largely determine how people perceive the evaluation process. If they are a part of its development and understand that its purpose is to improve coaching or whatever the task at hand, they will likely improve their performance. As an evaluator you must build the trust of those whom you are evaluating. Trust will come from your being fair-minded and having a positive attitude with coaches and support staff.

Many years ago I developed a procedure whereby coaches who had more than five years' experience would first fill out the evaluation instrument themselves as a self-evaluation tool. I did this to build their trust. One coach returned the evaluation with very poor marks, grading himself much lower than I had rated him. When we met to discuss his evaluation, I emphatically praised his strong points and made sound suggestions on how to improve in the weak areas. A few days later the coach came back to tell me he felt so good after the evaluation that he decided not to quit after all. I had no idea that he had been considering leaving; moreover, I found out that he had thought I was going to rate him low on the evaluation, and that was why he had marked himself down. Once he found out how good a coach I thought he was, his whole attitude changed about coaching.

## As Supervisor

The sport director must oversee the entire athletic department. Supervision includes (but is not limited to) knowing how effectively coaches work with athletes, overseeing fund-raising projects, developing inspection plans for all equipment and facilities, and assuring there are board of education–approved adult supervisors for all teams and activities that involve students. Of course, people other than the sport director carry out many functions of the athletic department. Coaches coach, bus drivers transport students to contests, custodians set up gymnasiums, maintenance personnel prepare athletic fields. The sport director, however, is responsible for overseeing all that these people do.

An effective supervisor allows coaches and support staff the room to do their jobs. At the same time it is your responsibility to know the kind of work the staff is doing. When a parent or principal wants to know what time the bus is arriving to bring back the basketball team, she expects you to know. As the supervisor it is your responsibility to know where people are and what they are supposed to be doing.

## As Educator

The sport director, above all, must be the consummate educator in the athletic department. Knowledge about sport is ever expanding, and as sport directors we are perceived to be the experts in our community's sports. We are expected to be the educational leaders in our athletic programs.

Preseason meetings for parents and athletes, speeches to booster clubs and community groups, updates to the administration and the board of education on new developments in athletics are a few of the methods sport directors use to educate their constituents. Effective sport directors always look for ways to upgrade their knowledge of sport, and they find ways to impart that knowledge to coaches, parents, athletes, administrators, officials, and support staff.

You can update and acquire knowledge on many current topics and issues by attending a conference or clinic. The National Federation of State High School Associations sponsors a conference for high school athletic directors every year in December. Most state athletic directors associations sponsor a state conference or workshop for directors of athletics. State athletic and activities associations are good resources for finding out where and when these workshops are offered.

# TEAMMATES IN PERSONNEL MANAGEMENT

As important as the sport director's role in personnel management is, there are other individuals who are critical to ensuring that policies are followed. The sport director must work with these individuals to implement an effective personnel management plan:

- School principals. If you are a sport director of a single school, you will work closely with one school principal; on the other hand, if your district has multiple schools, you will work with the principal of each one.

- District personnel director or human resources director. Particularly in large school districts you will work closely with a human resources director or personnel director, whose primary responsibility is to screen applicants for teaching or coaching positions. In smaller districts more of the burden of recruiting and interviewing will fall on the sport director's shoulders. Usually the human resources director will not be a part of the process to recommend a coach for a contract.

- Transportation director. When you need a bus for a contest or if your athletes left a mess on the bus the night before, you will be working with the transportation director or someone in that office.

- Director or supervisor of facilities and grounds. In small districts some of you will be lining and preparing the fields. In larger districts, however, this task is delegated to maintenance personnel who fall under the jurisdiction of the director of building and grounds, an individual in charge of all buildings and grounds.

- Head coaches. Most of your time will be spent communicating with head coaches who are the lifeline of your athletic program. Most athletic programs today have many coaches within a sport, and to help your program run more efficiently it would be wise to make head coaches responsible for communicating routine matters to their assistants.

## School Principals

In most schools a principal makes formal recommendations to the superintendent of the school district to hire coaches, advisors, or support staff. It is critical for the sport director to work closely with the principal, from recruiting through the interview and then to the final recommendation, to ensure that your organizational and personal philosophies are being satisfied. As sport director you should support the recommendations you make to the school principal with factual information obtained from applications, resumes, and personal interviews.

School principals in most states are also the voting members of the state athletic and activities association. As sport director you need to keep school principals informed about changes in rules and other sport information that would benefit the student athletes in your school. When the principal votes, he or she can then make an informed decision.

## District Personnel Director or Human Resources Director

Large school districts employ personnel directors or human resource directors to recruit and interview prospective teachers and coaches. Smaller districts may not have this position, and the duties will fall solely to sport directors and school principals.

If your district has a human resources director, you must develop strong communication lines with this individual to indicate the needs of the athletic department with regard to coaching openings. When openings occur, the personnel director can help in recruiting and interviewing prospective candidates. In large school districts, with districtwide personnel directors, there is always a need for input from local school personnel. If you have a districtwide personnel director, make an appointment to see that individual to delineate roles and responsibilities and assure good, open communication. The human resources director can certainly help you secure outstanding coaches from the ranks of the new teaching staff.

## Transportation Director

You should meet with the transportation director prior to the start of the fall season to develop guidelines for transporting teams. Union contracts may dictate by whom, when, and where athletic teams are transported. As sport director you must ensure as much as possible that bus drivers are qualified and understand their roles in the athletic department. You and the transportation director must generate discussions about how bus drivers, coaches, and athletes affect the efficient transporting of athletic teams from the school to the contest and back. Usu-

ally the transportation director assigns bus drivers. When problems arise involving transportation, the transportation director is the person you want to communicate with.

Years ago we had a trip on a Saturday across town to an all-day tournament. On the following Monday morning the bus driver called to report a list of violations the athletes and coaches had committed. The list included opening windows, using the rear door to exit the bus, insubordination, making too much noise, eating on the bus, and a lack of cooperation from the coaches. After listening to all the allegations, I assured the driver that I would talk to the coach, provide adequate education, and that certainly consequences for inappropriate actions would follow. I called in the transportation director and hockey coach, and we discussed the bus driver's concerns. Because of that meeting my coach and I became painfully aware of state laws and local policies that directly affected student athletes and their coaches while they were being transported to sports events. Then the transportation director and I devised guidelines (see box on page 10) for coaches and athletes and informed all coaches in writing of the guidelines and applicable laws. Once coaches became aware of the expectations, they could convey these expectations to players—and the problems were dramatically reduced.

## Director of Facilities and Grounds

You coordinate with the director of facilities and grounds to ensure safe facilities for play, proper maintenance of the facilities, and good coverage of events by custodial and maintenance personnel. You must develop inspection forms for each of your practice and playing facilities, as well as for athletic equipment. The director of facilities and grounds can help you in designing the forms and making sure inspections are carried out in a timely fashion. It is advisable to meet with the director of facilities and grounds in the late spring to go over all outdoor

## Transportation Guidelines

The board of education requires that all sport participants use school district buses to travel to and from athletic contests. If board-owned transportation is not available or if the trip is more than 150 miles, a public carrier properly insured and licensed in the State of Ohio may be used. Under no circumstances are students permitted to transport themselves or others to contests. In unusual or emergency situations athletes may be released to their parents or legal guardian for transportation home. Below are guidelines for student athletes who use transportation provided by the board of education:

1. Only students participating in the sport as players or in a support role are permitted to ride the bus.

2. A transportation request form must be filed 10 days before the date of the trip.

3. All individuals riding the bus must have an emergency medical form, completely filled out, in the possession of the coach or adult supervisor.

4. Students are not permitted to enter or exit the bus from the rear. This is an emergency-exit only.

5. Eating or drinking is strictly prohibited on the bus.

6. All individuals riding the bus must remain seated during the trip and when the bus is moving.

7. Inappropriate behavior, such as loud noise, limbs out the windows, disrespect to the bus driver, or failure to respond to the above guidelines will bring consequences ranging from detention or suspension to denial of participation in the sport or activity.

fields and indoor facilities that will be used in the summer and fall.

## Secretaries

Many larger athletic programs are fortunate to have secretaries to aid them in day-to-day operations. Today's athletic department secretaries perform hundreds of tasks, such as keeping records and files for the athletic director, typing schedules, and typing correspondence for the department. My secretary uses a computer every day, sending and receiving faxes, creating posters with use of a scanner, and printing at least some documents in color. With technology developing so quickly, the only limits a secretary experiences come from the equipment (and the training that goes along with it) she has to use.

Secretaries also answer the phone and greet visitors to your office. Your secretary is responsible for operating the office when you are not in. It will be important to have a thorough orientation for secretaries. This introductory program will focus on the need for patience, poise, and tact in dealing with people, but you should also be sure to relay the organizational philosophy and policies.

## Assistant to the Athletic Director

If you operate a large athletic department or a department with several schools, you may be fortunate to work with an assistant. Most assistants perform tasks that normally would be performed by the sport director. Some of those tasks include scheduling and contracting opponents, contracting officials, filling out box-office reports for contests, ordering tickets and keeping them in a secure place, and other duties that would assist you as the sport director.

Many assistant sport directors are teachers who arrange a free period or two that they can dedicate to their athletic duties. If you cannot arrange for free time for your assistant, you might offer a stipend for performing these athletic duties. If you are finding that the days are getting shorter and your "to do" list is getting longer, you should talk to your principal and discuss the possibility of securing an assistant athletic or sport director.

## Head Coaches

Many head coaches have programs that represent more than one team. It is not uncommon in team sports to have a team at the junior varsity, freshman, eighth-grade, and seventh-grade level. As sport director you want to involve your head coach as much as possible in the selection of assistant coaches and lower-level coaches. If your head coach understands your organization's philosophy and policies, then he or she will likely want coaches who believe in those philosophies and policies as well. Remember, the head coach is the architect of his or her total program and will be accountable to you through the evaluation process.

As you can see, as sport director you have many responsibilities in personnel management and must work closely with many people to operate an effective athletic program. Only with planning can you hope to bring together all these individuals and groups for the good of the athletes in your program. This planning and communication must take place long before the athletic season begins.

Typically, 75 percent of your planning will take place between the end of the spring season and the beginning of the fall season. In any one day it would be difficult to specify how much time you might spend in planning, promoting, scheduling, or other activities. Still, it is important to realize that more than 50 percent of your time will be spent on personnel issues. They include recruiting, interviewing, educating, evaluating, addressing complaints and giving praise, and, of course, mentoring.

## Summary

In Chapter 1 you learned that a sport director

1. must be fair-minded, knowledgeable, patient, tolerant, and organized, among other traits, in matters of personnel management;

2. plays varying roles in the school district, being directly responsible to the school principal, who is responsible to the school district superintendent (the elected school board is the ultimate authority in any school district);

3. leads, manages, mentors, evaluates, supervises, and educates people;

4. is a personnel manager who must develop a close working relationship with school principals, district personnel directors, transportation directors, directors of facilities and grounds, athletic secretaries, assistant athletic directors, and head coaches; and

5. has a multitude of responsibilities involving guidance, communication, supervision, planning, and assessing that are specific to the personnel with whom he or she works.

# *C*hapter *2*
## *Defining Goals and Policies*

A significant part of leadership is defining goals and creating policies that will help ensure meeting those goals effectively, efficiently, ethically, and fairly. Goals don't just exist in a world of their own. They grow out of a context. They are set for specific groups of people at particular times, and, if they are good, they have a recognizable purpose and can be measured. Goals don't just happen to be set—they emerge from missions. And they are achieved because of coherent, logical policies along with a lot of hard work.

In this chapter you will learn about these topics:

1. Why you should review your organization's and your personal mission and philosophy.

2. How to use your mission statement and philosophy to develop goals for the sport department.

3. How to create a handbook of policies about personnel and department activities.

# DEFINING A MISSION AND PHILOSOPHY

Sport exists for many reasons, ranging from providing entertainment to the joy of playing, from learning lifetime activity skills to developing elite athletes. Interscholastic middle school and high school athletics exist primarily to prepare student athletes to be better citizens. As sport directors we must never lose sight of this ideal. We must promote the concept of citizenship constantly among coaches, parents, and student athletes. Teaching young people to respect themselves, to respect others, to have integrity and be ethical, to be good sports, to work as a team, and to make a commitment is what it's all about.

We might call this ideal and purpose our *mission*. A general mission can be as simple as "to develop athletic skills and enjoy sport." Does your school district have a particular mission? Does your athletic department? If not, it's worth taking the time to formulate and communicate one. Can you state your mission in a few words or sentences?

A mission statement is a blueprint for your athletic department. It is a statement that tells you where you want to get to after this athletic experience. A mission statement should be measurable. It is where we want our athletes to be after they have been exposed to our coaches and competition. A good example of a mission statement is "provide an athletic experience that will enable our student athletes to become better citizens."

Keeping these thoughts in mind, we can add to them *values* we believe in personally and for the department. These values become our philosophy. A *philosophy* comprises statements that express what we believe in. A mission statement says where we want to be, and a philosophy is what we believe will get us there. A philosophy need not be complicated to have depth of purpose. In fact, stating a philosophy *simply* can help make it a valuable foundation for leadership. The American Sport Education Program (ASEP) has a simply stated philosophy: Athletes first, winning second. If you are not yet aware of your department's philosophy, see if it exists or formulate one in writing (see your princi-

pal for help in doing this). As you work in your position, undoubtedly you'll become more aware of how many aspects of your program you do have a personal philosophy about.

Once you are aware of the department's and your own personal philosophies, you can work to ensure that you approach personnel management in line with them. A first step is to surround yourself with coaches, parents, and support staff who believe, as you do, that these ideals must be the primary reason sport exists in our schools. When selecting or evaluating personnel, keep your mission and philosophy in mind. Let the mission drive your decisions and let your philosophy comprise the principles that keep you from straying from the mission. By now you might be asking yourself how to accomplish this. The answer is constant and continual education. In-service training for coaches and preseason meetings for young athletes and their parents are beginning points for all athletic programs today. A second step is to frequently remind yourself of your mission and philosophy as you work with people in your capacity as personnel manager.

Philosophies on personnel management vary from community to community. Sport directors play a major role in the direction that school boards and communities take in managing, supervising, evaluating, and mentoring their personnel. Do not expect to make major changes overnight; these important changes will take place over time. The box on page 15 depicts an example of the philosophical differences of a school district (the organization) and its sport director.

## School District's Philosophy of Personnel Management

Your school district's philosophy in regard to personnel management should be established by the principal and superintendent and approved by the local board of education or board of trustees. These kinds of philosophies will usually be printed in the *Board of Education Policy Manual*. The philosophy should also include a statement emphasizing the positive aspects of sport as an integral part of education.

## Personnel Management Philosophy of School District vs. Sport Director's Philosophy

**School district's philosophy**

Defines the purpose of sport programs in the educational process.

Describes the value of personnel management as part of the process.

**Sport director's philosophy**

Uses most positive values of program's purpose to identify types of coaches needed to reach objectives and goals.

Determines needs within each sport.

Determines what is not acceptable to the school and community in relation to personnel.

Uses personal preferences to determine which personnel to recommend for positions.

---

The school district's philosophy provides you with *general guidelines* for personnel management, not with specific directions for the program. You will develop many of the specifics, which may depend, however, on your school district's philosophy. Here are some examples of issues that you will face in personnel management:

- Will you recruit experienced or inexperienced coaches?

- Will you recruit staff coaches or "off-staff," walk-on coaches?

- Will you seek a balance of male and female coaches, as well as an ethnic diversity, in your program to match the makeup of the student body?

- Will you seek support staff (custodians, maintenance staff, bus drivers) dedicated to the athletic program and school district's philosophy?

- Will you promote individuals to leadership positions within the booster club who will concentrate on supporting the athletic program and its coaches?

- Will you seek to hire the best-qualified officials who are known also to promote sportsmanship?

## Personal Philosophies

You probably have already formed some personal philosophies about the types of coaches, parents,

Before beginning the recruiting process for a new boys' coach, I listed a few personal philosophies that I felt were important pertaining to the new coach. First, I wanted an individual who put sportsmanship, ethics, and integrity ahead of winning. Second, I wanted a coach who believed that following rules and policies was important not only for himself but also (as an educational tool) for his players. And I wanted a coach who understood the mission of developing athletes to become better citizens.

support staff, and officials you want to represent your program.

In applying your personal philosophy to personnel management, you may believe that not only the attributes a coach or a support staff possesses are important but also the willingness to model appropriate behavior when the pressure is on. It is important to determine for yourself what your personal philosophy is. Take a few minutes to fill out form 2.1, listing the attributes you seek in the various types of personnel you are responsible for.

## Combining School District and Personal Philosophies

Now that you have considered your personal views on personnel management, you need to put that in-

**Form 2.1**

# PERSONNEL ATTRIBUTES

Next to each personnel category list the particular attributes you look for in a person filling that position. Prioritize them, using 1 as high priority and 3 as low priority. These might be some attributes you list, for example: organized, student-oriented, personable, communicates well in writing and speaking, understands the philosophy of the program, understands his or her role in the athletic program, cooperative-style personality (rather than command or laissez-faire style), has philosophy of keeping athletes first and winning second. Do not limit your choices of attributes to the examples suggested—list those that will fit in with your athletic program's philosophy. The success of your athletic program depends on how well you match personnel with the attributes you feel are important.

| Position | Attributes you look for | Priority |
|---|---|---|
| Supervisory staff | **Example:** Good role model | 1 |
| | Loyal | 1 |
| | At least 25 years old | 2 |
| | Understands the sport | 3 |
| | Has experience supervising | 2 |
| | Gender matches students | 3 |
| Head coaches | | |
| | | |
| | | |
| | | |
| Assistant coaches | | |
| | | |
| | | |
| | | |
| Lower-level coaches | | |
| | | |
| | | |
| | | |
| Officials | | |
| | | |
| | | |
| | | |
| Bus drivers | | |
| | | |
| | | |
| | | |
| Maintenance staff | | |
| | | |
| | | |
| | | |
| Custodial staff | | |
| | | |
| | | |
| | | |
| Clerical staff | | |
| | | |
| | | |

formation to use. Form 2.2 asks you a series of questions to help you focus on the sport philosophy of your organization, the role of personnel management, and the responsibilities of your position. Form 2.3 asks key questions about your personal philosophy, helping you write down your philosophy and then tying it to the elements of form 2.2. Completing forms 2.2 and 2.3 is an important first step in developing your philosophy into a written document. To verbalize your philosophy is important, but it must be in writing for all to see and understand. Once your philosophy is in writing you can begin to identify goals and objectives for your program

## Form 2.2
# YOUR SCHOOL DISTRICT'S PERSONNEL PHILOSOPHY

To help you understand your school district's sport philosophy, answer the following questions:

1. What is the school district's philosophy regarding interscholastic sports?

_____

_____

2. How do athletic department personnel decisions affect that philosophy?

_____

_____

3. What attributes are the organization looking for in its athletic department personnel?

_____

_____

_____

_____

4. What attributes in athletic department personnel is the organization avoiding?

_____

_____

_____

5. What role does the organization want the sport director to play in personnel decisions?

_____

_____

_____

6. Based on the previous responses, what potential for conflict exists in the following areas?
   a. Within the organization

_____

   b. Within the community

_____

   c. Within the athletic department

_____

_____

7. How can those conflicts be resolved?

_____

_____

**Form 2.3**

# YOUR PERSONAL PHILOSOPHY
# OF PERSONNEL MANAGEMENT

To help you understand your personal approach to personnel management and how it relates to your organization's philosophy, answer the following questions.

1. What is my personal philosophy regarding interscholastic sports?

_____

_____

2. What is my personal philosophy regarding personnel management? (see form 2.1)

_____

_____

3. How does my philosophy have impact on the personnel management process?

_____

_____

4. Given the above, what potential for conflict exists in the following areas?
    a. Within the organization

_____

_____

    b. Within the community

_____

_____

    c. Within the athletic department

_____

_____

5. How can those conflicts be resolved?

_____

_____

_____

# DEFINING YOUR PROGRAM'S OBJECTIVES

Having a school district's and your own philosophy in mind can help you, the coaches, support staff, and parents assure that your athletes become better citizens. However, a philosophy in and by itself will not make this happen. You must also examine the goals and objectives, which are driven by principles your community believes in, to develop policies that will ensure that your philosophy is carried out by all who are a part of the athletic department.

Goals or objectives are measurable plans that help you reach your stated mission. Philosophies are principles or beliefs that keep you from straying too far from your mission. Athletic department goals should be evaluated and stated yearly. You can arrange a meeting with head coaches and the principal to accomplish this. In my school district, for example, we hold an all-day meeting with head coaches. The morning session is dedicated to establishing and evaluating goals for the athletic department. At this meeting head coaches are also asked to establish team and program goals for their particular sports as well as to establish plans that will help them reach their goals. This is a major part of a head coach's evaluation—the setting of goals and being able to achieve them.

A few years ago a coach stated that one of his goals was to increase the number of wrestlers in the program by 20 percent. One of his action plans was to conduct a wrestling camp for students from the third to ninth grades. Another action plan was to encourage each wrestler to bring a friend to the first practice. Yet another action plan was to promote wrestling, through the football coaches, among the football players. When we evaluated his goals, we looked at each action plan and tried to determine its effectiveness. Overall, the number of wrestlers increased by more than 30 percent. As we looked at the feedback from players and coaches, we determined that the camp and the recruitment of football players generated all but two of the new students, and we decided the plan to bring a friend did not generate many new wrestlers. This approach to planning works because it focuses on goals rather than individuals. Writing down both the goals and the plans to carry them out increases the chances of success. By putting them in writing you make a serious commitment and begin the process of achieving your goals.

The objectives of your personnel management as well as of your program should reflect your philosophy. Start by writing down those objectives so everyone can know them and you can ensure the objectives are carried out. Simply verbalizing objectives does not ensure they will be carried out. Unless you put them in writing and adopt action plans for carrying them out, you may never realize them.

## Prioritizing Your Objectives

Sport directors realize that they do not actively pursue many of the objectives they consider important. You must ask yourself whether, if these objectives are truly important to the program's success, you have created an action plan to accomplish them. For example, if an objective of your program is having coaches who are trained in the principles of first aid, do you

- offer them a training course prior to beginning their season?

- secure qualified medical personnel (doctors, certified trainers) to conduct a preseason first-aid clinic or workshop?

- include this prerequisite in the coaching application form or some document you give coaches prior to their beginning service for the school district?

Identify some objectives and next prioritize them by putting a 1 next to the objective that is most important, 2 next to the second-most important, and so on (see box below). Then actively pursue your most important objective; after you have accomplished the first objective, then actively pursue the second—and you are on the way to improving your program.

### Identifying Objectives

| List objective | Enter priority number |
| --- | --- |
| _____ | _____ |
| _____ | _____ |
| _____ | _____ |
| _____ | _____ |
| _____ | _____ |
| _____ | _____ |

## Short-Term and Long-Term Objectives

The difference between short-term and long-term objectives is important. All too often coaches, parents, and athletes focus so much on the short-term objectives that they lose sight of the long-term ones. Short-term objectives are for the length of a season or less. Long-term objectives are for more than one season. It's easy to neglect the distinction, but don't let it happen to you. It is essential that as the sport director you maintain the proper perspective about the short-term goals of the contest, for example, and the long-term goals of participation. A strong program philosophy will help you do that.

Ask yourself this: How much emphasis does your program place on achieving each type of objectives?

Do you spend most of your time planning to achieve the short-term objectives (like winning)? Do you hope the long-term objectives will just happen? Do you develop program policies that strive to provide balance in achieving both short-term and long-term objectives? As you can imagine, this is not an easy task—but it is one you must never lose sight of.

Consider the American Sport Education Program (ASEP) coaching philosophy, "Athletes first, winning second." It encourages every adult action to be based first on what is best for young athletes, second on what may improve the athletes' or team's chances of winning. This philosophy does not say that winning or, more accurately, striving to win is unimportant. Rather it says that winning should take a backseat to what is in the best interest of the young participants. Stated another way, the short-term objectives of winning the contest should never override the long-term objectives of participation and helping young people develop physically, psychologically, and socially.

## Achieving Consensus on Your Program Principles

Here are two approaches that you can follow to help your organization reach consensus on the program's objectives and principles. In Approach #1 you take these steps:

1. Call a meeting of the principal, superintendent, at least one board of education member, a male and female head coach, and at least one parent.

2. Discuss the need to have a program philosophy, with clearly stated objectives, principles, and policies.

3. Give each member copies of forms 2.2, 2.3, and 2.4 as self-study questionnaires.

4. Later call a second meeting, making sure each committee member has a copy of the others' self-study answers. Come to a consensus as a committee on your program's principles, objectives, and policies.

One method for reaching consensus in this second meeting is to break into groups of three to five people, having each small group gain its consensus. Then list on a board what each group agreed on and seek a consensus as a total group. You may be surprised by how much agreement exists in the small groups, and for the entire group to reach agreement then won't be so frustrating. As sport director you play a leadership role in this process by being the chairperson of these meetings and keeping everyone on task.

In Approach #2 you take these steps:

1. Based on your own self-study of forms 2.2, 2.3, and 2.4, write down your recommended list of program objectives and principles.

2. At a meeting of your organization's leaders, present your philosophy, including your objectives and principles for the program.

3. After these leaders review your presentation, guide them through each item to gain consensus. Allow input and feedback by all members of the organization.

4. Revise your program's objectives and principles based on what the group has developed.

Here again, as sport director you must lead the way. Encouraging your organization's leaders to give feedback and input will give them ownership in the program's objectives and principles. As facilitator of this process you cannot stifle this ownership process by disagreeing with comments that other people make. Everyone is entitled to an opinion.

# MOVING FROM PRINCIPLE TO POLICY

After you have established clearly stated program principles and objectives, you are ready to develop program policies for those objectives that affect personnel matters. Your policies must reflect your specific program needs. The approach will be to present different personnel topics and ask questions that help you formulate policies for those topics. Your policies should be consistent with the objectives and principles you and your organization leaders have already identified. You will develop them into a policy

## Form 2.4

# PRINCIPLES BEHIND OUR DEPARTMENT POLICIES

1. What would be in the best interest of students: participation or competition? What should be stressed?

2. What is more important: the development of athletic skills or performance in contests? Will you evaluate coaches on this?

3. How important is winning compared with having fun? Developing skills? Developing players physically, psychologically, and emotionally?

4. What role should parents play in sport? How does this relate to booster clubs?

5. When conflicts arise, how will they be dealt with and who will be responsible for dealing with them?

6. How important is the health and safety of the participants? What must be done to ensure the health and safety of all participants?

7. Who are our stakeholders ("customers")? What role will they play in the development of a mission statement and the development of athletic department policies?

manual. Keep in mind that *a policy manual is not static;* you should update it when policies are not working or as new policies need to be added.

Policies are rules, procedures, and plans of action. Correctly written and enforced, policies give a program a better chance to reach its objectives. It is well worth your time to develop an *Athletic Department Personnel Policy Manual.* We suggest you divide this manual into these three sections:

I. Program Objectives for Athletic Department Personnel

II. Program Principles for Athletic Department Personnel

III. Program Policies for Athletic Department Personnel

This policy manual is the most important document you will prepare for your department. It is imperative that you use your leadership skills to gain consensus for the contents of the manual—from the leaders of your school district and your athletic community, including the personnel that will be governed by these policies.

As sport director you must make sure that support staff and coaches have as much input into the development of the personnel policy manual as anyone else. Be sure to involve them and to reach consensus.

Back in the 1970s I represented teachers in some negotiations. At that time our personnel policies were contained in a document known as the "Memorandum of Understanding." This document spelled out the conditions of employment: what time you had to be at work, when you could use a sick day, how teachers were to be laid off, and even when and how they were to be evaluated. Our teaching staff was ready to strike because its members had absolutely no say about the contents of that memorandum. Feeling no ownership in the memorandum, the teachers concluded that the information in the document was not in their best interest and should not be taken seriously. I learned then that the people who have the most at stake must be a part of creating these kinds of documents

## Developing Your Organization's Personnel Policies

Once you have consensus on the principles and objectives regarding personnel matters, it is time to use these to develop policies that will enable you to reach your objectives. List the objectives and for each one of them ask questions that concern how you can attain it. Ask yourself, "Do we need a procedure or policy to make sure we reach our objective?" If the answer is yes, you need to write a policy. Let your principles or beliefs guide you in coming up with the right policy.

Next list the various personnel that will be affected by this policy manual and decide if the same policies will apply equally to all of them. Generally, you will write policies for head coaches, assistant coaches, support staff, and assistants to the athletic director. Ask yourself what are important areas of employment to cover? For example, is dress code important? How about the hours of work, overtime issues, conduct on the job, evaluation procedures, and terms of employment?

We will suggest some questions to start you off. This approach should point you in the right direction to formulate your policies on other personnel issues. You may use this same approach with other areas in the athletic department for which you would need to develop policies, including these.

- Program content
- Athletic participation
- Player selection
- Facilities usage
- Practice
- Contests
- Participant behavior
- Parent behavior
- Awards and recognition
- Health and safety

Here are some issues, followed by questions to consider, to help you develop policies.

### Policies Covering Eligibility to Coach

No single group in your program will influence how well you accomplish your objectives more than the coaches you recommend. You need to develop policies to clarify who is eligible to coach. Here are some questions you should answer to help you develop policies for a coach's term of employment:

1. What is the minimum age to be eligible to coach?
2. What coaching experience is necessary to coach? Is playing experience necessary to coach?
3. Do coaches need to go through a screening process to be eligible to coach? Is an application needed? Is a sports medicine workshop needed? Is CPR training needed? Is fingerprinting or a criminal check required?
4. Is any background in formal coaching-education programs (such as ASEP's Rookie Level, Coaching Young Athletes, or Leader Level workshops) to be required of coaches?
5. Is a parent of a player allowed to coach?
6. Is cross-gender coaching permitted (that is, a male coaching female sports or a female coaching male sports)?
7. If males are eligible to coach female teams, must a policy be developed requiring a female coach for locker-room supervision?
8. Are criteria for recommending head coaches different than for assistant coaches or lower-level coaches?

## Policies Covering Contest Officials

Game officials are necessary for our teams to compete. Here are some questions you should answer to help you develop policies for officials.

1. Are officials required to be certified by an officials' association or state athletic association? Are officials required to complete a training program provided by the school?

2. What experience, if any, is required to be an official?

3. How many officials are required to officiate at a particular contest or in a particular sport?

4. Will you permit a parent to officiate a contest that his or her child participates in?

5. Will you permit an employee to officiate a contest that his or her employer's team participates in?

6. Do you need policies to cover situations where officials fail to show for a contest or demonstrate poor sportsmanship?

## Policies Covering Support Staff and Parent Behavior

You can ask questions for other support staff similar to ones you did for coaches and officials to help develop written policies. You should think through the particulars of a given staff member's position, as well as parental involvement, and how these people interact in the process of reaching your program objectives.

1. What types of behavior by coaches, officials, bus drivers, and office staff are unacceptable? Cheating, violence, drug and alcohol use, harassment, smoking, derogatory language or gestures? Spell these out.

2. What policies may be needed to handle inappropriate behavior in practice? In a contest?

3. Should there be a policy to allow parents to file a complaint against a coach, an official, or another parent?

4. When unacceptable behavior does occur, should there be a policy to ban those adults from contests, practices, or the school grounds?

After you have drafted all the athletic department policies, be sure to secure the approval of your organization's leaders for them. Then publish your *Athletic Department Personnel Policy Manual*. Give a copy of the manual to every coach, official, and support staff person, including the athletic department secretary and assistant athletic director, on the first day of the individual's employment. However, this particular manual dealing with *personnel* should not be shared with parents or players.

With the information you have gathered you can begin the development of the *Athletic Department Program Policy Manual*. This manual will be the guiding light of your athletic department. Remember to *review it annually* to update and change policies as needed.

### *Summary*

In chapter 2 you learned to

1. identify the principles of your program philosophy;

2. develop personnel policies;

3. help determine your program's policies by reviewing your program's objectives and prioritizing them; and

4. create and distribute athletic department policy manuals to all appropriate personnel.

# Chapter 3
## Developing a Personnel Management Plan

In an interscholastic athletic department it is the sport director who is primarily responsible for the success of the personnel management plan. The process of creating a successful personnel management plan requires that the sport director understand all areas of a personnel department. In this chapter we explore many of the essential elements of an organized system of personnel management. Personnel in a sport program include the coaches, players, supervisors, parents, and support staff. It is important for the sport director to remember that people are the most important ingredient in any program; therefore, the personnel management plan must address the needs of personnel as well as of the organization.

In this chapter you will learn about these topics:

1. How to determine personnel needs.

2. How to develop a work schedule for personnel management.

3. What makes up a good job description.

4. What resources a sport director has, both internally and externally.

5. How to develop and maintain personnel records.

6. How to effectively plan for the evaluation process.

# ASSESSING NEEDS

People are the most important part of any athletic program. They include everyone who has a vested interest in the program, from the players to the parents to the ticket takers. For a program to be successful all of its participants must feel as though they have a part to play in its success. And they all are important to the success of its contests and other events. It is important to understand that if any of the "pieces of the puzzle" are missing, then the events won't run as smoothly or be as fulfilling as you intended for the students. By accurately assessing the personnel needs of the athletic program, including the personnel for running its events, you create a positive environment for the participants.

## Form 3.1

# SIZING UP THE ORGANIZATION

Fall sport: _____

    Varsity ___

    Junior varsity ___

    Sophomore ___

    Freshman___

    Total___          Male or female___

Winter Sport: _____

    Varsity ___

    Junior varsity ___

    Sophomore ___

    Freshman___

    Total___          Male or female___

Spring sport: _____

    Varsity ___

    Junior varsity ___

    Sophomore ___

    Freshman___

    Total___          Male or female___

## Sizing Up the Organization

The first step in staffing an athletic department is to determine what sports are offered, at what levels, and during which seasons. From this information you can determine what personnel needs exist. You do this by looking at the whole athletic program and then breaking the program down into individual sports (see form 3.1). As the sport director it is important to understand the role of each position and how the position fits into the overall program.

You must first determine the total number of sports the athletic program offers. Then divide the sports by season and level. Once the overall information is available, look at each sport individually. If you are the sport director for a multiple-school district, the number of schools in your district will obviously multiply the personnel you must find for each sport.

To establish what your personnel needs are answer the following questions:

1. How many games are played at home and how many home games are played at sites other than the school campus? Off-campus home games will involve securing additional personnel to cover the event. As an example, let's say you hold swim matches at a local recreation pool. You must hire security and lifeguards that you would not have to hire if you had your own pool.

2. How many students are involved in the program? This would include players, managers, statisticians, and so forth. For lower-level games, such as middle school games or ninth-grade games, students can fill such support staff positions as announcer, official scorer, or official timer. Usually, adults are used in these roles at varsity games.

3. How many coaches are necessary?

4. How many officials are necessary to run the contest?

5. What are the custodial and maintenance needs?

6. Are volunteers necessary? If so, what are their specific roles?

## Determining Personnel Needs

Once you have assessed what your personnel needs are, you can decide how many coaches you need, how many supervisors, how many officials, how many athletes per team, and so on. After making these decisions you must decide how many support staff will also be necessary to conduct games and operate the athletic program efficiently.

## Coaches

In establishing the number of coaches necessary to run a program your first consideration must always be the safety of the students involved in the program. There should always be enough coaches contracted to provide appropriate supervision of the student athletes. You may find form 3.2 helpful for keeping track of the coaches the program will need. Each sport should have a head coach.

The head coach is responsible for meeting the legal duties of coaches as well as for ensuring that all members on the staff are knowledgeable about and practicing the department's policies. Looking at federal, state, and local laws and at decisions made in court, coaches face a number of legal issues; they are accountable and they may be found negligent in their duties. Negligence can only occur if a serious injury happens because a coach neglected a duty or committed a breach of one of these legal duties. The responsibilities include the duty

- to plan,
- to properly instruct,
- to provide a safe environment,
- to provide safe and adequate equipment,
- to properly warn of the risk of participating in sport,
- to supervise,
- to properly match athletes, and
- to provide medical assistance when an injury occurs.

Several other factors also affect the number of staff members that should make up a coaching staff. These are some additional concerns:

**Safety.**   Can the number of coaches on a staff adequately perform the legal duties of a coach? Safety must be the primary concern.

**Number of student participants.**   The more athletes there are, the greater supervision and instructional responsibilities placed on the staff.

**League standards.**   At what levels do local leagues and area schools staff their various programs?

**Number of levels.**   How many different levels are offered at your school? Are there varsity, junior varsity, sophomore, and freshman squads? Does each squad require its own staff of coaches?

**Scheduling.**   Do the lower-level teams play home and away contests at locations and times that make it impossible for a coach to both attend the contest of one level's team and conduct a safe practice for the group not competing?

**Title IX.**   Is comparable consideration given both the males' and females' programs for staff, facilities, equipment and uniforms, playing and practice times, and so forth?

**Facility constraints.**   Are there special facility features that require additional staff, such as a soccer field that has two gates to supervise?

## Supervisors or Game Managers

The role of the game manager is to ensure that the activities at a contest which fall outside the realm of the coach's responsibility are dealt with in a safe and appropriate manner. The supervisor, or game manager, has these responsibilities, among others, at an event:

- Making sure the facility is prepared: the fields lined, P.A. system on, national anthem arrangements prepared.
- Handling of the officials; coaches should not be left to interact with officials after a contest.
- Securing the gate receipts and tickets for the contest.
- Instructing and placing security personnel in appropriate areas.
- Instructing and supervising gate help.

You should determine ahead of time how many supervisors or game managers are necessary for each contest. Base the number on the type of event, size of the crowd, type of relationship with visiting schools, number of functions the supervisor or game manager will be responsible for, and the level of the event.

## Game and Other Officials

Having competent game officials is a key to a successful contest. These officials actually wear the

**Form 3.2**

# DETERMINING PERSONNEL NEEDS

**Fall coaching staff**

| | | Coaches | | | | |
| --- | --- | --- | --- | --- | --- | --- |
| | | **Head** | **Assistant** | **Junior varsity** | **Freshman** | **Total** |
| **Football** | Last season | _____ | _____ | _____ | _____ | _____ |
| | Returning coaches | _____ | _____ | _____ | _____ | _____ |
| | New coaches | _____ | _____ | _____ | _____ | _____ |
| **Boys' soccer** | Last season | _____ | _____ | _____ | _____ | _____ |
| | Returning coaches | _____ | _____ | _____ | _____ | _____ |
| | New coaches | _____ | _____ | _____ | _____ | _____ |
| **Girls' soccer** | Last season | _____ | _____ | _____ | _____ | _____ |
| | Returning coaches | _____ | _____ | _____ | _____ | _____ |
| | New coaches | _____ | _____ | _____ | _____ | _____ |
| **Volleyball** | Last season | _____ | _____ | _____ | _____ | _____ |
| | Returning coaches | _____ | _____ | _____ | _____ | _____ |
| | New coaches | _____ | _____ | _____ | _____ | _____ |
| **Golf** | Last season | _____ | _____ | _____ | _____ | _____ |
| | Returning coaches | _____ | _____ | _____ | _____ | _____ |
| | New coaches | _____ | _____ | _____ | _____ | _____ |
| **Boys' cross-country** | Last season | _____ | _____ | _____ | _____ | _____ |
| | Returning coaches | _____ | _____ | _____ | _____ | _____ |
| | New coaches | _____ | _____ | _____ | _____ | _____ |
| **Girls' cross-country** | Last season | _____ | _____ | _____ | _____ | _____ |
| | Returning coaches | _____ | _____ | _____ | _____ | _____ |
| | New coaches | _____ | _____ | _____ | _____ | _____ |
| **Girls' Tennis** | Last season | _____ | _____ | _____ | _____ | _____ |
| | Returning coaches | _____ | _____ | _____ | _____ | _____ |
| | New coaches | _____ | _____ | _____ | _____ | _____ |

pinstripes or special clothing and referee the contest on the court, field, rink, or in the pool. The state athletic association often determines how many game officials are necessary for a contest. Typically a state athletic association will indicate the minimum number of officials necessary for a contest and the minimum licensing requirement for officials to work contests. Local conditions often require that more than the minimum numbers the state association has indicated be used in a game. For example, a state association might require two basketball officials, but a league official may feel that two game officials aren't enough and so hire a third, thus exceeding the state's minimum standard.

As you evaluate contest needs, you may find it is necessary to hire additional officials to perform functions other than officiating the contest. These officials could include scorers, timers, line judges, and so forth. Many of these officials are not licensed through a state association and do not have the same level of expertise as the contest official. So it falls on you as sport director to provide in-service training for these officials prior to the contest to assure they have the necessary skills to perform the functions you are asking of them. Because these officials can influence the outcome of a contest, it is a good practice to have adults in these positions whenever possible. My experience has been that adults must handle varsity contests. It is not uncommon for students to score or time lower-level contests. If you can secure competent adults, do it!

## Athletes

There is no exact science to determining the optimal number of student athletes for a squad at a specific level of play. In deciding on squad size, asking some questions can be helpful. If you haven't answered these questions before the season begins, your coach will be put in the position of making the decisions. Many coaches are not qualified to make these decisions without your help or the help of a good program policy manual. Here are the questions:

1. What is the purpose of the team? Is there a clearly defined philosophy and expectations for each level of team? Is it a grade-, developmental-, or skill-level team?

2. How many players are necessary? How many athletes are needed to field a team for contests? How many athletes are needed to adequately and safely practice the particular sport?

3. Are cuts necessary? How many athletes traditionally try out for the squad? What is the purpose of the cuts? Does the number of athletes trying out usually exceed the number that can reasonably be kept on the team? Do the student athletes who don't make the cut have other options for participation?

4. At what number of players does it become impossible for the coach to effectively manage the team?

5. How many teams will the school field? Will there be more than one per grade level or skill level?

6. How many coaches are available to instruct and supervise each team?

7. For each particular team, what do you believe is a safe and appropriate coach-to-player ratio?

By answering these questions and considering how they apply to the philosophy of the athletic program, you can clearly understand the impact of student participation in the athletic program.

## Support Staff

Adequate support staff is essential to a successful athletic program. Because of the expansion of programs and the number of facilities and teams that are monitored, it is now impossible to operate without a support staff. In determining personnel needs for support staff you must first review the program's operation. These are some areas in which you may want to use support staff :

**Clerical staff.**    With the growth of programs and the need to maintain accurate records on each athlete, clerical help is considered a must. Litigation is not uncommon in the athletic arena, and it is necessary that adequate records are kept, including the appropriate forms as requested by state athletic associations. Along with keeping records, athletic secretaries handle correspondence, provide required forms to the state athletic association, and perform literally a hundred other things to keep the athletic office running smoothly.

**Maintenance personnel.**    Facilities must be maintained in a safe condition for student athletes. The maintenance department handles this crucial function. Inspecting the facilities, bleachers, stadiums, playing fields, practice fields, and scoreboards should be done seasonally, annually, and even daily when appropriate.

**Equipment manager.**    The largest nonpersonnel item in an athletic budget is equipment. It is not uncommon for athletic departments to have an inventory worth more than $200,000 in uniforms and equipment. Having an equipment manager that checks out and maintains the equipment inventory is a plus for any athletic program. In the absence of an equipment manager, you should provide coaches with some assistance and training on how to control equipment and inventories.

**Scheduler.**    The sheer volume of the number of contests to schedule in a school can be overwhelming. In some schools the sport director employs an individual who has responsibility for scheduling the contests for the school. If you don't have a scheduler, then an assistant athletic director would be responsible for this. If you don't have either, then you're it!

**Trainer.**    We have an increased understanding of injury prevention these days, recognizing that a nationally certified athletic trainer may be the primary preventive agent against injury that a school can have. Many organizations now offer trainer services to schools for competitive fees. In the 1980s a certified trainer in your athletic department was a luxury—today it is a necessity. Trainers work closely with local doctors to ensure injured athletes do not come back to play before they are ready. Remember that the health and safety of players is a *legal duty* of a coach. Trainers help coaches make the right decisions.

My trainer came to me the Saturday after a varsity football game, concerned because a coach had played a linebacker who had shown signs of concussion during the game. He wanted me to know that he had disagreed with the coach's decision and had told the coach so. Needless to say, I had a serious discussion with my coach on a number of topics. First, he had failed in his duty to care for the health and safety of that player (thank goodness the boy didn't become seriously injured). Second, he violated our mission to develop athletes into better citizens, because the message he sent that boy and his team was that winning mattered more than their health. I was very concerned that my coach had ignored a trained professional's advice.

A trainer can be a tremendous asset to the athletic department, but be clear to coaches that the responsibility for the students' health and safety still rests with them. You might cover this in your *Athletic Department Personnel Policy Manual*. One caveat, however, is that you remind coaches that student trainers are not the same as *certified* athletic trainers. Coaches should never let students take the place of the trainer. The National Association of Trainers of Athletics suggests we call our student trainers "aides," so we do not give the impression that they are actually trainers.

## Balancing Needs and Resources

Most school districts have limited resources to fund their athletic programs. In fact, an alarming number of athletic programs must supplement gate receipts and fund-raising with fees from participants. Funding for sports will dictate how many coaches

you can hire, how many sports you can sponsor, and how many student athletes can finally participate. Sport directors soon learn that there are always more needs than there are available resources. This reality exists also in the area of personnel.

You must determine the personnel priorities for the athletic program. There are a number of facts to consider in making personnel decisions:

1. How many student athletes are participating in the sport?

2. How many teams are fielded in the sport?

3. For each team fielded what does the district believe is a safe and instructionally sound coach-student ratio?

4. How does the coach-student ratio compare to other schools locally?

5. Do you have funds to increase staff in one sport without decreasing staff in another sport?

6. If additional teams are to be added, are there adequate practice and contest facilities?

7. What is the cost per student athlete?

Fill out forms 3.1 and 3.2 to help determine how you will balance your program's needs and resources. Indicate in each blank the number of coaches necessary for next season. For each sport you should complete the coach's need form. You can use form 3.3 to help in planning for individual contests.

# SCHEDULING

Typically, staffing personnel for contests is done seasonally. Usually there are staff members that perform the same function from year to year, and they are slotted in for each season. You can determine the full staff prior to school being dismissed in the spring. The winter season is planned for in September and the spring season, in November.

# DEVELOPING JOB DESCRIPTIONS

The initial step in establishing a position within an organization is the creation of a job description. The

# Form 3.3
# UTILIZING RESOURCES TO MEET PERSONNEL NEEDS

Directions:  Complete the following form for each contest. The completed form will help you ensure that each position necessary for the contest is staffed.

Date and time _____     Opponent _____

Sport _____     Site _____

Level _____

| Position | Name | Phone |
|---|---|---|
| Coach | | |
| Official #1 | | |
| Official #2 | | |
| Official #3 | | |
| Official #4 | | |
| Official #5 | | |
| Ticket taker #1 | | |
| Ticket taker #2 | | |
| Ticket taker #3 | | |
| Ticket taker #4 | | |
| Scorekeeper | | |
| Scoreboard operator | | |
| Timer | | |
| Usher #1 | | |
| Usher #2 | | |
| Security officer #1 | | |
| Security officer #2 | | |
| Videographer | | |

job description defines the duties and responsibilities of the position you are creating (see figure 3.1 and 3.2 for samples).

## Maintaining Up-to-Date Descriptions

It is important that you keep job descriptions up-to-date. Job descriptions should be reviewed *annually*, during evaluations. The job description is the foundation from which the personnel management program will grow. Outdated job descriptions can become a burden to you in administering the sport programs. If the job description does not reflect the actual duties and responsibilities of the position, for example, a number of unwanted issues may surface related to evaluation and compensation.

The job description should provide the specific functions of the position. It should make clear what the employee will be held accountable for in all aspects of the job.

## Key Parts of a Job Description

Various models of job description exist. Most, though, have certain common components and key parts, which we will now outline.

### Job Title

The job title functions as a short descriptor of the position. The job title can be used to clarify the level of a position, such as a "head coach" or "assistant coach." It can communicate the role of the position, such as "equipment manager" or "athletic trainer."

---

**Job Description**

---

**Title:** Sport Director

**Evaluated by:** High school principal/middle school principal

**Responsibility:** Responsible directly to the high school and middle school principals

**Credentials:** Must possess a valid Ohio secondary principal certificate

**General duties:**
1. Direct and administer
   A. The interscholastic athletic program of the high school and middle school.
   B. All student activities, organizations, and programs.
2. Supervise all aspects of the middle school and high school program of cocurricular opportunities.

**Specific duties:**
1. Enforce the Ohio High School Athletic Association rules and by-laws and the regulations of the Southwestern Conference.
2. Represent all cocurricular activities at all high school department-chairperson meetings and middle school grade-level meetings.
3. Schedule all athletic contests and manage the school and student activity calendars, including assemblies, dances, etc.
4. Secure game officials for all contests.
5. Supervise all contracts for interscholastic games to eliminate conflicts and maintain a proper balance in all sports areas.
6. Prepare all athletic budgets and budget reports and supervise and/or delegate the keeping of all athletic financial records.
7. Arrange for the student physical examinations.
8. Supervise and approve purchase of equipment and medical supplies.
9. Supervise the maintaining of a permanent file of participants, medical examinations, insurance forms, injury reports, records, parent consent forms, payments, etc.
10. Maintain inventories of all athletic equipment, with the cooperation of the athletic coaches. Assume responsibility, with the cooperation of the athletic coaches, for the storage, issue, proper care, and disposal of all athletic equipment.
11. Direct the scheduling, availability and readiness of facilities for athletic contests.
12. Attend or designate representatives to attend athletic contests and appropriate cocurricular events.
13. Serve as the representative of the high school and middle school to all booster organizations.
14. Supervise and evaluate the coaches, directors, and advisors of all cocurricular and athletic activities.
15. Purchase and mail necessary tickets for all athletic events and direct the reserve-seat program.
16. Enforce good conduct and sportsmanship so as to promote the best interests of the athletic and cocurricular programs.
17. Supervise all personnel working with the athletic program in the secondary schools. This includes supervision of scoreboards, P.A. systems, police, transportation of teams, arrangements for officials and visiting teams, tickets, ushers, etc.
18. Plan and supervise all athletic banquets and awards programs.
19. Direct all financial aspects of the student activity program.
20. Develop and supervise a continuing staff development program for cocurricular staff.
21. Develop goals for and evaluate the athletic and cocurricular program.
22. Represent the entire cocurricular and athletic programs on the District Activities Council.
23. Manage the internal and external public relations activities of the athletic and cocurricular programs.
24. Administer appropriate student disciplinary policies.
25. Perform other duties related to the athletic and cocurricular programs as assigned by the high school and middle school principals.

**Figure 3.1**   Sample job description for a sport director.

---

**Job Description**

**Title:** Assistant Coach

**Responsibility:**
Responsible to the head coach as specified and to the high school principal

**General duties:**
Aids and supports the head coach in conducting the athletic program of the particular sport and the total athletic program.

**Specific duties:**
1. Observes and enforces the rules of the Ohio High School Athletic Association and the Southwestern Conference.
2. Assumes duties assigned him by the head coach pertaining to the overall athletic program of the particular sport.
3. Assists in teaching the basic fundamentals necessary for mastery of the sport.
4. Supports and remains loyal to the head coach.
5. Assumes partial responsibility for the performance of the players on the team.
6. Seeks to instill the highest concepts of sportsmanship, pride, and character in the players.
7. Sets a good personal example for the players, fellow coaches, and public.
8. Assists in providing for the greatest safety and welfare of all participants.
9. Assists in interpreting the athletic program to the public.
10. Performs other job-related duties as assigned by the superintendent.

Legal References
R.C. 3309.58
R.C. 3319.01
R.C. 3319.08

---

**Figure 3.2**   Sample job description of an assistant coach.

## Position Description

This provides a general description of the role the position plays within the sport program. Some of the roles identified in this area would include these:

a. The relationship the position has in regard to the sport program, such as head coach, assistant coach, assistant athletic director, or game manager.

b. The responsibility the employee has in the position as a representative to league, local, or state affiliations. Typically, specific job duties are not listed in this area; this description is a broad overview of responsibilities and duties.

## Qualifications

This is an important area within a job description. It is critical to understand the difference between *minimum* qualifications and *desired* qualifications. If, for example, a qualification for a head coaching position is previous experience as a head coach, you

may have to pass over a coach who demonstrates the necessary skills to be a successful head coach simply because the individual has never had a head coaching opportunity. Therefore, the coach doesn't qualify for the position. If a qualification is a *must*, say so. If a qualification simply is *desirable*, state it in that fashion.

You can sometimes use qualifications to motivate potential applicants. By your requiring completion of a coaching-education program to be a head coach, a coach pursuing that position will know such education is necessary within that sport program and will work toward completing it. Once again, however, you must be careful not to eliminate quality candidates with qualifications that they can attain at a later time.

## Supervisor

To whom is the person in the position responsible? It is critical for anyone seeking or considering a position to know who the boss will be. Typically the supervisor of the position is the person responsible for evaluations and other critical personnel decisions, as well as for acting as a mentor for the individual filling the position. In many situations coaches are responsible to the sport director, whereas, for example, the sport director is often responsible to the principal.

## Americans With Disabilities Act

In developing a job description, it is prudent to include appropriate statements regarding the Americans with Disabilities Act (ADA). For example, when you send a news release announcing a coaching position, it should mention that your school district is "an equal opportunity employer." School districts, through their legal counsel and professional organizations, should be able to provide a statement that meets the needs of the sports program.

## Title IX and Equity

You should also include a clear statement in the job description indicating that the program will give due consideration to all applicants and will not discriminate unfairly. The issue of Title IX (see appendix B for how to get the complete text and clarification or interpretations of Title IX) is a major force affecting interscholastic athletics. As sport director, you should ensure that the department is in compliance with Title IX in its hiring practices. You should familiarize yourself with the complete text of the title, which was printed in the *Federal Register* in volumes 44, no. 239 (December 11, 1979) and 45, no. 92 (May 9, 1980). In part it states,

No person shall, on the basis of sex, be excluded from participation in, be denied the benefits of, or be subjected to discrimination in employment, or recruitment, consideration, or selection therefore, whether full-time or part-time, under any education program or activity operated by a recipient which receives or benefits from Federal financial assistance.

Employment decisions, contracts, and employment preferences cannot be based on an individual's sex, and this applies to recruitment, advertising, hiring, promoting, termination, pay, assignments, leaves of absence, and other conditions of employment. Hiring the most qualified person is important, but attaining balance in staffing is also desirable.

## Duties and Responsibilities

This area provides a comprehensive description of the duties of the position. These are the responsibilities that should be performed on a regular basis, whether daily, weekly, monthly, or annually. If there is a recurring task, then it should appear on the job description. Typically the duties and responsibilities move from broad to specific. Examples of these duties and responsibilities should include supervision of student athletes. The supervision can range from general, such as overseeing warm-ups, to specific, such as overseeing a particular drill—making sure that a drill is run in a safe and educationally sound fashion. These are some duties that often appear on coaching job descriptions:

- transportation of athletes
- gathering and maintaining records
  1. physical forms
  2. emergency forms
  3. insurance forms
- attending parent meetings
- conducting practices
- contest management
- specific supervision responsibilities
- staff supervision responsibilities
- scheduling

# ATTENDING TO LEGAL ISSUES

Litigation is common in the sports profession, and sport directors not only must have an understanding of their legal responsibilities, they must also communicate what these legal responsibilities are to their staff and superiors. It is important that the lines of communication go up as well as down. Proactive, visible practices may not prevent a lawsuit, but implementing these preventive practices does create a perception of concern and preparedness in dealing with the question of negligence. These are some topics that you, as sport director, must be familiar with:

- Risk management

- Negligence
- Title IX
- ADA
- Due process
- Training and coaching education

It is sound practice for a sport director to document as much information as possible. If you discern that the potential exists for a lawsuit, be sure to gather and maintain documentation (or ask appropriate staff to do so). How long a time you must hold onto this information is not clear-cut. A person can bring legal action years after an event. Therefore it is prudent that you find a holding place for this type of information, in case there is ever a need. In most school districts the sport director can contact the district's legal counsel for advice and direction on what is appropriate in the maintaining of files.

During a football contest the middle linebacker is injured on a play. The injury is severe and results in partial paralysis. Attorneys for the player begin taking depositions five years after the incident occurred.

## Local Resources

You can find help locally in dealing with difficult situations. Most school districts maintain policies and guidelines that address how their employees handle situations. A sport director should be very familiar with any policies and guidelines that pertain to the department's operation. There are local authorities that offer assistance. Groups (such as police departments) and individuals (such as longtime coaches or central office administrators) can provide information to help your addressing difficult situations. You should realize that you are not the first sport director to face many of the problems that exist. It is important to develop a support base and a resource base to effectively address problem situations. Most districts have staff members who are expert in particular fields, such as personnel, financial, or public relations; these people are there as helpful resources for you.

The board of education has determined that the school district will implement a fee for the students participating in interscholastic sports. As the sport director it is your responsibility to inform players and parents. The first step in this communication is to sit down with the district's public relations officer and use his or her expertise to compose a letter to parents.

## Professional Organizations

In addition to local resources, many external resources exist. Almost all professional organizations now offer legal assistance. It is important that you join the available professional organizations for the liability insurance that may also be offered. These professional organizations provide up-to-date information and publications to assist members in the day-to-day operation of a sport program. They are invaluable sources of information, contacts, and documentation (for dealing with legal issues). As a sport director, you would benefit from belonging to these organizations:

- National Interscholastic Athletic Administrators Association (NIAAA)
- Your state's athletic directors association
- District and local athletic director associations

Membership in these associations not only provides valuable professional information, but also often includes liability insurance, newsletters, conferences and workshops, and other valuable benefits.

 KEEPING AND USING RECORDS

Gathering and maintaining information is necessary for ongoing assessment of personnel needs and for evaluating the personnel and the activities offered in the sport program. Your planning should include developing procedures for record keeping.

## Personnel Records

When an individual applies for a position, it is necessary to request information from a previous place of employment. This information can be quickly attained by the use of a fax machine or e-mail. In many states it is necessary for individuals seeking employment in a public school district to be fingerprinted and have a background check completed before they can be employed. Records must be kept on all those involved in the program—from the coaches to the athletes. It is important that employment records be maintained according to local, state, and federal guidelines. You probably will find yourself using employment records for many purposes, including

- directory information,
- determination of compensation,
- tracking training and qualifications,
- determining promotions,
- determining demotions,
- making annual evaluations,
- tracking the need for in-service training, and
- undertaking dismissal proceedings.

## Student Records

It is also necessary to maintain records on athletes who participate in the sport program. These records could include

- directory information,
- awards received,
- years in the program,
- medical history, and
- age.

If an athlete suffers an injury, it is important to collect and keep information about the occurrence in such a way that you or others can get to it at a later time. Injury claims are often made years after the event. The information in the file will be a valuable resource for the sport program should a legal issue be raised.

# INVOLVING KEY MEMBERS OF THE ORGANIZATION

You don't work alone in your role as sport director. Just as head coaches can typically look to their staffs as well as to the sport director for support, guidance, and leadership, you also have teammates. As the sport director it is important that you develop the team relationships that will provide for success. Inevitably you will be challenged about some decision you make. Perhaps one of your coaches or even someone above you in the organization actually made the decision. When the challenge comes, however, if you have developed a professional relationship—one in which you have already demonstrated integrity and competence—you will find stronger organizational support. So you must take the initiative in developing good relationships. This happens by meeting the needs, in a professional fashion, of those connected to the program. These needs and the individuals who have them are broad-based; you have professional relationships with supervisors, coaches, support staff, and parents.

## Supervisors

Supervisors are often in a position to assist as well as to evaluate the sport director. Providing regular updates regarding the sport programs is critical for a successful sport director. If you haven't yet established an effective method of communication between you and the supervisor, you should develop one.

Do not overlook the value of informal communication. If you are meeting your needs and the program's needs through informal communication, this may be all that is necessary. If, however, there appears to be a communication breakdown or gap, it may be wise to formalize communication. One way to accomplish this is to send a weekly memo, making sure you get it to the supervisor on the same day each week. The memo would update the supervisor on the various events that happened during the week. You thus provide documentation for yourself and consistent information to the supervisor.

## Coaches

Without doubt, coaches are on the front line in many of the decisions that get made. Either they make the decision or must carry out a decision others have made. Remember that it is difficult to support decisions when your input has not been sought. Therefore, if you expect coaches to support your decisions, make sure to involve them in the decision-making process. It is not necessary that you allow them to make the decision, but if your decision is in opposition to all the coaches, be sure to review it to know with certainty that you are on the right track. Involving your coaches demonstrates a respect for them, which promotes trust and a good working relationship.

## Support Staff

You have a wide range of individuals among support personnel. As with coaches, gaining their support and involvement in decision making can promote your working relationship for a successful sport program. No individual plays such an insignificant role that you should not ask for his or her input. In difficult times or when tough decisions must be made, the more people who understand the issues, the wider the support that can develop.

The support and involvement of the group of support staff can make the sport director's position more effective and lessen the stress. Many times support people have a great deal of contact with the community. And as they become experienced in their positions, they become more effective in the program's operation.

# PLANNING FOR EVALUATION

Evaluation is an integral part of a successful sport program. The purpose of evaluation is to improve the quality of coaching and instruction that student athletes receive. The focus in evaluation should be on development, improvement, and, in some situations, maintenance of the necessary skills. Often the evaluation process is part of the teacher's contract. Therefore, it is essential that you become familiar with the process as defined by the teaching contract.

## Preparatory Questions

*Preparing for* the evaluation is as important as actually doing the evaluation. Without the necessary preparations an evaluation will not accomplish the stated objective in an efficient and educational fashion. To begin the evaluation process, you should ask yourself several questions.

**Who will be evaluated?**   The list of potential evaluees should look similar to this:

- Head coaches
- Assistant coaches
- Support personnel
- Officials
- Others affiliated with the sport program

**Who will do the evaluating?**   You should have this question answered before the start of a sport season. It is common practice for the sport director to evaluate the head coach, for example, but who evaluates the assistant coach? In many areas the evaluation of the assistant coach is left up to the head coach. In some areas, however, all coaching evaluations are solely the responsibility of the sport director. Other people also are involved in the program. As the sport director do you ask for feedback from parents and players? Feedback is common, whether provided formally or informally. Depending on the situation, you should give this option due consideration. The broader the input a sport director receives, the clearer the picture becomes of how the employee is performing. When gathering a broad base of information, it is your responsibility as the sport director to sift through all the raw information or data to get access to the *substantive* information. If you read of or hear a student athlete complaining about a lack of playing time, you may not view it with much credibility, but if the student complains about inadequate instruction, you may want to discuss it with the coach.

**What tool will be used for the evaluation?**   Consistency is always an issue when dealing with evaluations. It is important that you create an evaluation form or "tool" if one does not already exist. This should be something with which both the evaluator and the person being evaluated are comfortable. By using the same tool annually, you can make the evaluation form an instrument that measures growth or a document of continued deficiencies. Evaluation is always a situation of potential litigation, so check with your organization's legal counsel to be sure the tool is acceptable to the organization.

**Does the person being evaluated know what they are being evaluated for?**   Personnel should know at the beginning of the season what criteria will be used in the evaluation process. It is critical that before people are evaluated, the person doing the evaluation discusses with them *what* they will be evaluating. Appropriate topics for discussion may include the

- job description,
- program or team philosophy,
- your and their expectations,
- communication,
- supervision,
- practice and game conduct,
- how to set goals, and
- individual goals set by the sport director and coach.

In setting goals for evaluation, it is important that you and the personnel members set goals that are measurable (see box). This is a sample of a measurable goal: "The head coach will develop and distribute to all team members and parents a team philosophy at the team's preseason meeting." By your creating measurable goals, both the employee's and your level of understanding (as the evaluator) increase, thus increasing efficiency and providing the greatest opportunity for success.

## Evaluation Timelines

Although evaluation is an ongoing process, it is necessary to establish benchmarks to review the progress you and your staff make toward accomplishing your goals. As already stated, the individual being evaluated must meet *prior to the season* with

---

**Sample Goal**

*My goal:* The head coach will develop and distribute to all team members and parents a team philosophy at the team's preseason meeting.

*How will I demonstrate its accomplishment?* With a written handout that I give team members and their parents and the sport director.

*By when will I accomplish this goal?* I will prepare the handout by August.

---

the person performing the evaluation to establish measurable goals. This should take place even before the first contact with student athletes.

Once the goals are established, the individual doing the evaluation should make *periodic checks* to ensure progress toward the goals is occurring. This demonstrates interest to the person being evaluated, and it creates credibility about the process. Periodic meetings or checks also enable the individuals involved in the evaluation to maintain communication, and if a problem arises they can immediately deal with it. Sometimes it is appropriate during the year to either change or restructure a goal, depending on the circumstances. At the conclusion of the season a culminating conference should take place in which you review the goals and measure the success in attaining those goals. At or after this meeting the initial goal-setting steps for the upcoming season should be established.

---

*Summary*

In this chapter you learned how to

1. assess and determine your personnel needs by reviewing individual sports, teams, events, sites, safety factors, and other information;

2. balance needs and resources by examining program priorities, numbers, and costs;

3. develop a job description by using common components and attending to legal requirements;

4. find information on important legal issues from local resources, publications, and professional organizations;

5. keep and use records for personnel, including students;

6. involve key members of the school district to help with your personnel management plan; and

7. plan for evaluations.

# Part II

## People Skills

# Chapter 4

# *Mentoring and Educating Personnel*

This chapter focuses on two areas that occupy sport directors during much of their time: mentoring people and educating them. Mentoring involves developing a caring and sharing relationship with individuals to help them reach their full potential, whereas educating is the act of imparting the knowledge necessary for staff members to perform their jobs properly. You must know when and how to mentor or educate.

## MENTORING

You already have an idea in your mind's eye of what mentoring is. If you were born before 1970, you

In this chapter you will learn about these topics:

1. The differences between mentoring and educating.
2. What skills to practice and avoid as an effective mentor.
3. When to educate rather than mentor.
4. Various methods to use to educate staff.

were probably influenced by the older, industrial-age mentoring model: big brother–little brother, big sister–little sister. This approach assumed the mentor was all-knowing and the person being mentored ("mentee") was an empty vessel waiting to be filled up. It did not allow for the mentee's having an active part in the relationship. In other words, the mentor really wasn't concerned about the mentee's needs. The focus in the old way was on career advancement. There were some good orientation programs to help a mentee learn basic skills and job knowledge, but attention wasn't given to what the mentee needed as a new coach or other staff member.

The term we use today, *mentor,* is not new. It dates back to ancient Greece and Homer's book *The Odyssey.* Mentor was an individual who was assigned the task of raising Telemachus, the son of Odysseus, King of Ithaca. While the king was gone for 10 years Mentor not only gave Telemachus the skills to become the next king, but he also gave of himself. He developed a nurturing, caring, sharing relationship that enabled Telemachus to become the best he could be. Mentor became the guiding light to Telemachus voluntarily—with no strings attached—the shoulder to cry on, the active listener, and the active questioner.

The information age that we are in has taught us that to be an effective mentor requires specific skills, that the mentee has needs that must be addressed to enable him or her to reach full potential, and that the relationship is a two-way street. The mentor can learn just as much from the mentee as the mentee can learn from the mentor. As we outline the skills necessary to be an effective mentor, you will see that not everyone has the ability to be a good mentor. If you establish a formal mentoring program in your athletic department, you should take care to match mentors and mentees so their strengths and weaknesses are complemented.

## Mentoring Is a Voluntary Contribution

All of us who work for a living perform duties or obligations in return for money, which puts bread on the table. Mentoring, however, transcends contractual obligations. It comes from inside our hearts, and it is a commitment to another individual,

whether or not he is aware of it, to provide a relationship that will enable that person to grow, develop, and solve his or her own problems.

Our staff of coaches, assistants, maintenance personnel, officials, bus drivers, and others receives money for services performed. Each employee has a contract that evidences payment for performance of services. Most staff members do a good job of following the contract to the letter. They come to work on time, they plan and organize their work, and they follow up-to-date strategies. Some of our staff go above and beyond their contractual relationships: they organize camps in the summer, work extra hours to be sure the gym is clean, dress well to set a good example, arrive early to officiate, or bring in big-name coaches or players to talk with the players. These staff people are the better employees that we hire. But they still can't all call themselves mentors because many of them go above and beyond for themselves—not for the participants or each other.

There is nothing wrong with being a good coach, official, custodian, or bus driver. But if you want to change lives or contribute to a young person's ability to become better, you must develop the skills to become an effective mentor. A mentoring approach is identified by the following attributes:

- A genuine caring attitude toward everyone you come in contact with in your department, an attitude of wanting everyone (participants, coaches, support staff, and parents) to be successful in accomplishing the program's objectives, an attitude of wanting to provide the support they need to be successful.

- Development of skills to work more effectively with people, including understanding these skills and practicing them every day.

## Behaviors and Skills to Practice

Some few of you already possess many of the skills it takes to become an effective mentor. You were fortunate enough to have had parents, teachers, coaches, and mentors in your life who influenced you enough that you learned to be like them. Most of us have some mentoring abilities, but need to practice to hone other basic skills of mentoring.

These are some of the mentoring behaviors and skills sport directors need to practice:

**Listening actively.** Coaches, players, support staff, and parents need for you to listen to them—and to give feedback that you are listening and understand their problems. Coaches need to learn to solve their own problems if they are to become effective coaches. You can do little things that let the other person know you are listening and want to clearly understand them, such as repeating what they say and asking questions.

**Providing information and exploring options.** You should know where coaches can find information to help them solve their problems. You should be familiar with publications and other resources that individuals can go to to help them solve their problems or get answers to their questions. Sport directors can help mentees explore options and brainstorm solutions.

**Being available.** Coaches, participants, support staff, officials, and parents are the most important people you deal with, and you must be available to them as necessary. You must be open-minded to their needs, provide encouragement when they are having difficulties, give emotional support when problems arise, and follow through on commitments you make to them.

**Using the Socratic method.** Socrates was noted for his teaching by asking questions. He knew people would learn more and remember it longer if they came up with the answer themselves. People come to us as sport directors with all kinds of problems, and we should learn to ask insightful questions to let them know we are listening and to allow them to solve their own problems. The next time a coach or parent or anyone in your department comes to you with a concern or problem, ask them questions like these:

- Why do you feel that way?
- How do you think the other party feels about this situation?
- If you were the other party (e.g., the parent or coach), what would you want to see happen?
- What do you feel would be agreeable solutions to both parties?

- What would you have to do to make this a win-win situation?
- Are you taking this personally?
- Can you separate the people from the issues?

**Confronting the mentee.** Sometimes you may have to confront a mentee to help him or her move forward. If you know that your mentee is going to make a bad decision or if you see the person is spiraling out of control, confronting him or her is the only way to bring the individual back on track. Be careful you do not confront individuals in a judgmental way. The best way to confront people is to tell them that you are concerned about them or their behavior and the direction they are going. Try to leave the responsibility to change with them. When you confront them, you are getting them to stop and think about what they are doing. To avoid being judgmental, use "I" statements: for example, "I am concerned that if you quit coaching, you won't be happy and the players will feel you are abandoning them."

I had a coach who was very upset with an official's call at the end of the game. The official allowed a three-point shot that the coach felt occurred after the buzzer. It was a tense situation because the fans were livid, the players were in shock, and the assistant coaches were upset, as was the head coach. My duty at the end of the game is to walk the officials to the dressing room. Coaches are not permitted in the officials' room after the game, and my coach was storming toward the room where the officials were dressing. I stopped him and looked him straight in the eyes as I said, "Coach, I'm concerned if you go in there, you will set the wrong example for the kids and will probably get a two-game suspension from the state and who knows what other consequences from me." It was enough to get him to stop and think. When he stopped, I told him to count to 10 and go back with the players, where he belonged.

## Behaviors to Avoid

Just as there are behaviors to practice to be an effective mentor, there are behaviors to avoid in order not to hinder the process. Some of these behaviors are difficult to avoid; we grew up thinking these were behaviors that helped people grow.

**Giving advice.** How can this be? Isn't giving advice the best thing you do? Many of you are wondering how or even why to avoid giving advice. People ask us for advice every day. Certainly, if someone asks you the best way to get somewhere or needs some other information that only you know, then you must give it. But often when individuals, such as coaches, players, and parents, come with problems and concerns, they want to tell you what is on their mind. Many times they want to bounce things off you because they respect you or your position. Be careful. Your first inclination may be to give advice and tell them how you would handle the problem or situation.

The problem with giving advice, however, is that it doesn't allow the mentee to solve his or her own problems. If you have teenage children, you know how they react when you as a parent give them advice. If you are paying any attention at all, you'll hear them say, "Never mind, you weren't listening anyway," or "You don't know what you're talking about." Generally, when parents, coaches, or players share their problems or concerns with you, all they really want is for someone to listen. If they don't want you to simply listen, then what they want is for you to solve their problems. Don't do it. There are more productive ways for them to solve their own problems, such as exploring options, brainstorming, or asking questions to come up with their own solutions.

**Rescuing the mentee.** As bad as giving advice is rescuing the mentee. Rescuing means you want to solve the problem *for them*. We often see this mechanism operating in education today. Johnny or Mary violates a rule or policy, and then mom or dad is in your office trying to make everything better. The parent tries to justify that it wasn't their son's or daughter's fault. We do the same thing with our own constituents. We have a new coach who violates policies or procedures, and we sweep it under the table. We don't want to see them make mistakes so we take care of it for them.

**Criticizing.** No matter how constructive you think criticism may be, it still is judgmental and perceived to be threatening by your mentee. One of our basic needs is to survive; criticism threatens that basic

A coach on my staff forgot to fill out the transportation request form for his team over the holidays. The coach knew that it was his responsibility to make a request 10 days before the trip, but because he was disorganized or lazy, he failed to do it. Rather than make a big issue, I instructed my secretary to smooth things over with the transportation department and do the request for the coach. Guess what? The next year the same thing happened. I learned that when you rescue people, they don't learn to handle their own responsibilities. If you don't hold them accountable, then they are not learning to be responsible individuals. You must learn to confront people in a positive way when they fail to perform their duties. If you bail them out instead, you will be the one responsible. Remember, "What you permit, you promote."

need. As educators, we know that criticism lowers self-esteem, and it doesn't matter who receives it. Even the strongest people may doubt their abilities when someone, particularly someone they respect, is criticizing them.

I'll never forget my first evaluation as a business education teacher. The instrument was a checklist, and I was being rated from 1 to 5, with 5 being the highest. All of my marks were 4s and 5s except one. I received a 3 on the appearance of my classroom. The evaluator told me in the evaluation meeting that he wanted to see more visual charts, color, and items that students could view in the room. As good as my evaluation was, I had difficulty getting past the comment that my classroom appearance needed improvement. Interestingly, as I looked back years later, had the evaluator asked me what I thought of the appearance of my classroom in relation to those standards, I would have probably rated myself lower than he did.

**Promoting or protecting.** I don't mean you shouldn't help your mentee climb up the ladder to gain recognition or promotions. But you shouldn't show favoritism. Let the person's talent earn them recognition and promotions. If others perceive you to be a protector of the chosen few or someone showing favoritism, it will hurt your credibility.

**Building walls.** Sometimes sport directors erect barriers between themselves and coaches, parents, officials, participants, or other support staff without intending to do so. You may not like what people are saying to you and you may not like how certain people dress or who they hang around with, but as mentor and sport director you must be above all of that. Your job is to make people feel you are friendly, relaxed, and approachable. You need to build a reputation as a fair and honest person.

**Diminishing someone's value.** Sometimes we "blow off" or ignore a mentee's abilities, interests, or willingness to try something new. An official for the ninth-grade level, for example, may tell you that she would like to become a varsity official. Don't discourage her from setting goals that you might think she can't reach. Let the mentee find out on her own, one way or the other. As another example, perhaps a mentee asks you, "Why?" Your reaction may be to answer him, "Don't worry about why; just trust me and do it." The question *why?* has to be answered if at all possible. The answer to the why question may be the key that allows the mentee to go forward and understand something or gain the insight to solve a problem.

**Considering mentoring mandatory.** Mentoring must be voluntary. To be effective, a mentor must operate voluntarily, above and beyond contractual obligations. As soon as contracts, obligations, or remuneration are introduced, mentoring ceases to exist. The mentoring attitude must be voluntary or else it may damage the relationship with the people you work with.

## Mentoring and Evaluating

As the person responsible for evaluating athletic department staff, you may be wondering how you can evaluate and mentor the same individual. If you are having difficulty wearing both hats, you will probably have some trouble being an effective mentor. Don't look at evaluation as a negative process but rather as a positive one: it gives you the opportunity to help your staff grow and develop. If you approach the *evaluation* by looking at the process *with a mentoring attitude,* you will increase your chances

of helping the individual improve, and the individual will look to you as a person who cares and wants him or her to be the best employee and individual possible. You must develop trust and credibility with your staff to help them move forward. Mentoring is the approach that will help you get there.

# EDUCATING

Education is another key role you have as the sport director. The more ways and time you can find to educate staff, the more problems you will avoid in the future. Educating, or imparting the knowledge to do a better job, is a major responsibility. In today's athletic departments we must educate coaches on the skills and the legal duties and responsibilities of coaching. We must educate parents and student athletes about our athletic department philosophy, rules, and regulations as well as about our expectations of them as sport parents and participants. We should educate our officials in the role of sportsmanship and their responsibilities as referees for our contests. And we need to educate our support staff on their duties and the expectations we have of them as they work in our athletic departments.

## Types of Educational Tools

You have many tools and resources at your disposal. You must use them all to help your athletic personnel do their best. These are the most common and effective tools to educate coaches, support staff, parents, and participants:

**In-service training.** This type of training is done in-house. Your school district provides it through your office. As sport director you may conduct an in-service meeting to update coaches on rule changes in their sport, for example, or educate them on Title IX or requirements of the Americans with Disabilities Act. You may bring in an expert (such as another sport director, an official, or a lawyer) to educate your staff on ways to recruit more athletes, on recent rule changes, or about their iegal obligations as coaches and support staff. You should build a library of books, magazines, videotapes, and articles that you can make available to employees when they need them.

**Conferences and workshops.** Associations of sport directors, coaches, and officials sponsor workshops and conferences covering topics that will help us perform our jobs better, handle stress better, or find useful sport-specific information on strategies or skills. There are other profit-making organizations that offer workshops in almost every major city on "how to" almost any topic you can think of. Sending staff to these workshops and conferences will cost the athletic department or booster clubs money, but their value is hard to deny.

**Individual meetings.** When an individual staff person needs to know how to improve in a skill or to become aware of a better way of doing something, a face-to-face meeting can be the most efficient approach. These meetings are personal and are like tutoring. A lot can be accomplished in a short time.

**Department meetings.** Most of us have preseason meetings with coaches or support staff to go over expectations, duties, evaluation procedures, and general information. The problem is finding a time and place to conduct these meetings so everyone can attend. If the meeting is shorter than a half hour, try holding it in the early morning, before work. If you plan a longer meeting, use an evening but provide food—and *stick to the agenda*. I have been fortunate to be able to hold an all-day meeting for head coaches once a year. The board of education pays for a substitute, and we inform the off-staff coaches about it long enough in advance that most of them also can arrange to attend. These meetings are dedicated to evaluating mission, changing policies, and dealing with major coaching issues.

**Orientation meetings.** It seems that you are always preparing a new staff member to perform special duties or a new coach to begin next week! It is important to schedule orientation meetings for new coaches and support staff people. Try scheduling them before the school year, at least once before each season begins. Orientation meetings give the staff the information they need to perform their duties and comply with the policies set by the athletic department and board of education. If you are meeting with new coaches, the orientation would include responsibilities before, during, and after the season; rules changes; mission, philosophy, and policies of the athletic department; information on the evaluation process; and a discussion of the coach's role and relationship with student athletes.

An orientation for support staff would include setting out the athletic department's expectations, the staff member's duties and responsibilities (the tasks to be performed), discussion of the evaluation process if there is one, and discussion of the role that staff members play with student athletes.

# COMPARING MENTORING WITH EDUCATING

A sport director needs many skills, competencies, and resources to deal effectively with the personnel in his or her athletic department. We have presented some information and examples of effective mentoring and how to best educate your staff. You may now be wondering when you mentor and when you educate. There are no strict rules, but in general when you are conveying competencies, skills, or knowledge to help personnel perform their job or duties well, you are in the education mode.

> The requirements for coaching had changed in Ohio, and the state's Department of Education now required each coach to hold a valid CPR card and take a preapproved, four-hour sports-medicine clinic. When the edict came down, I called a meeting to educate my coaches as to their responsibilities and the time lines this new requirement would impose.

When you want to improve personal development, enable your staff to reach full potential in their work and as people, or create a better place for your staff and the students to live and work, then you are in the mentoring mode. Sometimes mentoring and educating overlap. Keep in mind that you are a role player and you must decide when, where, and how to perform the many roles you play.

> A coach who has just been confronted by an irate parent and is feeling frustrated by a losing season needs to be mentored—not educated.

*Summary*

In this chapter you learned

1. the difference between a mentor and an educator;

2. how to be an effective mentor by practicing such skills as active listening, exploring options, using the Socratic method, and constructive confrontation—and avoiding such behaviors as giving advice, rescuing and criticizing, protecting, and diminishing; and

3. about various educational tools to use for educating your personnel, including in-service training, conferences and workshops, meetings, and library resources.

# Chapter 5
## Communicating and Resolving Conflicts

The style in which we communicate will in large part determine how well we resolve conflict. This chapter deals with the components of communication and how they relate to solving problems and making decisions. We'll also look at the 14th Amendment and Title IX of the Education Amendment of 1972 and discuss their impact on an athletic department.

## COMMUNICATING

Any experienced sport director will tell you that significant time is spent in communicating. Information is communicated or transmitted, of course.

In this chapter you will learn about these topics:

1. The components of communication and how they relate to your style of communication.
2. Problem solving with a team or group.
3. Listening skills that can help you resolve conflict.
4. Conducting a meeting.
5. How the 14th Amendment to the Constitution grants equal protection under the law to groups and how Title IX of the Education Amendment of 1972 guarantees gender equity.
6. Due process and how to ensure it in the athletic department.

Communication also is an essential part of solving problems, reaching consensus on decisions, and resolving conflicts within the athletic department.

## Opening Lines and Opportunities to Communicate

Clear lines of communication must be established to minimize the occurrence of disagreements and misperceptions that can easily emerge from our emotional profession of sport. Once you have established communication guidelines, put them in writing. Then make sure they get distributed to coaches, athletes, and parents. You can also use preseason meetings as opportunities to explain and promote communication guidelines.

Figure 5.1 provides a sample of good guidelines for communication, in this case focused on interactions between parents and coaches. The preseason meeting is an excellent event at which to present and explain these kinds of guidelines—and to encourage coaches, athletes, and parents to follow them.

## Components of Good Communication

Most communication is nonverbal. Give or take a few points, only 10 percent of a message someone receives is verbal; 60 percent is nonverbal and 30 percent is tonal. This is worth rephrasing. As listeners, only 10 percent of what we understand of a person's speaking comes from the verbalized words. The speaker may be talking all night long, but we may not be receiving those spoken words. What we are perceiving are the nonverbal indicators, such as posture, facial expressions, hand movements, touching, and head movements. We are also receiving the sound or tone of the speaker's message, which speaks volumes more than the verbal words. Remember the old adage "It is not what you say as much as *how* you say it that counts."

Sport directors must be empathic listeners. We need to listen with empathy, being sensitive to the cues that the speaker gives in body language and tone. The art of reading these nonverbal cues is one of the keys to effective communication.

What we receive as a message depends very much on what we see and hear. To be good listeners or receivers of messages we have to give the sender our attention and, in some way, confirm what the message is that we are receiving. My coach screamed

> I remember a coach I had in high school who seemed to constantly scream and yell at his players. Once he became frustrated and commented to the team that he didn't understand why no one listened to him. "What's the problem?" he asked us. Well, no one volunteered to tell him, but we all heard him—not his words, but the veins popping out of his head, his roaring, and his flailing arms.

at me to "Concentrate!" The message I received was that he was angry with me; I didn't receive the same message he thought he was sending.

Just as we must become decoders of nonverbal and tonal messages, we must become more aware of our own tendencies or ways we use to express ourselves. Do we say what we mean and do our actions agree with what we are saying? Do our nonverbal and tonal messages convey what we want them to say? If we want to get a point across to athletes, for example, we send verbal, nonverbal, and tonal messages. How many different ways can you send the message that you don't agree with something someone said?

## Communication Style

How we communicate varies, some people demonstrating great control and others showing great emotion. We all know people who—like CP30 in *Star Wars*—are calm, cool, and collected. Other individuals—such as George Costanzo in *Seinfeld*—exercise little control in their communication. In reality, people's communication styles can fall anywhere along the continuum between those two extremes.

Identifying a person's style is important to you as the sport director who interacts with the individual. People under control usually are seekers of information, whereas people expressing emotion are givers of information. It is sometimes hard to get information from people under control, and it is often difficult for emotional people to listen.

Consider these styles:

- Expressive—talks for the joy of talking and to be accepted.

- Reserved—speaks only when asked, contemplates things, perhaps is shy.

- Amiable—uses communications to develop relationships.

## Parent and Coach Communication Guidelines

### Parent-coach relationship

Both parenting and coaching are extremely difficult vocations. By establishing an understanding of each position, we are better able to accept the actions of the other and provide greater benefit to children. As parents whose children are involved in our athletic program, you have a right to understand what expectations are placed on your child. This begins with clear communication from the coach of your child's program.

### Communication you should expect from your child's coach

1. The coach's philosophy.
2. Expectations the coach has for your child as well as all the players on the squad.
3. Locations and times of all practices and contests.
4. Team requirements, i.e., fees, special equipment, off-season conditioning.
5. Procedures we follow should your child be injured during participation.
6. Discipline that results in the denial of your child's participation.

### Communication coaches expect from parents

1. Concerns expressed directly to the coach.
2. Notification of any schedule conflicts well in advance of the practice or event.
3. Specific concern in regard to a coach's philosophy and expectations.

As your children become involved in the programs at their high school, they will experience some of the most rewarding moments of their lives. It is important to understand that there may also be times when things do not go the way you or your child wishes. At these times we encourage discussion with the coach.

### Appropriate concerns to discuss with coaches

1. The treatment of your child, mentally and physically.
2. Ways to help your child improve.
3. Concerns about your child's behavior.

It is very difficult to accept your child's not playing as much as you may hope. Coaches are professionals. They make judgment decisions based on what they believe to be best for all students involved. As you have seen from the list above, certain things can be and should be discussed with your child's coach. Other things must be left to the discretion of the coach.

### Issues not appropriate to discuss with coaches

1. Playing time.
2. Team strategy.
3. Play calling.
4. Other student athletes.

There are situations that may require a conference between the coach and the parent. These are to be encouraged. It is important that both parties involved have a clear understanding of the other's position. When these conferences are necessary, the following procedure should be followed to help promote a resolution to the issue of concern:

### If you have a concern to discuss with a coach,

1. Call to set up an appointment.
2. The their high school telephone number is 123-4567.
3. If the coach cannot be reached, call the Activities Director, Mr. Allen. He will set up the meeting for you.
4. Please do *not* attempt to confront a coach immediately before or after a contest or a practice. These can be emotional times for both the parent and the coach. Meetings of this nature do not promote resolution.

### What can a parent do if the meeting with the coach did not provide a satisfactory resolution?

1. Call and set up an appointment with the Activities Director to discuss the situation.
2. At this meeting the appropriate next step can be determined.

Research indicates a student involved in sport activities has a greater chance for success during adulthood. Many of the character traits required to be a successful participant are exactly those that will promote a successful life after high school. We hope the information provided within this pamphlet makes both your child's and your experience with the high school athletic program less stressful and more enjoyable.

**Figure 5.1**   Parent and coach communication guidelines.

- Analytic—carefully compares and contrasts what is said to what is known as fact; may challenge the speaker.

## Credibility

Credibility is crucial in your role as personnel manager. You can achieve credibility by consistently following certain principles. Of course, you first must present valid or true information. Provide reliable information that can be counted on in all situations. Use a dynamic, open style with people to communicate the information. Make sure that your nonverbal and tonal messages agree with your verbal message. Admit it when you make a mistake.

Be a cooperative style leader by becoming an active listener. Don't just be a talking head, but rather stay open to comments or questions from those you are giving information to and communicating with.

## Sending and Receiving Skills

These are some examples of sending and receiving skills that you as sport director must develop for yourself. Furthermore, you would do well to educate your coaches in them:

- Develop credibility.

- Be positive. Encourage your staff, and give praise when it is deserved.

- Try not to be judgmental with your staff. There is a difference between being judgmental or critical and being supportive and helpful

- Be consistent in your communication. Do what you say. Try not to continually change your mind or remake decisions.

- Don't dominate conversations. You may think you're important, but believe me—the receivers of your messages will turn you off sooner or later if you don't give them an opportunity to speak or reply. Effective communication is a two-way street.

- Use your nonverbal skills to communicate positive messages. Give a smile, a wave, or a wink to let people know that they're doing a good job and that you acknowledge them.

- Don't send mixed messages. If someone violates a policy or procedure, deal with it and don't let it pass. Don't deal with some staff and

not with others; this, too, delivers a mixed message and you may lose credibility. Trust is difficult to establish—but easy to lose.

- Listen carefully and try not to interrupt.

- Ask questions for clarity, which confirms that you are listening.

- Acknowledge feedback, using such comments as "I understand," "OK," "Uh, huh."

# SOLVING PROBLEMS

Most of the communication that you do in personnel management is one-on-one problem solving, as you work with student athletes, coaches, parents, and support staff. Sport directors also need expertise, however, in working with groups. You work with committees, coaching teams, boosters' clubs, athletic teams, and parent groups. In this section we cover some basic duties that enable you to plan and prepare for a meeting to solve problems. Next, we discuss some tips for conducting a meeting and for dealing with conflict if it arises or with an impasse if one is reached. Then we suggest some methods you can use to reach a decision when you're working with a group of people.

## Basic Leadership Duties for Meetings

Before the meeting begins, keep the following points in mind. Your role is to guide the discussion toward the achievement of goals and the solution of problems, not to allow personal ideas or agendas to dominate. Be receptive and thankful of members' opinions. Also be sensitive to members who have difficulty expressing themselves. Help them draw out their ideas, especially those who are reluctant to talk. You should be familiar with parliamentary procedure. Use your knowledge of parliamentary procedure to brief the group on the fundamentals and how they will be used.

## Tips for Conducting Meetings

The following points will help you in conducting a meeting with any size group:

- Introduce members of the team; possibly have a warm-up activity.

- Give a verbal overview of the agenda, purpose of the meeting, topics, methods, and adjournment time.

- Develop ground rules for conducting team meetings with members of the group (when people can speak, use of the microphone, limiting the time spent on a single topic, whether the individual must stand and state her name, residence, etc.).

- Seek alternate points of view or additional information before making a decision (this could be a ground rule); this helps prevent making snap decisions.

- Cover one agenda topic at a time and stick with it; don't allow members to get off the topic. Stay focused and on task.

- Involve all team members whenever possible. Even if all members don't add to the discussion, you can insist that everyone vote.

- Stimulate discussion by
  a. encouraging individuals to speak,
  b. interceding when several members are holding their own discussion,
  c. remaining neutral when disagreements develop,
  d. seeking explanation when Yes or No answers are used,
  e. summarizing various or divergent points of view or asking others to do so,
  f. ensuring each member's chance to participate (staying actively aware of who is dominating or sitting back and not discussing), and
  g. controlling discussion length by moving to the next topic.

## Resolving Arguments and Breaking Up Impasses

Many times disagreements occur or a group reaches an impasse and cannot seem to reach any decisions. You do have options for dealing with these problems. Here are some suggestions:

- As the chairperson you may move for a vote. This makes people take a stand.

- You may table the topic or decision for further study or discussion.

- You can appoint a subcommittee to study the problem or conduct research.

- You might invite two protagonists to remain after a meeting to discuss their points of view in greater depth. Don't waste everyone's time when only two people disagree.

- When an individual dominates the committee, ask the group whether it has enough information on that topic that would allow moving to another point of view or another topic; see the individual privately and ask him or her to allow greater committee participation.

## Practical Methods to Reach Decisions With Teams or Groups

Many techniques have been developed by social scientists to help leaders work with groups to reach decisions. Here are four of them that you might find useful and wish to experiment with or study further.

**Affinity diagrams.** List a particular problem in the center of a poster board or chalkboard. List the contributors to the problems around the edge and show reactions to the problem with various types of lines or colors (e.g., dotted line is partially related; a solid is directly related; red is a contributor; blue is a resolution). This diagramming helps to place in perspective what the focus of resolution needs to be.

**Interactive digraphs.** A special form of affinity diagram is called an interactive digraph, wherein two particular positions or viewpoints are drawn with similar relational lines as in the affinity diagram. The digraph helps show the support systems for the two points of view and the ways these can be brought closer by changing the support mechanism.

**Interactive matrices.** A matrix is a rectangular listing, using rows and columns, of the components or elements of a problem or situation. List various forces or viewpoints down the vertical axis of a matrix, and repeat them across the top. Have the group vote on merits of the comparisons within each cell (e.g., A vs. B; A vs. C; A vs. D; B vs. C; B vs. D; C vs. D).

**Collaborative negotiations.** Try to find the common ground as you compare each point of view.

Then build on those commonalties. Disallow degrading commentary about any point of view.

# RESOLVING CONFLICTS

Remember that sport can be very emotional, which will lead to disagreements between parents and coaches or athletes and coaches. Your coaches need your leadership and support to cope with these types of problems. When a crisis exists, it is difficult if not impossible to solve problems or concerns at just that moment. One of the most important points in communication is for coaches to avoid meeting with *parents in the heat of the moment*. Strongly encourage them to follow this point.

It is sad but true that there is more violence directed from parent to coach, parent to parent, and parent to official than ever before. Granted there are more sports and more participants, but physical violence in sport is becoming all too common. The only cure is to educate participants and set clear expectations.

> Several years ago the junior varsity football coach came into my office after a Saturday morning game to tell me a father had punched him in the stomach. The father was blaming the coach because the son didn't play that day when all his relatives were there to see him. When something like this happens in your athletic department, you had better be prepared to deal with it because reactions abound. Usually the reaction is not helpful to resolving the problem. In this case, charges were not filed, but the father was banned from school grounds for one year.

As sport director you will be involved in many conflicts that arise from how parents, players, and coaches perceive situations. The most common conflicts come from parents' perception about playing time allotted their sons or daughters, how the coach treats athletes, the strategies the coach uses in practices or games, and whom the coach selects for the team. Today, more than ever, parents expect coaches to be knowledgeable in the skills of effective coaching. Parents also want more opportunities to communicate their concerns to coaches. Because of these high expectations sport directors must become more skilled in how to communicate effectively and how to resolve conflict.

## Working With Individuals

If you have some knowledge of how to effectively resolve conflict and a willingness to be proactive, you can use various effective strategies to develop better communication lines in the department. First, remember that conflict is natural and normal. There will always be some conflict. If you develop your skills in dealing with conflict, you will not want to avoid it at all costs. Most sport directors are nice people who hope in general to avoid conflict. Think of dealing with conflict as a role, however, one that you play just as you play the role of father, husband, or coach. When you look at resolving conflict as one of your roles, you will be able to step away from it personally. And the more practice you get at doing this, the more effective you will become at reaching solutions.

Conflict can be dealt with in positive or negative ways, and it is up to you to decide which path to take. Many sport directors are coaches or former coaches, and former athletes. We are very competitive by nature and experience. To resolve conflicts, however, we must fight the urge to win at all costs. The only time that anyone wins is when everyone wins.

You are responsible and can solve your own problems. Mentor coaches to be responsible as well and to solve their own problems. Recall the behaviors and skills that you must practice and avoid to help your mentee reach their full potential (see chapter 4).

It is also important that you separate the people from the problem. Be easy on the people—and go after the problem. Get all parties involved to promise that they will make things better. People sometimes dwell on blaming or punishing someone, on getting their just due or their vision of justice. The wish for due payment gets in the way of resolving conflicts.

In attempting to identify the problem, be an active listener. Clarify what you are hearing and repeat it back to help you and others reach the real issues. Do not be judgmental or critical of others—

Having sat in on many meetings to resolve conflicts with coaches and parents, I can tell you the biggest barrier is the inability to deal with the *issues* or problems, rather than with the people. We need to practice identifying the problem and not allowing the people involved (whom we may not like or whose beliefs we may not agree with) to get in the way of seeking solutions. Let's be honest. When a parent comes into your office and is upset, 9 times out of 10 he wants a "pound of flesh": the coach's job or at least that someone is reprimanded. That approach never works in the direction of agreeable solutions because it deals with people, rather than with issues or behaviors.

and ask the other parties in the conflict to do the same. When people are judgmental and critical, they prevent themselves from making things better and getting to agreeable solutions.

Someone greets you by saying, "You don't look well today. Are you sick?" Regardless of how you felt before hearing that comment, this person made a judgment about you that could easily ruin your day. Sometimes you make judgments about people without even being aware of doing so. Whenever you tell someone else how he feels, how she looks, how she behaves, or what he's thinking, you are being judgmental.

Brainstorm possible solutions. As the sport director you must mediate this aspect. Help people find solutions. Offer an apology if appropriate. Take notes and make a list.

Once the list is completed, evaluate the solutions. Pick one (or prioritize more than one) solution. Look for win-win solutions.

To implement the solutions be sure to determine the who, what, where, and when—so all parties are clear and "on the same page." This is an important step toward avoiding problems. You don't want any party coming back later and saying, "That was not what we agreed on." Be sure to follow up on what was agreed to. You do not want the process to break down because someone failed to follow through with responsibilities.

Perhaps the most important strategy bears repeating. Don't forget to deal with problems and behaviors, not people. If you focus on the people, you will find it difficult to find acceptable solutions.

## Using Listening Skills

Here are a few tips to help you be a better listener, an active listener. When you start becoming a better listener, you are on the road to solving problems and resolving conflicts.

- Concentrate and focus on the person with whom you are communicating. I personally have a difficult time talking with my wife when the television is on or I'm reading a book. I need to stop what I'm doing and focus on what messages she is sending me.

- Affirm or summarize the communications in total or by components. You might simply say, for example, " I want to make sure I can restate what you've said."

- If you're confronted, listen for the larger message rather than refuting small parts of it. If someone contends that you were 15 minutes late, for instance, don't argue that it has really been only 10 minutes. The larger message is your tardiness.

- Don't interrupt. Instead nod, affirm, take notes. Then ask the other person to do the same. Interrupting is rude, and it sends the message that you are not listening. It seems to imply that "I am right and you are wrong." Interruptions make it difficult to reach solutions.

- Respect your adversaries. No matter how you feel about them personally, you must demonstrate courtesy and acknowledge their opinions and their positions or authority.

## Characteristics of a Good Decision

Whether you are trying to resolve a group's or an individual's conflict, you can tell it is a good decision if these two main characteristics are true:

*The process takes into account relevant facts and uses them well.* How many times have you come to a decision only to find out later that you based the decision on information that was not true or not complete? Getting the complete story from all parties, asking questions to clarify parties' positions, and examining as many solutions as possible will help you reach more lasting resolutions.

*The decision has the commitment of those who will carry it out.* This decision must be win-win. Both parties must feel they gave up something but also gained something. If parties are not in agreement, it will be difficult (if not impossible) to gain the commitment to carry it out.

# INFORMAL OR FORMAL MEETINGS

When do you take the time to set up a formal meeting with coaches and parents? When do you take time to have only an informal meeting? Much of this will depend on your management style and what you and your staff feel most comfortable with. As a general rule, if the subject has to do with athletic department policies, impending or perceived crises, or disagreements, you should make every effort to schedule a formal meeting. At a formal meeting you have more control and can generate a calmer approach. The heat of the contest can be left outside the meeting. You can state ground rules and expectations at the beginning of the meeting.

Informal meetings occur spontaneously every day. For example, parents, athletes, and coaches stop by your office to ask a question, you talk with a parent at a contest about a booster project, or an athlete stops you in the hall to ask what the prerequisites are for trying out for a particular sport. You might call for a formal meeting after the chance, informal meeting to bring parties together to improve matters.

# FAIR TREATMENT

Sport directors must be fair in their personnel management and interactions. They need to be familiar with the 14th Amendment to the United States Constitution, Title IX of the Education Amendment of 1972, the concept of due process, and with fair disciplinary procedures.

# Equal Rights Protection and Title IX of the Education Amendment of 1972

Under the law, there is a clause in the 14th amendment that prohibits states from enacting laws that would deny any person equal protection under the law. Elements of the 14th amendment that are most important to our profession are contained in the following excerpt:

> No state shall make or enforce any law which shall abridge the privileges or immunities of citizens of the United States; nor shall any state deprive any person of life, liberty, or property without due process of law; nor deny to any person within its jurisdiction the equal protection of the law.

A legitimate challenge must show that a group of people is being treated differently than everyone else without justification. In other words, criteria would cover groups based on gender, race, and national origin.

Combine the equal rights protection with Title IX of the Education Amendment of 1972, which provides statutory authority for similar protection, and you have the basic power to enforce sexual discrimination claims. Title IX of the Education Amendment states:

> "No person in the United States shall, on the basis of sex, be excluded from participation in, be denied the benefit of, or be subject to discrimination under any education program or activity receiving Federal financial assistance."

The 14th Amendment protects groups such as females from being treated differently than the total population, and Title IX provides the authority to seek redress and even penalties if it is determined that an institution did discriminate against such groups.

Most state athletic and activity associations provide information to schools to help them evaluate equity issues in athletic departments. These are some of the areas that should be evaluated to determine that females (both employees and youth participants) are given equal opportunity and provisions:

- Selection of sports and levels of competition to effectively accommodate the interests and abilities of members of both sexes

- Equipment and supplies
- Scheduling of games and practice times
- Travel and per diem allowances
- Assignment and compensation of coaches and tutors
- Locker rooms and facilities for practice and competitions
- Medical and training facilities and services
- Housing and dining facilities and services
- Publicity

Be proactive in providing equal opportunity for all of your students. You can be proactive by evaluating your department and determining whether you are assuring males and females the same type of athletic program. An excellent resource that can guide you through a self-review is *Gender Equity in Interscholastic Athletics* by Dr. Deborah Moore, published by the Ohio High School Athletic Association in 1997.

## Due Process

Another major element of the 14th Amendment is its due process clause. There are two types of due process: substantive and procedural. *Substantive due process* limits the state regulatory powers by making sure that legislation bears a reasonable relationship to the purpose and is not arbitrary or capricious. This clause has received a lot of notoriety in Roe v Wade 1973, which protects a woman's right to terminate her pregnancy. *Procedural due process* is a clause that gives the individual the right to be heard. Here is where we, as sport directors and coaches, must be careful. This clause assures our athletes and our athletic personnel of fair treatment.

An athlete gets under the coach's skin at practice. The coach gets so upset that he yells at the athlete, "You are off the team; don't ever come back. I've had it with you." If this has happened in your athletic department, your coach obviously has never heard of procedural due process or doesn't understand it.

Understand that it is a privilege to be an athlete, and the courts are still supporting the fact that indi-

viduals do not have a right to be an athletic participant. But once you select a student athlete for your team, that athlete is guaranteed procedural due process before being removed. In the same way, personnel whom you evaluate and supervise are guaranteed the same protection.

## Disciplinary Process

Many times the sport director is involved in situations demanding that discipline be levied against a student, coach, or parent. The most common reasons for enforcing discipline procedures are these:

- Violation of an athletic department policy, such as training rules or school rules, or of an athletic conference policy.
- Violation of a team rule that is being contested.
- An athlete becomes ineligible academically.
- A parent violates sportsmanship expectations.
- A coach violates the contract or other athletic department or school board policies.

Regardless of the situation, when someone is being disciplined, you should call a formal meeting with all the parties involved. Due process procedures should always be followed to ensure that the party receiving the discipline has an opportunity to be heard and is treated fairly. You should be aware of these steps in following procedural due process. Individuals (student athletes and athletic department personnel) have a right to the following:

1. Being informed of all charges and complaints brought against them. If an athlete violated a training rule then you must at least verbally inform the student athlete.

2. Having a hearing. You may inform the student of the charges at this hearing. I suggest you invite the parents—if you don't, I'm sure you will hear from them later.

3. Securing counsel. The counsel may be a lawyer, the parents, a neighbor or a friend.

4. Adequate time to prepare to respond to the complaint. In your due process steps you should give a minimum of 24 hours (or whatever is agreeable between the two parties).

5. An opportunity to present their side of the issue. This is the main element in due process.

The point is that before you can remove an athlete or an employee, you must be fair and give the party an opportunity to respond to the allegations. (See box for an outline example of guidelines for disciplinary procedures.)

Nothing is more embarrassing or frustrating than having to inform a coach that he must reinstate an athlete until every step of the due process procedure has been followed. It is important to include the steps to due process in your athletic department handbook or policy book. Make sure you cover this procedure with all new coaches and support staff at the preseason orientation meeting. Consult with your school district's attorneys to be sure you include all the necessary steps in your due process procedure. Urge your staff to be sure to put decisions and actions in writing and distribute them to all involved parties.

Following due process guidelines is another way for your athletic department to show its professional foundation. Although it is a privilege to be selected as an athlete, once that individual is chosen for a team, the person does have the right to be treated fairly. As a sport director you should pledge to guar-

According to the athletic policy handbook for our department, a coach can remove an athlete from the team without notice for a 24-hour period. If the coach wants to remove the athlete from the team or suspend the athlete for a longer period of time he or she must do all of the following: inform the athlete and his parents within 24 hours of the emergency removal of a time and place for a hearing; hold a meeting to state the allegations being made against the party(ies) committing the violation; give the party the opportunity to explain his or her side of the story; make a decision about the removal or any other disciplinary action and ask if the party understands the action; give the party an opportunity to respond to the action; give the disciplined party options for recourse if they do not agree with the action; be sure to put the decision and action in writing and distribute it to all parties. For example, if the coach is conducting such a meeting she may tell the violating party that he can appeal to the sport director or the building principal.

antee due process to all of your participants, coaches, and support staff—granting them the protection they are afforded under the law.

*Summary*

In this chapter you learned that to communicate and resolve conflicts effectively, you should

1. pay special attention to the nonverbal and tonal components, both in sending and receiving messages;

2. use team and group meetings to reach decisions;

3. use listening skills to resolve conflict; and

4. learn the relevance of the 14th Amendment to the Constitution and Title IX of the Education Amendment of 1972 to your role as sport director, making sure to promote fairness, equal protection, and due process for constituent groups and equity for both genders.

# Chapter 6
## Selecting Staff and Evaluating People

Personnel problems are our thorniest issues to deal with, so it is imperative to begin with good staff. Unfortunately, many a sport director is strained for time when the season is about to start if he has not yet selected a coach or when the game is that night and she does not yet have an official scorer. Sometimes you must simply force yourself to take time, however, even if it means delaying the start of the season, so you can avoid selecting personnel who don't agree with your department's philosophy or understand its mission. If you make a mistake as you hurriedly scramble to find staff, you will find it then becomes too late to go back and do it right. You must not only make time to find good personnel, but develop your skill in assessing people's performances, both in interviews and on the job.

After you have selected staff, you owe it to them and the participants to help them grow and develop on the job. People are not static; in other words, they can change their beliefs and behaviors in positive ways. As the sport director *you* can make that happen by using evaluation tools that encourage staff members to grow.

In this chapter you will learn about these topics:

1. Recruiting, screening, and interviewing coaches and support staff.

2. Developing an evaluation plan for coaches and staff.

3. Informing staff of the evaluation process and setting time lines for implementing evaluations.

4. Suspending, releasing, and not retaining personnel when necessary.

# SELECTING STAFF

A major role the sport director plays is to recruit new head coaches, assistant coaches, and support staff. How well you perform in this role will affect how well your department can reach its program goals. Providing an outstanding interscholastic athletic program for the youth depends on having excellent personnel. Achieving an outstanding staff takes good judgment about people, good planning, and skill in eliciting from job applicants the information you need to find the best people to work with the youth and other personnel in your department.

## Announcing a Position Vacancy

Many states require that you first consider certified on-staff personnel when a vacancy occurs. It is a wise policy to post the coaching vacancies to certified personnel first. After all, they are trained to work with students, are easier for you to communicate with, and there is a better chance they will stay in coaching for a long time. Plus, your staff's morale stays higher when they know there is opportunity for advancement.

If there are not qualified certified staff, then solicit noncertified staff that are qualified candidates. If there are no qualified, noncertified candidates, you might advertise in area media for certified staff to become coaching candidates. You can accomplish this with a phone call to the local newspapers or community bulletin boards. If a certified teacher from a neighboring district does apply, give the sport director of that school district a call as well, to avoid potential hard feelings. You do not want people in a neighboring school district feeling that you are pirating their coaches.

You may want to call the sport director of a local college or university to obtain some referrals of potentially qualified students, athletes out of season, former athletes, or former college coaches. There may be other sport programs in your community (such as YMCAs, YWCAs, CYOs, elementary schools, or youth and recreation programs) that have coaches who, depending on the level of expertise required, could be successful at the interscholastic level.

Once these avenues have been thoroughly tested, then—and only then—you might go public to solicit coaching candidates. The best sources for advertising coaching vacancies are

- local newspapers,
- coaching associations,
- electronic bulletin boards,
- national coaching publications, and
- professional conferences or workshops.

When advertising coaching vacancies publicly, you probably will find it helpful to follow these tips:

1. Keep the advertisement short and to the point.

2. State the requirements (experience, qualifications, if there are teaching positions available, the area of certification you are seeking).

3. State how and where applicants should apply. Be sure to include an application deadline.

4. Whether you indicate salary is optional. You may want to delay discussing it until later (and in person).

5. You may want to mention that your school district is an "equal opportunity employer."

Remember, how you solicit vacancies will determine the number and quality of your applicants. Spending time on this phase of recruiting will make the task of final selection much easier.

# Screening Applications and Preparing for Interviews

After you have publicized and solicited candidates, you must have a screening process that will direct you toward the selection of a coach or other personnel. You may want to accept complete responsibility for screening applications, to work with your principal or personnel director, or to form a screening committee made up of coaches, parents, former athletes, administrators, and other stakeholders. How you handle this screening depends on the hiring responsibilities in your school district and the importance of the vacant position in the community.

Regardless of how you do the initial screening, remember to protect the confidentiality of the candidates. At this point in the process it is no one else's business who has applied. You certainly do not want any candidate to get in trouble at home for showing interest in the position. As the process nears completion, that issue will have to be dealt with.

There are five phases to the screening, and we will devote a section to each of them.

## 1. Evaluating Credentials

You first select the candidates to interview by evaluating the candidates' credentials (application, letters of recommendation, resumes, etc). Evaluating credentials will save you a lot of time later, especially if you have numerous applicants for the position. Form 6.1 is a typical coaching application form and form 6.2 is a review form and checklist to help evaluate candidates' applications and resumes. Note that the application form solicits only that information you feel is important to qualify this person as a *candidate*.

In evaluating applications and resumes you must decide if the candidates possess the requirements for the position (see form 6.2). If a candidate does not possess the requirements, there is no point in going further with the individual. At this point, you would no longer consider the person a candidate, but as a courtesy you should immediately send a letter thanking the candidate for taking time to apply and indicating that you are no longer considering this person a qualified candidate. An example of an appropriate rejection letter can be found in figure 6.1 .

## 2. Interviewing Candidates

Once you have screened out the candidates who do not possess the necessary qualifications for the position, you can determine the type of interview setting you will have for this particular coaching position. Interviewing can be one-to-one, two-to-one, or range up to a large, diverse committee of interviewers representing all segments of the school and community. Only you—with your principal—can determine the setting and number of interviewers for the particular coaching position. Traditionally, the more visible the sport is in the community, the greater the likelihood you have to form an interview committee. Here are a few tips for organizing and preparing an interview committee:

**Form a diverse committee.**   Make up the committee from all segments of the school and community. Some possible interviewers might include a building administrator, a teaching staff member, a male and a female coach, a parent of a past player in that sport, a former player in that sport, a respected official, or a former coach in that sport.

**Inform the committee about the candidates.**   By sending them applications and resumes in advance of the interview.

**Inform the committee of its role in the process.** You may find yourself writing memos and letters in connection with the selection process. You will find a few simple examples in figure 6.2 of letters that you may be responsible for writing. Usually the committee asks predetermined questions, which you and the principal can help them develop. Later you and the principal can use the feedback from the questions to rank the candidates. Make it clear that the final decision on which candidate to recommend to the board of education rests with the school administration. You should avoid giving that much responsibility to the interview committee.

The sport director and principal should rank the candidates (from most to least desirable) based on the qualifications, credentials, interviewers' feedback, and reference checks of the candidates. Before making an announcement or recommendation, it is important that you and the principal determine if the most desirable candidate is willing to accept the position if it is offered. If the most desirable

 **Form 6.1**

# COACHING APPLICATION FORM

1000 Burns Road, North Thoreau, IL 60999  (217) 987-6543

Please return form with teaching application or mail to the above address.

Date _____   Social Security No. _____

Name _____
|    Last    |    First    |    Middle or maiden name    |

Present address _____   Home phone ( ____ )_____

_____   Work phone ( ____ )_____
|    City    |    State    |    Zip    |

Sports and coaching level for which I would like to apply:

_____

Teaching certifications: _____

**Coaching experience** (list the most recent first)

| Sport | Employer/address | Phone | Direct supervisor |
|-------|------------------|-------|-------------------|
|       |                  |       |                   |
|       |                  |       |                   |
|       |                  |       |                   |

Have you ever been discharged or requested to resign from a coaching position?   ( ) No   ( ) Yes
If so, please explain _____

_____

Have you ever been convicted of a felony?   ( ) No   ( ) Yes

Please list your experience as a participant in organized sports:

| Sport | Level played | Honors, awards |
|-------|--------------|----------------|
|       |              |                |
|       |              |                |
|       |              |                |

Please list other significant experience relating to your application for a coaching position:

_____

_____

_____

_____

_____

_____

Please list 3 personal references (Name, Address, Phone Number):

_____

_____

_____

## Form 6.1 *(continued)*

Tell us your reasons for wanting to coach: _____

_____

_____

I hereby authorize the high school to obtain from my former employers all data needed to support this application. I certify that all the information on this application is true and complete to the best of my knowledge and I understand that any withholding or falsification of information on this application is grounds for dismissal.

| | |
|---|---|
| Applicant's signature | Date |

## Form 6.2

# RESUME REVIEW CHECKLIST

**Directions:** Check the appropriate rating to help you evaluate the quality of the coaching applicant in relation to the position you are seeking.

| Coaching qualification | Minimum requirement | Based on resume applicant | | |
|---|---|---|---|---|
| | | Is not qualified | Meets qualifications | Exceeds qualifications |
| 1. Minimum age to coach | 21 years | | | |
| 2. Experience necessary | 3 years | | | |
| 3. Playing experience | High School | | | |
| 4. Coaching education | ASEP Rookie | | | |
| 5. Specific gender | Female | | | |
| 6. State requirements | Sports-medicine CPR | | | |

7. Other:

Based on the evaluation of the resume this applicant does ___ does not ___ (check one) qualify for the coaching position.

candidate is unavailable or withdraws, then the second-most desirable one must be approached, and so on. If all qualified candidates turn out not to be available or withdraw, the process must start from the beginning. Do not accept a candidate who is not qualified just to fill the position; such a decision will more than likely come back to haunt you.

### 3. Evaluating Professional and Personal References

Evaluate the candidates also by checking references, both professional and personal. If the candidate does not provide professional references in a resume, then it is appropriate to ask for some. Keep in mind that these references are more than likely individuals who will point out only the positive aspects of the candidate. Regardless, you should prepare several questions that would indicate whether the candidate possesses the qualities you are looking for. Call the professional references and ask questions. Here are a few questions that you may ask a friendly reference:

- What are the candidate's strong and weak points as a coach? As a person?

- What kind of rapport does the candidate have with athletes, parents, officials, opposing coaches, and the sport director? How does the candidate demonstrate this rapport?

---

**Rejection Letter**

May 12, 1999

Prospective Basketball Coach
1 Basketball Lane
Basketball, U.S.A.

Dear Prospective Basketball Coach:

The Washington High School Athletic Department wants to thank you for taking the time to apply for the position of Boys' Basketball Coach. Thirty-two individuals have submitted information for our consideration.

A committee has interviewed four applicants who have certification in an area in which we have a teaching opening and have had at least four years of successful coaching experience.

We want to thank you for applying. Even though you were not selected for an interview, your qualifications are very good and will hopefully enable you to secure a head coaching position in the future.

Sincerely,

Tim Flannery, CAA
Athletic Director

TF:mao

---

**Figure 6.1**   Rejection letter.

- Has the coach ever demonstrated poor sportsmanship?

- What motivates the candidate to want to coach?

- What is the candidate's philosophy? Does she have a strong coaching philosophy that puts athletes first and winning second as demonstrated by the coach's behavior?

Do not rely solely on "friendly" references. As sport director you should follow up with personal references as well. These types of contacts tend to be more objective and therefore help you evaluate the true qualities of the candidate. Personal references might include, but not be limited to, the following:

- The sport director or head coach, principal, personnel director, or superintendent of the candidate's last coaching assignment

- A friend or professional acquaintance who worked with the candidate

- Coaches on your staff who have coached against or with the candidate

These are some questions you might ask the personal references:

1. Would you hire this person?

2. Should we continue our search for this position?

3. Would this candidate, in your opinion, be successful in our school district?

4. Can you compare this candidate with someone else whom we are both familiar with?

Take comprehensive notes of your conversations with references. These notes will come in handy when you're making your final recommendation.

### 4. Additional Job Requirements

After selecting the most desirable finalist, you must advise the individual of what requirements must be met before the person could be granted a contract and begin coaching. In other words, tell the person what prerequisites there are to begin coaching in your district. Some possible prerequisites are

---

**Personnel Letters**

---

To: Mary Thomas, Devon Jackson, and Cassandra Suarez
From: Kent Reel
Date: May 22, 1997
Re: Interview for the position of girls' tennis coach

Because we have several on staff who are interested in the Girls' Tennis coaching position, the athletic department will conduct interviews to determine the most qualified candidate. Please stop by to make an appointment with me by Tuesday, May 27. The interviews will be concluded by June 3, 1997. You should allow 15 to 30 minutes to answer several prepared questions.

After the interview we will make a recommendation to Dr. Harvey for the 1997 season. If you have any questions about this process please see me.

cc: Dr. Harvey

---

To: Head Football Coach Committee Members
From: Henry Woolsey
Date: February 8, 1995
Re: Head Football Coach

Thank you in advance for taking your valuable time to help us select our next head football coach. Your charge is to give important feedback to the administration to enable them to choose the best candidate for our athletes and our program.

It is imperative that you familiarize yourself with each candidate before the interview. Please read the packet of information very closely and make notes where appropriate. We want our next coach to exemplify all the characteristics necessary to be successful. We have enclosed

1. possible questions,
2. resume—support material supplied by candidate, and
3. characteristics sheet—to be used for your note taking.

If you have any questions, please contact the chairman of your committee, Phil Natividad, Principal Katie Patterson, or Athletic Director Tony Callihan. The high school and its athletic department are very appreciative of your efforts.

---

To: Charles Petit
From: Andrew Smith
Date: May 25, 1995
Re: John Doe and Jane Sunshine

John Doe has coached wrestling for the past two years. He is a state champ from St. Edward's and is certified in social studies (7-9) and history (9-12).

Jane Sunshine has coached track for the past two years. She could also coach basketball. Jane is certified in elementary physical education. She has taught one year in the parochial system.

Both of these individuals are outstanding young people, and they both have resumes on file in your office. Please allow them to interview if a position opens for which they are qualified. If there is anything else I can do to enable this to happen let me know.

cc: John Doe
     Jane Sunshine

---

**Figure 6.2**   Sample personnel letters.

- fingerprinting,
- a background check by the local or a federal law enforcement agency,
- completing a sports-medicine or first-aid workshop,
- completing a coaching education requirement from college or a qualified program (or the willingness to take coaching education within a specified period of time after the coaching assignment begins), and
- having had medical exams, tests, or vaccinations.

These prerequisites are referred to as the *self-selection process*. If the candidate does not have the time or the desire to achieve these prerequisites, then the person automatically excludes him- or herself from consideration. If this occurs, the sport director and principal must go to the next most desirable candidate.

> In Ohio a coach must have a valid CPR card and have taken a four-hour sports-medicine clinic approved by the State Department of Education. Our board of education requires a tuberculin test, fingerprint check, and criminal background test. Recently I informed a candidate that she was a finalist for a coaching position and of the requirements that must be met before she could coach in our school district. She looked at me as if to say, You must be kidding. She thanked me for my time and said she was no longer interested in the position because she didn't have the time to meet those requirements. I still don't know whether she was afraid of something or if she really didn't have the time.

### 5. Making the Final Recommendation

Working closely with the building principal, make your recommendation for employment or approval. After the applicants have been evaluated to determine who will be interviewed, the candidates interviewed, the professional and personal references checked, and the best available candidate has agreed to all the job prerequisites, it is time to make the final recommendation. Usually, the sport director recommends to the principal, the principal recom-

mends to the superintendent, and the superintendent recommends to the board of education. Regardless of the chain of command, the final authority will be the board of directors, board of trustees, or the governing body of the institution.

To make the task of recommending a candidate easier, it is advisable to include all of the information on the candidate that you have accumulated up to this time. The following information may be included with your recommendation:

- Application, resume, and any other information presented by the candidate
- Feedback from interview committee
- Notes on conversations with friendly and objective references
- A written statement or checklist of the candidate's willingness to present or perform the prerequisites of coaching.

# EVALUATING PERSONNEL

One of your primary roles is to evaluate staff. The more effective you are, the more influence you have on the quality of the athletic program. Many sport directors look at the evaluation function as an unpleasant task, but evaluation can be a very positive experience. It helps to keep this positive side in mind as you approach evaluations and the myriad procedures involved with them. Evaluation is a tool to improve quality for the students in the school district.

## Director's Role in Evaluating

Make no mistake about it—you must take a leadership position in developing a personnel evaluation system. However, there is nothing wrong (and lots right) with seeking advice from staff members you know who already do well in their positions.

Keep in mind that the athletic department's goals and objectives for coaching evaluation must be satisfied in the process. You should consider having the coach receive feedback from athletes and parents to be sure the objectives of the coach and the athletic department are being accomplished. When weaknesses are identified in the evaluation process, you should ensure developing a mutually agreed on strategy to strengthen the area and setting a reasonable time to improve. Then you must follow through as a supervisor by ensuring that the strategy is implemented.

## Using Evaluation Tools

Giving personnel input into the construction of evaluation instruments or forms allots them some ownership and diminishes their potential distrust or anxiety. A good evaluation system uses three main types of written tools. The first is checklists (called *summative tools*). Remember that summative tools are nothing more than checklists, which are useful in determining competencies in many areas. See examples of a few summative evaluation tools in the checklist for evaluating a head coach (form 6.3) and an assistant coach (form 6.4), as well as the general coaching checklist (form 6.5). Make checklists an important aspect of the evaluation system. Checklists enable the sport director to efficiently gain information on critical components of a staff member's role in working with young athletes, such as safety issues and coaching competence, or with other department personnel and office needs.

The second type of tool (called *formative tool*) in the case of evaluation uses goal-setting items. Formative tools are more open-ended questions, asking staff members to set specific goals and their own action plans to attain those goals (see an example of a formative evaluation tool for coaches in form 6.6). The formative tools do more to help staff grow and develop.

Still a different, third type of tool you must provide is a *timeline* for meetings, observations, and appraisals. You should discuss the timeline and have parties agree to it before the season begins. This evaluation timeline should be an agenda item at your coaching preseason meeting.

## Components of Evaluation

Evaluation procedures are usually most fully developed for coaches, but they may be adapted to other positions as well. These are the components you should consider including in your evaluation system for coaches and at least some other staff members:

1. A preseason meeting with each person to discuss the evaluation process.

2. A coach's or staff member's self-evaluation.

3. A head coach's role in evaluating assistant coaches and lower-level coaches; a staff member's (possibly a supervisor's) role in evaluating co-workers.

4. Players' feedback about coaches and perhaps other appropriate staff members.

5. Parents' feedback about the program.

6. Conveying feedback and expectations to returning personnel.

7. Procedures for releasing or not retaining personnel.

Some of these components will be discussed in more detail in the next few chapters, particularly for the coaches.

### Writing Out Goals

Be sure the staff member and you discuss written goals (formative tools) for the season. You can help the employee by being sure the goals are measurable and attainable. Winning a specific number of games or titles is not within the control of the coach or players, for example, and should never be accepted as a goal for the season. Goals should focus on skill improvement, the work ethic, and citizenship skills, such as sportsmanship. Remind people that these goals will be revisited at the end of the season.

### Conveying Feedback

Your evaluation checklists should be developed with the help of experienced, successful staff members. The checklists should enable you to communicate how strong or weak a department member is in particular job skills and duties. The form should be to the point and easy to fill out. The instrument should allow you the ability to give written feedback on the areas that need improvement, but also the areas in which the employee is performing extremely well. If you or the employee identify weaknesses, then suggestions for improvement should be made.

## Retaining and Releasing Personnel

If you are going to recommend this staff member for the next season and you have pointed out areas that need improvement, then you must also take time

 **Form 6.3**

# HEAD COACH EVALUATION FORM

Sport: _____    Evaluator: _____

Coach: _____    Date: _____

1 = Effective        2 = Needs improvement        3 = Unsatisfactory        4 = Unable to observe

| | 1 | 2 | 3 | 4 |
|---|---|---|---|---|
| **A. Professional and personal relations** | | | | |
| 1. Rapport with players | | | | |
| 2. Rapport with coaches | | | | |
| 3. Rapport with parents | | | | |
| 4. Rapport with athletic director | | | | |
| 5. Appropriate dress at practice and games | | | | |
| 6. Public perception | | | | |
| 7. Public relations with media | | | | |
| 8. Sideline conduct at games | | | | |
| 9. Commands respect by example in appearance, behavior, and language | | | | |
| 10. Upholds athletic department policies, rules, and regulations | | | | |
| 11. Is open and receptive to constructive criticism | | | | |
| 12. Implements recommended changes | | | | |
| 13. Adheres to stated procedures and chain of command | | | | |
| 14. Develops and distributes an appropriate program philosophy | | | | |
| 15. Demonstrates the implementation of the program philosophy | | | | |
| **B. Coaching performance** | | | | |
| 1. Thorough knowledge of his/her sport | | | | |
| 2. Prompt in attendance at practice, games, and meetings | | | | |
| 3. Exercises self-control | | | | |
| 4. Is innovative; uses new coaching techniques and ideas when appropriate | | | | |
| 5. Keeps abreast of new trends in his/her sport or particular area | | | | |
| 6. Shows poise | | | | |
| 7. Supervision of athletes in the locker room and training room | | | | |
| 8. Practice and game organization | | | | |
| 9. Teaching performance on the athletic field | | | | |
| 10. Has developed a system and a philosophy and has implemented it in various levels of our program | | | | |
| 11. Has performed satisfactorily the duties contained within the job description | | | | |

| | | | | |
|---|---|---|---|---|
| 12. Has promoted the concepts and values of citizenship/sportsmanship | | | | |
| **C. Coaching responsibilities** | | | | |
| 1. Compliance with meeting deadlines | | | | |
| a. Equipment inventory | | | | |
| b. End-of-season reports | | | | |
| c. Eligibility lists | | | | |
| d. Team rosters | | | | |
| e. Physical cards/emergency medical | | | | |
| f. Program information | | | | |
| 2. Care of equipment and facilities | | | | |
| a. Issue and storage | | | | |
| b. Organization of storage areas | | | | |
| c. Removal of equipment from lockers at the conclusion of the season | | | | |
| 3. Knowledge of state eligibility rules and sport rule changes | | | | |
| 4. Attendance at state-sponsored rules interpretation meeting in his/her sport | | | | |
| 5. Discipline and control of athletes at games and practice sessions | | | | |

| Coach's record | Overall | S.W.C. | S.W.C. Place | Tournament |
|---|---|---|---|---|
| 1997-98 | | | | |
| 1996-97 | | | | |
| 1995-96 | | | | |
| 1994-95 | | | | |
| Overall | | | | |

Comments:

Athletic director's signature: _____ Date _____

Coach's signature: _____ Date _____

**Circle one:**

Effective:            To be recommended for continued assignment.

Needs improvement:   To be recommended for reassignment provided an understanding can be reached in areas where improvement is suggested.

Unsatisfactory:       Not to be recommended for continued assignment.

 **Form 6.4**

# ASSISTANT COACH EVALUATION FORM

Sport: _____    Head coach: _____

Assistant coach: _____    Date: _____

1 = Effective          2 = Needs improvement          3 = Unsatisfactory          4 = Unable to observe

|  | 1 | 2 | 3 | 4 |
|---|---|---|---|---|
| Position: |  |  |  |  |
| 1.  Loyalty to head coach |  |  |  |  |
| 2.  Follows the chain of command |  |  |  |  |
| 3.  Knowledge of sport |  |  |  |  |
| 4.  Teaching ability |  |  |  |  |
| 5.  Ability to motivate |  |  |  |  |
| 6.  Rapport between coach and players |  |  |  |  |
| 7.  Intensity of interest in coaching this sport |  |  |  |  |
| 8.  Supervision of players in locker room and other areas |  |  |  |  |
| 9.  Rapport between coach and rest of coaching staff |  |  |  |  |
| 10.  Accepts duties given by head coach |  |  |  |  |

11.  General evaluation of this coach (narrative).    Years experience in this position.

12.  Comments:

Head coach's signature: _____    Date _____

Athletic director's signature: _____    Date _____

Coach's signature: _____    Date _____

**Circle one:**

Effective:              To be recommended for continued assignment.

Needs improvement:      To be recommended for reassignment provided an understanding can be reached in areas where improvement is suggested.

Unsatisfactory:         Not to be recommended for continued assignment.

**Form 6.5**

# COACHING EVALUATION FORM

**Directions:**

A. Rate each item under the major heading based on the following scale: 5 = Excellent, 4 = Good, 3 = Acceptable, 2 = Needs improvement, 1 = Unsatisfactory, N/O = No opportunity to observe, N/A = Not applicable.

B. Total the score and divide by the number of items under the major heading. If you use either N/A or N/O for any item in a category, subtract that item from the total and then divide to obtain the average.

C. Record the overall rating score under the evaluation summary.

D. Comments must be made for any item given a rating of needs improvement or unsatisfactory. Comments for outstanding performance are encouraged.

**Communications:**

_____ 1. Maintains open communication lines with athletes, parents, officials, coaches, etc.

_____ 2. Submits reports on time.

_____ 3. Keeps the athletic director informed about the sport.

_____ 4. Communicates recruitment, tryouts, and selection procedures to students and parents in advance.

_____ 5. Communicates with parents during the season.

_____ 6. Develops a rapport with fellow coaches, athletes, parents, and administrators.

_____ 7. Clearly communicates athletic department goals and objectives to student athletes.

_____ Total divided by 7 = ☐

**Knowledge of sport:**

_____ 1. Is familiar with the fundamental philosophy, skills, and techniques to be taught in that particular sport.

_____ 2. Uses a variety of methods to teach, analyze, and correct skills.

_____ 3. Demonstrates a working knowledge of the sport.

_____ 4. Remains current in knowledge and techniques of the sport.

_____ 5. Applies knowledge of sport when developing workouts or practices.

_____ Total divided by 5 = ☐

**Methods and organization:**

_____ 1. Has activities planned and organized.

_____ 2. Provides positive feedback to each athlete.

_____ 3. Clearly states goals and objectives.

_____ 4. Is prompt in meeting the team for practices and contests.

_____ 5. Provides proper supervision and administration of locker and training room before and after practices or contests.

_____ 6. Demonstrates care of equipment, uniforms, and facilities.

_____ 7. Adheres to the regulations relative to bus trips.

_____ Total divided by 7 = ☐

**Used for evaluation of head coaches with assistants only:**

_____ 1. Establishes the fundamental philosophy, skills, and techniques to be taught by staff. Designs conferences, clinics, and staff meetings to ensure staff awareness of overall program.

_____ 2. Trains and informs staff; encourages professional growth by attending clinics, coaches association meetings, etc.

*(continued)*

# ◤◣ Form 6.5 *(continued)*

_____ 3. Delegates specific duties, supervises implementation, and analyzes staff effectiveness and gives feedback to athletic director on all assistants.

_____ Total divided by 3 = [       ]

**Motivation:**

_____ 1. Provides positive feedback to each athlete.

_____ 2. Exhibits a positive attitude.

_____ 3. Deals with athletes in a positive manner.

_____ 4. Makes individuals feel they are an important part of the team.

_____ 5. Encourages a maximum effort from each athlete.

_____ 6. Uses good team discipline and control (respect not fear).

_____ Total divided by 6 = [       ]

**Professional, ethical, and personal behavior:**

_____ 1. Sets a good example for athletes to follow.

_____ 2. Is cooperative with game officials and those responsible for the operation of the contest.

_____ 3. Exhibits self-discipline.

_____ 4. Exercises leadership power appropriately.

_____ 5. Demonstrates honesty and integrity.

_____ 6. Develops rapport with athletic coaching staff.

_____ 7. Upholds OHSAA, league, department, and school policies, rules, and regulations.

_____ 8. Has good relationship with personnel from other schools.

_____ Total divided by 8 = [       ]

**Evaluation summary:**

| | Average points | *Can best be described as |
|---|---|---|
| Communication | _____ | _____ |
| Knowledge of sport | _____ | _____ |
| Methods and organization | _____ | _____ |
| Methods and organization (head coaches section) | _____ | _____ |
| Motivation | _____ | _____ |
| Professional, ethical, and personal behavior | _____ | _____ |
| Total | _____ | _____ |

*The coaches evaluation can best be described as (check one: excellent, good, acceptable, needs improvement, unsatisfactory).

**Specific strengths:** _____

_____

_____

**Specific recommendations:** _____

_____

_____

Evaluator's signature _____ Date _____

 **Form 6.6**

# GOAL-IDENTIFICATION FORM

Name _____ Date _____

You play a vital role in our athletic program's ability to develop athletes to their greatest potential. At the same time, we believe that our program should place you in a position that encourages and assists you in growing professionally. To ensure that we take the steps necessary to promote your professional growth, we would like you to answer the following questions, which will help you set goals for the coming year.

As you think about your goals, consider areas of your performance that you would like to strengthen as well as areas you would like to learn more about. Once you have completed the form, we will meet to discuss your goals and how we can work together to reach them.

**First step:  Identify areas of professional growth.**

List at least three areas of your professional responsibilities that you would like to improve during the course of the coming year. The following are sample responses that might be appropriate for coaches: motivating athletes, zone defense, parent involvement, community involvement.

1. _____
2. _____
3. _____
4. _____

**Second step:  Identify specific goal statements.**

Examine each of the areas you identified in the first step, and use the space below to rephrase each of your responses in the form of a goal. The more specific you can make your goal statements now, the easier it will be to judge your achievements. For example, if you had written "motivating athletes" on the first line, you might write the following goal statement on the first line below: "to motivate athletes to give 100% effort in every practice." What are your goals?

1. _____
2. _____
3. _____
4. _____

**Third step:  Identify actions to take in pursuit of goals.**

For each of the goals you have written in the second step, list two specific actions you will take to reach your goals. For the example given in the second step, you might list these actions: Action 1, "Read a book about motivating athletes;" Action 2, Observe Coach Rodriguez's practices." What actions might you take to reach your goals?

First goal: _____

Action 1: _____

Action 2: _____

Second goal: _____

Action 1: _____

Action 2: _____

Third goal: _____

Action 1: _____

Action 2: _____

Fourth goal: _____

Action 1: _____

Action 2: _____

to allow the individual to discuss the suggestions you made on the evaluation. The likelihood of improvement will be greatly increased if the person agrees with your suggestions or is permitted to make his or her own suggestions. It would be appropriate at this time to indicate whether the areas of weakness are major or minor. That is, if particular weaknesses do not improve, will the individual be in jeopardy of being released the next season?

School districts may have various expectations about how personnel are informed of being recommended for a position, retained for the next season, released for the next season, or disciplined. Sport directors in multischool districts are usually responsible for all the correspondence about such notifications. Directors of single schools will have more varied responsibilities. Some athletic departments don't have any responsibilities in these matters, for example, the responsibility instead shifting to principals or personnel directors. Other departments may have the responsibility for all matters, just as the sport director has in the multischool districts.

Releasing an employee is different from not retaining them. We might consider releasing or suspending a coach, for example, during the season or abruptly should any of the following conditions exist:

- The person is a physical danger to the athletes or him- or herself.

- Evidence of a felony is presented.

- The person knowingly violates athletic or board policies after previous violations have occurred.

With any of these occurrences you should *consider suspending the individual with pay* until an investigation can be conducted. Be sure to familiarize yourself with due process to be able to handle the situation fairly. You should consider the following courses of action if you or your department is made aware of any serious violations that a department employee commits:

- Ask questions of those making any serious allegation to obtain as much information as possible. Write the information down so you don't lose or forget any facts.

- Inform the building principal and superintendent. It will be their responsibility to inform the board of education.

- If the situation warrants it (e.g., sexual imposition or abuse with athletes), solicit the help of the local police department.

- Determine if questions should be asked of anyone else who might have knowledge about the allegations. You might consider asking questions of those who are directly involved in the situation or who might have special knowledge of the situation, such as the board of education's lawyers.

- Call a meeting as soon as possible, after information is gathered, with the individual in question, his or her counsel, the principal, the board of education counsel, and anyone else suggested by the lawyers.

- Follow due process steps with regard to informing the individual of the charges, allowing the person to respond to the charges, and informing the employee of the right to appeal your decision if he or she disagrees.

- Be sure to take notes along the way, and save the notes and any written communications in case of future lawsuits.

Not retaining a personnel member for the next season is an altogether different situation than releasing an individual. If the evaluation process is working properly, the person should realize long before your telling him or her that things are not working out. Every employee has weaknesses, but the reality is that most staff members, such as coaches, possess strengths that far outweigh their weaknesses. When someone has a preponderance of weaknesses or doesn't seem able to improve in key job skills after much help and support from the sport director, then it is time to prepare the person for the inevitable.

We should consider not retaining a staff member if the following conditions exist:

- Weaknesses, which have been pointed out in the evaluation process, are not improved after a strong effort has been exerted to suggest ways to improve on the weakness.

- The person puts winning and selfish goals before important goals of the program.

- The person refuses to improve in significant job competencies or to adhere to the philosophy of the athletic program.

- The person exhibits inappropriate behavior in the presence of students.

- The person does not perform his or her legal duties and exposes him- or herself and the school district to lawsuits.

Always keep in your mind that the student athletes must come first. Personnel must understand and practice the job skills and philosophies that help students develop physically, psychologically, or socially. Hopefully, coaches and other personnel that you recruit and recommend understand and put into practice the philosophy that your athletic program subscribes to. And usually personnel work out well in their positions if you have been careful in the selection and evaluation processes.

***Summary***

In chapter 6 you learned to

1. recruit coaches and staff from within the department and by using the media and other sources;

2. screen applicants, interview them carefully, review their references with probing questions, and come to a final selection;

3. lead in developing and implementing an evaluation process;

4. use both summative and formative tools, as well as players' and parents' feedback, in the evaluation process;

5. understand how releasing, suspending, and not retaining personnel are distinct and to pursue each course when appropriate and necessary; and

6. follow fair procedures for retaining, suspending, releasing, or not retaining personnel.

# Part III

## Management Skills

# Chapter 7
## Setting the Tone for Sport Participants

At the center of any school athletic program are the student athletes. You should design your program so that the primary focus is on the student athletes, with all other aspects of the program growing from that focus. The sport director of a single school, with an office located in the building, will have a tremendous amount of contact with student athletes, interacting over such topics as eligibility, discipline, extrinsic motivation, recognition, and just plain getting to know them. Such a sport director will see and communicate with students during the day, at practices and games, and also at other school activities (dances, plays, musicals, etc.) In

multischool districts, however, the amount of contact is much more limited because the sport director's office is usually located at a central office building away from the school.

Various levels exist in an interscholastic program, and as students progress through the program, your expectations for them change. The higher the level of program, the greater the commitment and skill development that are required to participate.

In assessing your department's offerings for student athletes, you should have a broad-based program that meets the students' interests and needs. An interscholastic athletic program permits student athletes to develop skills and grow as individuals. Middle school teams are traditionally maintained at grade level: for example, a school will field a seventh-grade-only girls' basketball team. This limits who can play on the team and the level of competition the team faces.

Keep safety, skill level, and maturity level as the main focuses. Lower-level teams introduce skills and begin creating an understanding of the positive values of commitment. Some of the appropriate concepts that are taught at these early levels are the value of daily practices, appropriate physical conditioning, and a healthy, balanced diet. From these lower teams, in which maximum participation is encouraged, the program grows to an advanced level. The transition begins when student athletes move from grade-level teams, such as a freshman team, to skill-levels teams, such as a junior varsity team on which athletes from more than one grade level can participate. The skill-level teams focus more on skill development and commitment from the student athletes.

In this chapter, you will learn about these topics:

1. How important it is to supervise participants and staff.

2. How to monitor student academic progress.

3. At what level to resolve conflicts among students.

4. How to meet participants' needs.

5. What you need in a code of conduct and how to implement the code.

# YOUR RESPONSIBILITIES TO THE STUDENTS

You oversee all areas of the athletic program and have the responsibility of seeing that policy is being followed in all aspects of the program. You also are responsible for ensuring that participants are receiving quality coaching, using safe facilities, and using equipment that meets all recommended safety standards. With the enforcement of policy it is nec-

essary for the sport director to be aware of potential litigious situations as they relate to policy development and implementation. Appropriate policies should be in place to ensure proper program implementation. You should also have policies in place to address such concerns as hazing, youngsters' disabilities (consider the ADA), and equitable opportunities (consider Title IX). These should all appear in a department handbook that is distributed to each student in the school.

If any player is not following the approved program policy, it is the sport director's responsibility to take appropriate action to ensure compliance. It is important to understand that if a policy exists, it is your responsibility to see that the policy is enforced. If the policy does not accomplish what it was intended to accomplish, change the policy. *Do not ignore the policy.*

The board of education has a policy that anyone who rides school transportation to a contest must return by that same transportation. The conference track meet is scheduled for the same day as the state band contest. Sally is the top 100-meter sprinter in the conference—and first-chair flute in the band. She can't get to both events riding the same transportation. Sally is going to have to make a choice.

It is also important to make sure all participants are aware of and knowledgeable about the athletic department's philosophy, objectives, and expectations. Many schools give student athletes a folder or handbook with this information, along with illustrations of team mascots, policies, and schedules, and other reminders. Such printed materials might follow these typical outlines:

• Cover, containing mascot, school name, motto, and perhaps the names of sports and coaches

• Athletic department philosophy, goals, and objectives

• Code of conduct and participant responsibilities

• Definition of sportsmanship

• Rules of attendance and participation; schedule conflicts

- A calendar of contests; addresses of and directions to other "competitor" schools
- Academic eligibility
- Other rules on eligibility, including age, residency, and physical examinations
- Rules on alcohol, steroids, or other substance abuse
- Discipline procedures
- Policies about equipment, travel, dress, college recruitment
- Awards and varsity letter requirements

# PARTICIPANTS' RESPONSIBILITIES

Participants must accept the responsibility that comes with being a part of a sport program. As participants, athletes must meet their responsibilities to *continue* to participate. You should provide the participants with discussion in a program handbook (see the sample in figure 7.1) that outlines the philosophy and expectations of the program. You might develop specific flyers for particular sports that discuss philosophy and expectations. Figure 7.2 shows an example developed for cheerleaders.

There should also be communication from the coach to the players. The coach must let players know what he or she expects from each participant, as well as the coaching philosophy. This information should be shared not only with the participants but also with their parents to ensure open communication and understanding among all involved.

Certain areas are typically considered to be the responsibility of the participants, although these may vary from area to area. Examples of some of the participants' possible responsibilities include

- meeting attendance requirements at school and practice,
- fulfilling academic requirements,
- maintaining appropriate behavior,
- notifying the involved parties of a schedule conflict (having a game or practice the same time as a band concert),
- carrying out the participant's role on the team, and

- maintaining good nutrition, getting enough rest and exercise, and staying healthy.

By the coach and you clearly defining the responsibilities of the student athlete, the participant, parent, and coach all will have the increased likelihood of successful experiences during the season.

# ACHIEVING ACTIVE PARTICIPATION

Communicating opportunities and a welcoming atmosphere are crucial to running a successful program. As part of setting a welcoming tone, coaches should get to know the students personally so they can evaluate the needs of the individual students who are already involved or interested in becoming involved in their programs.

If students do not want to be part of a sport program, the sport director must take the initiative to determine why. You can do this by interviewing students or by using surveys. Surveys can be helpful to determine student interest and in your addressing Title IX concerns. A potential participant who does not feel welcome or comfortable in the environment that the team or program offers is unlikely to take the risk of participating.

## Recruiting

In announcing team tryouts or signups, you and the coach must use all the means you have available. For example, these are vehicles you probably have available for announcing tryouts or signups:

- Public address announcements at school
- Public address announcements at contests
- Newspaper advertisements (including school newspapers)
- Local radio or school radio spot announcements
- Local-access television stations

When you make the announcements, there is basic information you should be sure to include for those who might be interested in trying out or signing up to be a participant:

### Athletic Department Goal and Objectives

**Our goal**—The student athlete shall become a more effective citizen in a democratic society.

**Our specific objectives**—The student athlete shall learn teamwork. To work with others in a democratic society a person must develop self-discipline, respect for authority, the spirit of hard work and sacrifice, and to place the team and its objectives higher than personal desires.

1. To be successful.   Our society is very competitive. We do not always win, but we succeed when we continually strive to do so. You can learn to accept defeat only by striving to win with earnest dedication. Develop a desire to excel.

2. Sportsmanship.   To accept success and defeat like a true sportsman, knowing we have done our best, we must learn to treat others as we would have others treat us. We need to develop desirable social traits, including emotional control, honesty, cooperation, and dependability.

3. To improve.   Continual improvement is essential to good citizenship. As an athlete, you must establish a goal and you must constantly try to reach that goal. Try to better yourself in the skills involved and in those characteristics set forth as being desirable.

4. Enjoy athletics.   We acknowledge the personal rewards we derive from athletics and strive to give sufficiently of ourselves in order to preserve and improve the program.

5. To develop desirable personal health habits.   To be an active, contributing citizen, it is important to obtain and maintain a high degree of physical fitness through exercise and good health habits.

### Responsibilities of a High School Athlete

Being a member of an athletic team fulfills an early ambition for many students. The attainment of this goal carries with it certain traditions and responsibilities. A great athletic tradition is not built overnight. It takes the hard work of many people over many years. As a member of an interscholastic squad, you have inherited a wonderful tradition—a tradition you are challenged to uphold.

Our tradition has been to win with honor. We desire to win but only with honor to our athletes, our school, and our community. Such a tradition is worthy of the best efforts for all concerned. Over many years our squads have achieved more than their share of league and tournament championships. Many individuals have set records and won all-state, all-conference, and all-American honors.

It will not be easy to contribute to such a great athletic tradition. To compete for your school may mean that you will have to say **"no"** to pleasures an athlete cannot afford. When you wear the colors of your school, we expect that you not only understand our traditions but also are willing to assume the responsibilities that go with them.

### Responsibilities to Yourself

The most important of these responsibilities is to broaden yourself and develop strength of character. You owe it to yourself to get the greatest possible good from your high school experiences. Your studies and participation in other extracurricular activities as well as in sports prepare you for your life as an adult.

### Responsibilities to Your School

Another responsibility you assume as a squad member is to your school. Jefferson cannot maintain its position as an outstanding school unless you do your best in whatever activity you wish to engage. By participating in athletics to the maximum of your ability, you are contributing to the reputation of your school.

You assume a leadership role when you are on an athletic squad. The student body, our community, and other communities judge our school by our conduct and attitudes both on and off the field. Because of this community pride, make Jefferson proud of you and your community proud of your school by your faithful exemplification of these ideas.

### Responsibilities to Others

As a squad member, you also bear a responsibility to your home. If you never give your parents anything to be ashamed of, you will have measured up to the ideal. When you know in your heart that you have lived up to all of the training rules, that you have practiced to the best of your ability every day, and that you have played the game "all out," you gain self-respect and your family can be justly proud of you.

*(continued)*

**Figure 7.1**  Sample philosophy and expectations.

## Conduct of an Athlete

The conduct of an athlete is closely observed in many areas of life. It is important that your behavior be above reproach in all of the following areas:

**On the field**—A real athlete does not use profanity or illegal tactics, and learns fast that losing is part of the game. You should be gracious in defeat and modest in victory. It is always courteous to congratulate the opponent on a well-played game after the contest, whether in defeat or victory.

**In the classroom**—A good athlete becomes a good student. A person cannot be a classroom laggard and think he or she can be an outstanding athlete. If you are lazy in class, you will be lazy on the practice field or floor and will never reach your full potential. As an athlete, you must plan your schedule so that you give sufficient time and energy to your studies and achieve acceptable grades.

In addition to maintaining good scholarship, an athlete should give respectful attention to classroom activities and show respect for other students and faculty at all times. Horseplay and unnecessary boisterousness are not approved habits of behavior.

A healthy athlete should have a good attendance record. Never cut classes or school.

The way we act and look at school is of great importance. Athletes should be leaders, and fellow students should respect and follow them.

**Figure 7.1**   *(continued)*

## (Your School) Cheerleader Philosophy

The primary goal of cheerleading is to develop the sportsmanlike support for athletic teams in the school setting. When we enter competitive events we strive to win; this is why athletes spend hours of their time practicing and why coaches provide knowledge and skills to help achieve that goal. Team unity is a vital component of our program.

Winning is not our only goal, nor is it the measure of a successful program. Win or lose, building character in each of our players is the ultimate goal of our program because character extends beyond the field or court and into everyday life. There are three major areas that cheerleaders can experience personal growth through participation in athletics.

### Self-Development

Cheerleaders gain confidence from continuing to improve and eventually mastering each skill. Cheerleaders learn how to encourage and work together with other members of the team, even if they are not friends away from school. Cheerleaders learn to be responsible by attending practice, being on time, and maintaining good academic standing. Cheerleaders must be accountable for their behavior in and out of school. Performing skills incorrectly, not giving 100 percent, and violating team rules are detrimental not only to the individual but the entire team.

### Overcoming Adversity

If athletics teaches us nothing else, it teaches us that life is not fair. Many decisions do not go our way, and a cheerleader's response to these situations can either push a team toward success or guarantee its failure. You can try hard or quit. You can make your teammates better or complain about decisions that did not go your way. Learning to respond positively will help you to overcome adverse situations in athletics, academics, and in future life.

### Keeping Failure in Perspective

Most teams will not win state championships. Every cheerleader, no matter what the skill level, will make mistakes. It seems that failure is inevitable. Yet most athletes choose to continue competing and practicing rather than to quit. They refuse to become complacent or drown in self-pity. By keeping failure in perspective, they have learned to reflect, not dwell, on mistakes and to evaluate—win or lose—the successfulness of each performance.

It is the coaches' desire to build a successful cheerleading program. It is also our desire to help our athletes develop qualities that will enable them to achieve success, not only in sport but in future endeavors as well.

**Figure 7.2a**   Philosophy for cheerleaders.

---

## Cheerleader Expectations

There are five major characteristics that we expect our cheerleaders to strive for and improve upon: academic excellence, commitment, teamwork, team pride, and self-discipline.

### Academic Excellence

We expect our athletes to pursue academic excellence. Education, not cheerleading, will be the driving force in determining the future success of the individual. We expect our athletes to inform us if they are having difficulties in any of their classes so that we can work with them to improve their academic standing.

### Commitment

We expect our athletes to be committed to cheerleading. This may involve some sacrifice of time away from other activities, such as a job or a vacation. This commitment is necessary for the athlete to improve her skills. Commitment means coming to all practices, arriving on time, and being dressed appropriately.

### Teamwork

Cheerleaders are expected to work together as a team. We are one team composed of cheerleaders with varying skill levels. It is expected that everyone will support each other.

### Team Pride

We expect our cheerleaders to display a positive attitude. This includes practicing good sportsmanship at all times. You represent not only our school but our community. You also represent your parents, coaches, teams, and most importantly yourselves. We expect you therefore, to demonstrate pride and self-respect in and out of school. Appropriate behavior is required on the bus traveling to and from events. Interactions with all opposing coaches, cheerleaders, fans, and judges will occur in a respectful manner.

### Self-Discipline

We expect athletes to practice self-discipline. This includes following all school and team rules. Self-control must be exhibited in emotional situations. Cheerleaders must apply themselves and work hard to continually improve skills in season and out.

---

**Figure 7.2b**   Expectations of cheerleaders.

- The name of the team that is announcing the tryout (for example, varsity girls' basketball)
- The name of a contact person
- A phone number for the contact person
- The time of the initial meeting
- The location of the initial meeting

### Sample Announcement

The Bay High School girls' basketball team will be holding a meeting for all girls interested in participating in basketball in the upcoming school year. The meeting will be held at 3:30 P.M. in the west gym bleachers. If you have any questions about the meeting, please contact Coach Smith at 555-5555.

It is also important to know the audience to whom the announcement is being made. If there are ethnic groups in your community that speak English as a second language, it may be wise to publish your announcement in the appropriate languages for the various ethnic groups. By communicating openly and, when appropriate, in the participants' first language, you create a feeling of trust. This is an initial motivator in getting potential participants in place.

## Motivating

In the initial meeting coaches should take the opportunity to explain the value of participation. You might help coaches formulate a list of benefits if they haven't done so already. Participants in the sport program, for example,

- develop relationships with teammates,
- do better academically, in general, than do nonparticipants,
- have fewer behavioral problems, in general, than do nonparticipants
- miss less school, in general, than do nonparticipants, and
- have fun, develop physical skills, and augment social skills.

# BALANCING ATHLETICS, ACADEMICS, AND OTHER ACTIVITIES

It is important that all parties involved in the sport program recognize that academics provide greater opportunities in life than athletics will. As we know from reviewing information developed by the National Federation of State High School Associations, the number of students choosing to participate in sport is increasing. That means that your monitoring the academic progress of student athletes becomes an ever-larger task simply because of the increase in the volume of students. Therefore it is important for you to use the available resources efficiently and effectively to address the academic progress students make. The resources include people—counselors, teachers, parents, and tutors.

## Monitoring Academic Progress

In using resources for review, it is important that you understand what standards are being used to monitor the student athlete. Most state high school athletic associations maintain a minimum academic standard for student participation. Many local school districts have additional requirements for students to meet. You must be familiar with all standards that affect the student athletes. If there is a question, you should contact the high school athletic association as well as the appropriate person in your district for establishing academic standards among student athletes.

An important key to monitoring academic progress is to communicate to participants, coaches, and parents what the standards are in your particu-

lar district and state association. It is also helpful to explain who will monitor student progress. This may vary from school to school. In some schools coaches monitor their students, whereas in others the sport director may have a formal program in place. This information should be readily available to the community and frequently published.

## Preparing for the Future

In addition to the academic standards that are required at the state and local level for participation, there are also standards that should be understood if a student is interested in competing at the collegiate level. Many resources are available, and as the sport director you should make this information available. You should communicate to coaches what is available and work with them to ensure students and parents have access to the information. The National Interscholastic Athletic Administrators Association publishes the *Guide for College-Bound Students*, which is updated yearly. It outlines recruiting rules for colleges, the questions prospective students should ask, and even study habits. It clearly states the criteria to be eligible for college athletics, from the NCAA Division I to national junior colleges. It describes the NCAA Clearinghouse for prospective college athletes, and the booklet contains information students can use to deal with college coaches.

# CODE OF CONDUCT

Young people involved in sport programs need to understand the rules and expectations that govern their participation. And they want to know that these rules and expectations are applied equitably and consistently. A *code of conduct* should exist in all sport programs. The code of conduct (see sample in figure 7.3) clearly establishes and communicates policies and procedures for participation.

## Procedures for Retaining and Suspending Participants

Within the code of conduct there should be a procedure for denying participation. That suspension procedure should include the following:

---

**Student Activity Code for High School**

### I. Definition

This code is applicable to students in any elective student activity. An elective student activity is any activity that meets, performs, or practices at times other than, or in addition to, the regular school day and school year. Activities that are required as a part of the regular school curriculum are excluded.

### II. Philosophy

We believe that elective school activities make school life richer and more rewarding and that adherence to certain behavior codes enhances an individual's pattern of living.

While students have no absolute rights or requirement to participate in elective student activities, including athletic and other extracurricular programs, it is a privilege encouraged by the school system and the community.

We believe that the harmful effects of chemical use are well documented. The dangers of chemical use are taught throughout the health courses in our schools and this behavior is consistent with our district's philosophy and curriculum.

### III. Activity Behavior Code

During the school year, defined to include all vacations, and the duration of the activity (which may include summer vacation), no student at any time or in any location, shall

a. possess, use, sell, offer to sell, deliver, conceal, consume, or be under the influence of any drugs of abuse, including alcoholic beverages or any counterfeit drugs of abuse;

b. instigate or conspire with others to sell, deliver, conceal, consume, or be under the influence of any drugs of abuse, including alcoholic beverages or any counterfeit drugs of abuse;

c. use, conceal, sell, purchase, accept, or transmit any substances reasonably thought to be drugs of abuse, sold as drugs of abuse, or inferred by the seller or buyer to be mind-altering substances or drugs of abuse;

d. possess, use, transmit, or conceal any item designed for use with illegal cannabis or drugs of abuse;

e. violate any federal, state, or municipal law or ordinance governing conduct not described in paragraph a through d above where the student should have reason to understand that such violation has or is likely to have a negative impact on the school or the school community;

f. possess, conceal, sell, transmit, or use tobacco in any form, or conspire with others to conceal, sell, transmit, or use tobacco in any form on school property or while in attendance at a school-sponsored or school-related activity;

g. be suspended from school, assigned to in-school suspension, or be expelled from school for violation of the Student Discipline Code (5130).

### IV. Disciplinary Action

a. For activities that have a schedule of public playing dates or activities, a first violation of the Student Activity Code will result in removal from participation in 20 percent of the next scheduled public playing dates or activities. For activities that do not normally have a schedule of public playing dates or activities, a first violation of the Student Activity Code will result in removal from participation in the equivalent of 20 percent of the next scheduled activities, publications, events, or meetings, such equivalent to be determined by the advisor of the activity and the assistant principal.

b. A second violation during any school year will result in the removal of the student from participation in all extracurricular activities for the balance of that semester and the loss of the right to receive any awards that might result from the student's prior participation.

c. A third violation during any school year will result in the student's exclusion from participation in any school activities for the remainder of the school year.

*(continued)*

**Figure 7.3** Code of conduct.

## V. Students Voluntarily Seeking Help

A student who voluntarily seeks help with any situation covered by this code prior to the imposition of any discipline under the schedule set forth above, at the discretion of the assistant principal may be excused from full imposition of discipline, provided that the student voluntarily and fully participates to the satisfaction of the assistant principal in a program designed to help the student avoid such situations in the future. A current list of available programs will be given to each student found in violation of this behavior code.

## VI. Procedure for Implementation of Discipline

a. Any participant in an extracurricular activity, including athletics, who is suspected of violating the Student Activity Code will be given written notice of the suspected violation and afforded the opportunity for a meeting with the head coach or advisor of the activity. In that meeting the student will have a chance to respond to the charges. If the student admits a violation of the Student Activity Code, the coach or advisor, in accordance with the schedule set forth above, shall inform the student of the voluntary help options and of the duration of the participation exclusion should the student refuse to seek such help.

b. If the student denies a violation of the Student Activity Code, he or she shall be afforded the opportunity for a hearing before a Review Board. The Review Board shall consist of the assistant principal, the athletic director, and one other faculty member appointed by the principal. The assistant principal shall arrange for a hearing to be conducted within no more than two school days of the meeting with the coach or advisor. The student is entitled to be accompanied by his or her parent or guardian at the hearing. The Review Board will consider arguments made on behalf of the student as well as evidence which supports the discipline. The decision of the Review Board shall be made in writing to the student and his or her parents within 72 hours of the hearing.

c. Any student may appeal a decision of the Review Board to the principal within five school days of receipt of its decision. The principal shall meet with the student, his or her parents or guardian, and the coach or adviser and make a decision based upon the information presented. The principal may affirm, reverse, or modify the ruling of the Review Board. The principal shall inform the student and parents or guardian of the decision in writing within 72 hours of the hearing.

### Risk of Participation

All athletes and their parents must realize the risk of serious injury that may be a result of athletic participation. The school district will use the following safeguards to make every effort to eliminate injury:

1. Maintain a continuing education program for coaches to learn the most up-to-date techniques and skills to be taught in their sport.
2. Instruct all athletes about the danger of participation in the particular sport.
3. Conduct a preseason parent/athlete meeting prior to the start of the season to fully explain the athletic policies and to advise, caution, and warn parents/athletes of the potential for injury.
4. Maintain safe equipment and facilities.

**Figure 7.3** *(continued)*

- Notification of the participant.
- Notification of the participant's parent or guardian
- Explanation for the denial of participation.
- Opportunity for the participant to explain his or her side.
- Opportunity for appeal of the decision to deny participation.

All sport directors should be sure they check with their legal advisors to ensure due process is allowed where necessary.

## Keeping Records

It is valuable for coaches to maintain information in regard to students. Coaches should keep statistical information that may be used later in college recruiting or for league honors. It is also necessary, for awards purposes primarily, that the sport director maintain a student file. In addition, you should keep records, as mentioned earlier, of a student's medical history as it relates to athletics.

# RECOGNIZING PARTICIPANTS' NEEDS

Too often coaches do not assess or consider the needs of sport participants. Young athletes have important needs, however, when they come to us. In a quality program the students' needs come first. These are common aspirations and needs that student athletes experience: to be part of a team, to be recognized, to feel good about themselves, to be better athletes, perhaps to be involved in an activity to get into West Point or some other institution, to learn the skills necessary to be an outstanding citizen in our society. Student athletes need to develop physically, psychologically, and emotionally.

## Quality Coaching and Environment

The most important contact in any sport program is that between the coach and the player. As the sport director, you must ensure the validity of that relationship. You can do this by hiring qualified, competent coaches who have demonstrated the professionalism necessary to be successful with young people in the sport program. This begins by your understanding what credentials are necessary for the coach to be successful. Long gone are the days when coaches were expected to roll the ball out on the court and let the kids play. Coaches today must be trained in a wide variety of areas, from first aid to child abuse.

## Opportunities for Community Service

Community service is an excellent way for young people to grow and develop dramatically in a short time. It is a mentoring device that allows coaches to expose their players to real-life situations, where the youth can use skills they learn in sport. Student athletes are often asked to support community ac-

tivities. This is an opportunity for them to reach out to the community and demonstrate appreciation for the support the community has given the team and the sport program. Some philanthropic projects that sport participants become involved with include

- giving blood,
- recycling,
- community reading programs,
- coaching youth teams,
- construction for Habitat for Humanity,
- working with the elderly,
- mentoring elementary or middle school students,
- collecting food and clothing for the needy,
- mowing lawns or raking leaves for those that cannot, and
- painting a house or garage that needs it.

## Safe Environment

One of the largest areas of litigation in sport programs is over the negligence of coaches, sport directors, and school districts with regard to unsafe facilities, fields, or equipment. Earlier we mentioned that sport directors and coaches have the responsibility to provide a safe environment to athletic participants. Some people raise their hands and ask, "How can I ensure that all fields, facilities, and equipment are safe?" The truth is that you and your coaches have an obligation to provide a safe environment. Your attention to this important standard will make sport safe for young people. Choose to look at this and all your legal duties as positive standards that make sport safer for young people.

Prior to each season you and the coach for each sport should conduct a facility check of equipment, fields, and any other areas that the team will use. You want to guarantee that participants will have a safe and secure environment in which to participate. If a problem is discovered, you should immediately forward a written report to the appropriate individual in the district to correct the problem. In many instances problems can be anticipated and planned for, and a proactive position is the best position for a sport program.

You must also be open with participants and par-

## Form 7.1

# BASKETBALL END-OF-SEASON EVALUATION

Please answer all questions honestly and fairly.

I. Rank players in order. (Best player = 1, second best = 2, etc.)

| | |
|---|---|
| 1. | 8. |
| 2. | 9. |
| 3. | 10. |
| 4. | 11. |
| 5. | 12. |
| 6. | 13. |
| 7. | |

II. Awards. (Vote for the player most deserving of each award. You may *not* vote for yourself.)

   a. MVP Award (most valuable player):

   b. Carl Weir Award (person who puts most time and effort into improving):

   c. Captain's Award (person you'd want to represent the team):

   d. Best defensive player:

   e. Coaches' Award (person who does little things to make team better):

   f. Sportsmanship Award:

III. Questions

   a. Do you think you were well-prepared as a team for games? Explain.

   b. As a team we shot poorly this season. What can we do to improve shooting?

   c. Do you think off-season activities were helpful for our program? (Open gym, team competition, summer league, weight room) Why or why not?

   d. As a team we had difficulty thinking through basketball situations. What can be done to improve this?

   e. What suggestions do you have to improve the basketball program?

   f. What needs to be done by the players to make our program competitive again? Explain.

   g. After Christmas break (17 days off) we played 5 games in 10 days. Do you think this needs to be corrected? Explain.

   h. Add any comments needed to be made about anything in the program:

ents about the risks of playing sports. Although a coach can do his or her utmost to supervise practices and games, the use of equipment in good condition, and a safe playing field, injuries still occur on occasion. Students must also be alert to their keeping in good condition and using common sense in their participation, all the while realizing that injury is a possibility.

## Awards Program

In assessing a sport awards program you should review certain basic requirements. First, all participants should be recognized. Second, the awards format should be progressive. The recognition should be based on longevity and skill. An awards program may follow this sample sequence:

1. First-level award   Certificate
2. Second-level award   Chenille letter
3. Third-level award   Sport pin
4. Fourth-level award   Plaque

Within the awards program special awards can be developed. These special awards can promote individual accomplishment or recognize outstanding behavior. Some schools have numerous awards for various sports. These are a few types of special awards that many schools present:

- Most Valuable Player
- Outstanding Defensive Player
- Sportsmanship Award

Some schools give participants a part in recognizing their peers. Form 7.1 shows an example of a questionnaire you might use to solicit feedback from the athletes on both on how they thought the season went and how their colleagues performed.

*Summary*

In this chapter you learned to

1. identify many of your responsibilities to sport participants;

2. prevent (or resolve when necessary) conflict with the use of such tools as a student code of conduct; and

3. recognize the students' needs for quality coaching, community service projects, a safe environment, and recognition through awards and other means.

# Chapter 8
# Mentoring Coaches

Coaches are vital to the athletic department's ability to reach its stated objectives. This chapter will describe the responsibilities and relationship of coaches and sport directors, and it will provide many forms to assist you in the performance of your personnel duties. As sport director you should adopt a mentoring attitude toward the coaches in the athletic department, helping create an atmosphere in which coaches can become the best that they are capable of.

In chapter 8 you will learn about these topics:

1. What responsibilities the sport director and coach have in complying with department policies regarding supervision; how the mentoring role is appropriate with coaches.

2. How to recruit qualified coaches to your program.

3. How to develop an effective coaching education program to assist coaches do their best for the good of the student athletes.

4. What records to keep for coaches.

5. How to evaluate coaches in order to improve their effectiveness.

6. How to help motivate coaches and recognize them for a job well done.

7. How to determine which coaches should be retained or released.

# SPORT DIRECTOR'S RESPONSIBILITIES TO COACHES

The sport director is responsible for coordinating all aspects of personnel management among the coaching staff. These tasks represent your key responsibilities with coaches:

- Recruiting competent coaches and educating them in the mission, objectives, and policies of the sport program.

- Providing professional information to them and guidelines for safety, legal responsibilities, conduct, and effective communication.

- Establishing a recognition system to motivate coaches to be effective with student athletes.

- Developing an evaluation system to improve coaching effectiveness.

- Establishing guidelines and policies for retaining and releasing coaches.

The role that you play is as important as the responsibilities you perform. Some people think a sport director should be all things to all people. This perception is wrong and should be discounted immediately. Your main role is to implement an athletic program that follows the policies of the athletic department in an effort to accomplish the mission and objectives of the program. In your interactions with coaches you are primarily a mentor (see chapter 4).

To mentor coaches effectively you should convey a genuine caring attitude, an attitude of wanting the coach to be successful in accomplishing the program's objectives. This attitude helps you to provide the necessary support a coach needs to be successful. You want to be an *active listener*. Coaches benefit by your listening—and giving feedback that you are listening and understanding their problems. They do not need you to give them advice on how to solve their problems, even though at times they might ask for your advice. By giving advice you become responsible for their problems. Coaches must learn to solve their own problems if they are to become effective coaches.

Develop strategies for coaches to solve their own problems. If you criticize a coach, no matter how you sugarcoat it, you will put the coach on the defensive and lessen your ability to help him or her improve. Develop an approach that uses nonjudg-

mental language and allows the coach to deal with his or her own behavior—rather than having the coach angry with you for criticism.

> Here are some statements and questions that are not judgmental. Your using them allows coaches to deal with their own behaviors.
>
> - "I understand that you used strong language with the official last night. What did you say? Do you feel it was appropriate? How does your language last night qualify you for your role as a model for the players? How else might you have handled that situation?"
>
> - "Inventorying uniforms is your responsibility, and there are still 10 players who have not turned theirs in. What are you planning to do to retrieve those uniforms by Friday?"
>
> - "Tell me what happened with Mr. Smith last night after practice."
>
> - "I understand the bus was late last night for the game with Bay. Tell me how you handled the situation. Was your behavior appropriate? Why?"
>
> - "You changed the home baseball game with Amherst to an away game and did not inform our office. We did not order a bus, the parents were not informed, our trainer was waiting at the field with the officials we contracted, the local newspaper was at our field to do a story on the game, and maintenance personnel prepared the field for a game that wasn't played. We cannot tolerate not being informed. We are all part of the athletic department team. We succeed and fail together. Do you want to be part of the team? To us you are an important part of the team. Let's go on from here, and remember that you are part of a team that relies on your doing your part."

You should and can provide information, however, and explore options with your coaches. You must keep up to date about where coaches can get information to help them solve their problems. Familiarize yourself with publications and other resources that coaches can go to for help in solving their problems or getting answers to their questions. Help coaches explore options, such as brainstorming solutions.

Coaches are the most important group you deal with directly, and you must be available to them. If your leadership style is cooperative, you might feel comfortable with an open-door policy. If an appointment is necessary, be sure your coaches understand that expectation. Stay open-minded to coaches' needs, provide encouragement when coaches are having difficulties, provide emotional support when problems arise, and follow through on commitments you make to them.

To mentor effectively you must not place yourself above the coach. Let coaches explain their needs, and be willing to switch roles at times. In other words, the coach may possess skills or values that *you* can benefit from. Your relationship is a two-way street; you both can benefit from it. You want to help coaches reach their full potential. A good relationship, developed through the mentoring approach, often permits you and the coach to overcome roadblocks and unlock potential.

The Socratic method of questioning is an excellent mentoring tool. It enables you to help coaches by *not* giving advice. A number of years ago one of my best coaches informed me that he was not going to return to coaching because the parents were too demanding, the amount of time was too much, and on and on and on. Not wanting to lose one of our best coaches, I felt that I had to convince him to stay. Instead, however, I did two things. First, I listened with empathy and agreed with the way he was feeling. Then I asked him a number of questions to get him to think about why he went into coaching in the first place: What do you like about being with the kids? What were the great moments you had in coaching? Where are kids going to learn commitment, teamwork, and responsibility, if not from you? Are other coaches having the same types of concerns? Who can handle these kinds of problems better than you? I asked him to take a few weeks and think about the answers to these questions. Needless to say, he decided to stay with coaching because that is where he belonged. He was too good to leave the kids, who needed him.

## Assisting Coaches in Following Policies

Once your organization's leaders and you create the policies for the athletic department, it is imperative that you *explain these policies* and assure that the coaching staff understands them. The coaches will be responsible for conveying the policies to and enforcing them among their teams.

It is important that you *meet with the entire coaching staff at least once a year*. In addition, you should *meet individually with each coach before, during, and after the season*. The preseason meeting for parents and athletes is the appropriate time to go over the athletic department's policies. You may want to distribute copies of guidelines on safety, communication with parents, or other coaching responsibilities (see example in figure 8.1). Give the coach time at that meeting to also indicate the *team's policies*. The discussion should center on the purpose of the policies as they implement the athletic department's overall philosophy, and it should include how violations of policy are to be handled (i.e., their consequences). You must take the time with the coaching staff to be sure each member understands and knows how to convey these messages to parents and athletes.

A good brochure for new coaches includes a mission statement; the athletic department's goals and objectives; the coaches' responsibilities before, during, and after the season; coaching expectations; a list of the legal duties coaches have; and a preseason meeting agenda. See appendix C for a sample of this brochure.

## Orientation for New Coaches

Spend extra time with first-year coaches. You want to make sure new coaches get off on the right foot. Before the first practice at the beginning of each season, conduct a one-hour, in-service meeting for all new coaches about athletic policies. You should meet with the coach to identify their coaching responsibilities and go over the athletic department's expectations for conduct. This meeting will get you and the new coach off to a positive start and ensure that the coach is aware of department policies and expectations. Don't forget the brochure for new coaches to bring them up to speed regarding philosophy, goals, objectives, coaching expectations, legal duties, and the preseason meeting agenda. The detailed job description, including its listing of coaching responsibilities, can be a good starting

---

**Coaches' Safety Checklist**

---

Prior to each practice, game, or organized activity all coaches, assistant coaches, and others in charge of an activity should develop the habit of a safety check.

Coaches must go to games and practices thinking about safety.

The season includes practices, games, playoffs, and tournaments. Coaches will average 7 to 8 hours per week with the team or about 192 hours per year. The coach has care, custody, and control of someone else's child and has the moral and legal obligation to see that the safety of each player is part of the everyday routine.

**Emergency plan**

____ Locate nearest telephone.

____ Find ambulance facilities.

____ Know location of nearest health care facility.

**Field conditions**

____ Goal posts anchored?

____ Edges rounded on goal posts?

____ Posts welded properly?

____ Glass and foreign objects removed from field?

____ Sprinkler heads seated properly?

____ Corner markers covered?

____ Cracks filled in field?

____ Playing area free of ruts or hills?

____ Benches and stands set back from field?

____ Restraining line 3 feet from touchline for spectators?

**Medical information**

____ Know special needs of players.

____ Obtain authorization to have player treated.

____ Insist on having parent's group health information.

**Schedule**

____ Practice begins.

____ Practice ends.

____ Arrange for supervision of players without rides.

____ Arrange supervision prior to practice.

____ Arrive early enough to police fields.

____ Supervise locker rooms before and after practice.

**Team conditions**

____ Train and warm up properly.

____ Prohibit unacceptable activities or behaviors (rowdiness).

____ Place players of similar ability, size, and age together.

**Equipment**

____ Covered shin guards on each player.

____ Jewelry removed.

____ Shoes adequate for conditions.

____ Ball in good condition.

**Weather**

____ High winds (suspend activity if over 30 m.p.h.).

____ Approaching rain or thunderstorms (suspend activity).

____ Lightning is seen (suspend activity).

____ Heat: light clothing, water (consider changing time of activity or suspend activity).

____ Cold: proper dress (same as heat).

**Coach's kit**

____ First aid.

____ Emergency medical forms.

____ Parents' phone numbers.

**Coach**

____ Understand the rules of the game.

____ Understand the role of the referee and linesmen.

____ Communicate the rules clearly to players.

____ Attend coaching clinics (CPR and sports medicine as required by state department of education).

____ Have balanced attitude—athletes first, winning second.

**Parents**

____ Communicate with parent, especially after injuries.

____ Let parent know schedule of games and practices.

____ Recruit their help in supervision.

____ Discuss your philosophies with parents.

**Tournaments and travel**

____ Are drivers aware of liabilities and responsibilities?

____ Have small adult-to-player ratio.

____ Plan out all activities.

____ Pack medical cards for emergency.

____ Understand medical and liability policies.

____ Know your legal and moral responsibilities.

*(continued)*

**Figure 8.1** Coaches' safety checklist.

**Negligence and a coach's legal duties**

The risks of the game (called inherent risks) are acceptable as long as a coach acts prudently and the inherent risks are known, appreciated, understood, and consciously accepted by the participants.

**Negligence**

Failing to act in a manner in which a reasonable and prudent coach would normally act in a similar situation.

**Four factors in determining negligence**

(All four must be present to prove negligence.)

1. The presence of a duty: Do you owe the player a duty or duties?
2. Breaching the duty: Failing to act necessarily or acting wrongly in the performance of a duty.
3. Cause of the injury: Your breach of duty?
4. Extent of injuries.

**Legal defense**

(When charged with negligence there are defenses.)

1. Assumption of risk: Players must know, understand, and appreciate those risks. You must tell them.
2. Contributory negligence: The player acted negligently and contributed to the injury.
3. Comparative negligence: Negligence of both parties compared on a percentage basis.
4. Other defenses: Act of God or technical defenses.

**Ten legal duties of a coach**

1. Adequate supervision: General and specific to the game.
2. Sound planning: Progress of skills is essential.
3. Plan instructions and drills. Don't move too rapidly by forcing improvement.
4. Inherent risks: Repeat warnings to player and parents of dangerous risks and dangerous techniques.
5. Safe playing environment.
6. Provide safe field, gym, or equipment.
7. Evaluating athlete's disabilities: Evaluate player's injuries and incapacities to determine limits of participation. This includes mental, physical, and even child-abuse situations.
8. Matching or equating opponents: Match to size, age, and physical ability. More body contact requires closer attention.
9. Emergency first-aid procedures: Establish procedures for an emergency. Where is help and a phone? Don't assist in first aid unless qualified.
10. Keep accurate records, especially in case of injuries.

Respect the civil rights of your players on and off the field. Consider the factors of the game as it relates to officials and spectators. Be aware of problems concerning transportation. Carry adequate personal liability insurance. Accepting money for transportation sometimes voids personal auto liability insurance.

**Figure 8.1**   *(continued)*

point for discussion when you meet with the coach (see figure 8.2).

This meeting is also the time to go over athletic department expectations for coaches' conduct. In figure 8.3 you can examine a sample code of conduct for coaches to follow.

A good supplement to the code of conduct for coaches is the NFICA Code of Ethics (see figure 8.4). Spend time on each point, making sure the coach understands all of them. Be sure to give the coach a copy of both codes. It is not a bad idea to

have the coach *sign* a copy of the codes to keep on file. This confirms to the coach that you regard these codes as truly important.

## COACHES' RESPONSIBILITIES

Coaching responsibilities vary from school district to school district. What you as sport director expect

**Coaching Duties and Responsibilities**

**Qualifications**—Please check appropriate line(s) below.

\_\_\_\_ Have valid state teaching certification in _____.

\_\_\_\_ Employed in school district.

\_\_\_\_ ASEP/NFICEP–certified.

\_\_\_\_ Years of coaching experience.

**Professional**

1. Know the game and be able to instruct participants in fundamental skills and strategies.
2. Know league, state, and national regulations for the particular sport.
3. Pursue knowledge that is sport-specific or related to skills of coaching.
4. Join coach organizations at local, state, and national level to improve professionally and to recognize student athletes. Attend clinics and conferences.

**Personal**

1. Assure that students receive instruction to enable them to improve physically, psychologically, and socially.
2. Become a role model for student athletes both in and out of the school setting and promote good citizenship. Treat students with respect. Be positive with players.
3. Remind athletes of the importance of grades.

**School-Related**

1. Maintain accurate records of physicals, insurance forms, medical emergency forms, parent consent forms (warning of risk of participation), etc.
2. Be supportive of other school teams, programs, and activities, both outwardly and behind the scenes.

**Community**

1. Maintain two-way communication with media, booster club, parents, and officials.
2. Become a positive and visible force in the community.
3. Promote your sport within the community.

**Administrative**

1. Submit budgets, rosters, physical cards, transportation requests, and awards to sport director on time.
2. Maintain a written inventory of all uniforms and equipment.
3. Report all injuries to the sport director; do not allow injured athletes who are under the care of a doctor to participate without a release.
4. Meet with sport director to be evaluated.
5. Supervise athletes both on the playing field and in the locker room.
6. Be knowledgeable about due process and use it to discipline athletes or when it is necessary to remove athletes from the team.
7. Document any unusual event, such as vandalism, an angry parent, or suspension.

**Other**

1. Always do what is in the best interest of the athletes.
2. Insist on integrity from athletes.
3. Coaches will take an active part in preventing the use of drugs, alcohol, and tobacco.

**Figure 8.2**   Sample coaching responsibilities.

---

**Coaches' Code of Conduct**

---

Coaches are role models and mentors for student athletes in the school setting. The school district and athletic department expect coaches to adhere to the following code of conduct:

1. Model positive and appropriate language and behavior at all times, especially when dealing with young people.
2. Abide by all rules, guidelines, and policies of the board of education, athletic department, National Federation sport's rules, and Southwestern Conference League.
3. Practice the skills of an effective mentor to provide student athletes the opportunity to develop physically, psychologically, and emotionally and reach their full potential as athletes and people.
4. Respect and treat students as you would want people to treat you and members of your family.
5. Put the health and safety of each team member ahead of anything else. Make decisions that protect young people.
6. Communicate with athletes and parents the philosophy and expectations of the team and the athletic department throughout the season. Adhere to the communication guidelines as set forth by the athletic department and insist that parents do the same.
7. Promote academic excellence in the school setting and monitor athletes' grades for eligibility purposes. Work with other staff members on behalf of the student athletes to help make them better students.
8. Encourage student athlete to fulfill family responsibilities, community service projects, and responsibilities in other school activities.
9. Work in the best interest of the student athletes to resolve conflicts that arise with other student activities (e.g., band trips, school dances, community service projects).
10. Model behavior and make decisions in the best interests of student athletes based on our motto, "**Athletes first, winning second**."

**Figure 8.3** Coaches' code of conduct.

of your coaches probably depends on the size of the school, whether you work in a single-school or multiple-school district, and what has been the tradition of the particular sport.

Just as you wear many hats and coordinate many groups of people, so do your interscholastic coaches. Encourage coaches to adopt a mentoring attitude with their constituents. Coaches must effectively communicate and coordinate with

- the sport director;
- the student athletes on their teams;
- the parents of the student athletes and the adults in the booster organizations;
- the support staff, including bus drivers, custodians, an athletic department secretary, contest supervisors, scorers, timers, and statisticians; and
- the school's administrative staff, certified staff, noncertified staff, and the student body.

Let's examine the key responsibilities coaches have with each group of their constituents.

## Sport Directors

A coach has many responsibilities to the sport director. Here are some of the main ones.

**Report information to the sport director.** A coach must keep you informed about the team and program in many key areas. This information will help you compile programs, eligibility lists, recognition-night material, directions to contests, and rosters, and to keep data on hand for opposing schools and the news media. All this information must be given to the sport director before the first contest, and a coach should update it during the season. (Note also that athletes must turn in copies of sport physicals and emergency medical forms before the first practice.) These are the key items of information a coach should forward to the sport director to keep you abreast of the program:

- Names, jersey numbers, grade, and other vital information of team members
- A list of student athletes who have proper physicals and emergency medical forms

---

### Coaches' Code of Ethics

---

**National Federation of Interscholastic Coaches Association**

The function of a coach is to educate students through participation in interscholastic competition. An interscholastic program should be designed to enhance academic achievement and should never interfere with opportunities for academic success. Each student athlete should be treated as though he or she were the coaches' own, and his or her welfare should be uppermost at all times. Accordingly, the following guidelines for coaches have been adopted by the NFICA Board of Directors.

**The coach** shall be aware that he or she has a tremendous influence, for either good or ill, on the education of the student athlete and, thus, shall never place the value of winning above the value of instilling the highest ideals of character.

**The coach** shall uphold the honor and dignity of the profession. In all personal contact with student athletes, officials, athletic directors, school administrators, the state high school athletic association, the media, and the public, the coach shall strive to set an example of the highest ethical and moral conduct.

**The coach** shall take an active role in the prevention of drug, alcohol, and tobacco abuse.

**The coach** shall avoid the use of alcohol and tobacco products when in contact with players.

**The coach** shall promote the entire interscholastic program of the school and direct his or her program in harmony with the total school program.

**The coach** shall master the contest rules and shall teach them to his or her team members. The coach shall not seek an advantage by circumvention of the spirit or letter of the rules.

**The coach** shall exert his or her influence to enhance sportsmanship by spectators, both directly and by working closely with cheerleaders, pep club sponsors, booster clubs, and administrators.

**The coach** shall respect and support contest officials. The coach shall not indulge in conduct which would incite players or spectators against the officials. Public criticism of officials or players is unethical.

**Before and after contests,** coaches for the competing teams should meet and exchange cordial greetings to set the correct tone for the event.

**A coach** shall not exert pressure on faculty members to give student athletes special consideration.

**A coach** shall not scout opponents by any means other than those adopted by the league and/or state high school athletic association.

---

**Figure 8.4** Coaches' code of ethics. (Used with permission from the NFHS.)

- Transportation request forms to all away contests

- Names of athletes who have quit, moved away, or joined the team after the start of the season

- An inventory of equipment and uniforms and where they are stored in the off-season

- A list of home and away scrimmages

- Names of videographers, statisticians, scorers, announcers, and timers for the game program

- Notification of equipment or facilities that need repair or to be replaced

- Names of student athletes who are being removed from the team for rule violations (re-

member to follow the steps of due process when removing team members)

- Names of student athletes and the awards they earned during the season

**Use evaluations to improve as a coach.** A second area of responsibility the coach has is to use the evaluation process to become a more effective coach for the good of the student athletes in the program.

**Seek help when appropriate to resolve problems.** When problems with players or parents occur, the coach should use the sport director as a sounding board.

**Recommend other coaches for employment.** A coach should inform you of possible assistant coaches and lower-level coaches to consider for employment.

**Inform you of practice schedules and contest schedules.**   You may find yourself fielding questions about personnel or participants, and you must know how practices are scheduled and what people are where at given times. Sport directors get too many phone calls from parents confused as to the time practice starts and ends. Remind coaches, too, that they lose credibility when they tell parents practice ends at 5 P.M. and they don't let the athletes go until 5:30 P.M.

**Meet on a consistent basis** (at least weekly) to update you on the day-to-day concerns of the program.

## Student Athletes

Coaches have many responsibilities to the athletes on their teams. They will be most effective with student athletes by modeling the ASEP philosophy "Athletes First, Winning Second." We also believe that our most effective coaches are *mentors* to the student athletes they coach. Coaches who mentor go beyond the contractual obligation of coaching. Our best coaches make coaching a labor of love. Mentors make the most of teachable moments to help players become better citizens in society. These are other key responsibilities and legal duties coaches have to student athletes:

**Instruction of sport skills.**   Sport skills should be planned properly and taught in a progression from simple to complex.

**Ensuring a safe environment.**   Inspect facilities and equipment daily for practices and contests. Match athletes by size and ability, especially in contact sports or sports where balls are thrown or caught.

**Familiarity with first aid.**   Coaches must ensure that the young athletes are being supervised by an adult who knows what to do if an injury occurs.

**Providing emergency medical treatment to an injured athlete.**   If a student is injured during participation, the coach has a legal duty to help. Coaches are usually the first to respond to injured athletes, and it would be wise to plan ahead for emergencies by having a fully stocked medical kit, a phone nearby, and a plan to contact professional emergency personnel if a serious injury occurs.

**Evaluating athletes for injury or incapacity.**   A coach must be able to handle three situations: making sure an athlete is in good enough health to play the sport, determining if illness or injury will prohibit an athlete from playing in practice or contests, and making sure that athletes are healthy enough to return to play after illness or injury.

**Supervising all athletic activities.**   These include practices, contests, and the locker room, where coaches must ensure athletes are safe and are not involved in horseplay.

**Warning athletes and their parents of the risks involved in playing sport.**   Coaches should warn the athletes verbally and in writing that playing sports can cause serious injury and even death.

Keep in mind these are not just key responsibilities of coaches to athletes but also *legal duties* they have in interscholastic programs. In other words, if coaches are not prepared for these situations and do not act in a prudent manner, they may be found negligent in their duty. In cases where negligence is charged, not only will the coach be sued but also the sport director, principal, superintendent, and, most likely, the board of education. With this in mind, sport directors, principals, and superintendents have a legal obligation to recommend and train competent coaches. This legal principle is called *respondeat superior*.

## Parents

Coaches have important responsibilities to parents, which are best met by their being proactive. If coaches have a mentoring attitude toward athletes, then they will intuitively understand that what the parents really want is for a coach to care about their child as an athlete and young person. To demonstrate to parents that they truly care, coaches must communicate effectively before, during, and after the season.

*Before the season* begins the coach should conduct a preseason meeting to let the parents know what the philosophy and expectations are and how he or she operates the program. The communication guidelines should be explained at this time. That is, the coach should explain when communication should take place, where it should take place, and what subject matter is appropriate (what can and cannot be discussed; see chapter 5).

*During the season* the coach should not hesitate to communicate with parents if there is difficulty with an athlete's grades, behavior, or commitment. In addition, when an athlete is injured or ill at practice or at a contest, the coach must immediately call parents to inform them of the situation. Coaches should be open to discussing parents' concerns as long as parents follow the coach's or athletic department's guidelines.

*After the season* coaches must solicit help from parents in several areas: planning the banquet or recognition night, returning uniforms or equipment, and discussing future plans for the athlete. The coach of today must look at parents as allies, rather than keeping to the old notion that parents have no business getting involved. Being proactive with parents will reap more benefits than being reactive will.

## Support Staff

Like the sport director, coaches rely on many individuals to operate a successful sport team or program. Support staff (assistant athletic director, athletic department secretary, custodians, bus drivers, contest officials, and scoring officials) can make the difference between having an enjoyable season and one that is not so enjoyable. At the preseason meeting the coach and the sport director must decide who will be responsible for securing support staff. It is not uncommon for the coach and sport director to share this important function. The coach must assist the sport director in the following activities having to do with support staff:

- Communicating in writing the practice schedules and contest schedules, with time, date, and site.

- Using forms or memos to explain the duties and expectations at contests or practices and the time frame for completion.

- When schedule changes occur, notifying all the individuals in writing who play a part in the event.

- Training and in-servicing individuals on the athletic department's policies or any rule changes in specific sports, operation of equipment, and performance of duties.

Many of these tasks can be delegated, but remember that if coaches are willing to share the responsi-bility with the sport director in all aspects of the program's operation, the chances for having an efficient, well-run department are much greater.

## School

The coach is viewed by the student body, staff, and school community as a visible extension of the school. Therefore, a coach must represent the school at all times as a positive ambassador. You must help the coach understand and perform many roles and responsibilities that are part of the position as it relates to the school in general. If the coach and you win over the student body and community, you will reap overwhelming support and enthusiasm, which are tremendous benefits for your events.

Some of a coach's responsibilities to the school community are these:

**Being a positive role model** for athletes and all the students in the school. The student body will enthusiastically support a coach whom it likes and respects. Remember that our actions speak louder than words.

**Being positive with the news media.** A coach should never criticize officials, opposing players, or the team's own players. Negative comments are embarrassing and portray a poor image.

**Promoting the team and program** in the school setting. This includes recruiting athletes, working with the sport director on game promotions, and representing the team in staff and community organizations. The coach should also promote the team and school in the media.

# RECRUITING AND HIRING GOOD COACHES

The success of an athletic program stems largely from the quality of the coaches on staff. As the sport director you must develop a recruiting plan that can attract the best candidates. Understand that it doesn't mean you will always be able to hire the best coaches, but you can recommend the best coaches available. Most athletic programs need between 30 and 100 coaches to fill all the positions that have been established by the board of education. When the best coach is not available, you must seek the candidate with the most potential to be an effective coach, one who understands and models the philosophy of sport in your school district.

## Governing Body Guidelines—Who Can Coach

Does a governing body (the state department of education, state high school athletics and activities association, board of education, sport's national governing body) require coaches to know cardiopulmonary resuscitation (CPR), sports medicine or sports first aid, or coaching education before they can coach? Do coaches need to have a tuberculin test, a fingerprint check, or a law enforcement background check before they can be recommended? Check with your governing bodies to determine the requirements your coaches must meet before they can coach. See appendix A for a complete list of sport-specific national governing bodies.

For example, the Ohio State Department of Education requires each coach to possess a current certification card for CPR (you should also check the requirements of American Red Cross and American Heart Association) and a four-clock-hour workshop in sports medicine, once every three years. At least one clock-hour of the workshop must be presented by a medical doctor or nationally certified trainer (ATC). These workshops must have prior approval, assuring that the subject matter falls within the guidelines set by the state.

In West Virginia, as another example, all coaches not on the teaching staff must have completed the ASEP Leader Level coaching principles clinic before they are permitted to coach. Check the requirements in your state to be sure your coaches meet all of them. Failure to comply with these requirements may prevent your school from competing in the state tournament and it may mean also having to pay a stiff fine.

Local boards of education may require coaches to be fingerprinted, have a background check, have a tuberculin test, or be vaccinated against hepatitis. Don't look at these requirements as an administrative nightmare but as another way to ensure your athletes that the athletic department is selecting the most qualified coaches available. Inform coaches that as the sport director you will be responsible for verifying their having taken CPR, coaching education, and sports-medicine clinics. The personnel department (or human resource department) will be responsible for verifying their meeting requirements for a tuberculin test, fingerprinting, and background check by the police. Meet with your principal or personnel director to confirm who is responsible for verification of these requirements.

## Walk-On Coaches

A coach who is not a member of the school district staff is called a *walk-on* coach. These are individuals who generally are not teachers but who "walk on" to our campus to coach from outside the school district. Some local school boards require walk-on coaches to undergo a law enforcement background check. One of the most difficult situations for a community or a sport director to deal with is a coach who has a record of abusive or illegal behavior. If the board of education attempts to determine this possible background of abuse, it will take some pressure off the school and the athletic department in case an allegation does arise.

Find out as much as you can about a walk-on coach to be sure the person shares your department's philosophy. Use your personal contacts to verify the kind of role model and the type of coach this candidate is. You can be held liable for negligent acts of the coaches you recommend under the legal doctrine of *respondeat superior*. In other words, be sure the person you are recommending is a good citizen and has potential to be an effective coach.

Be sure to hold the walk-on coach to at least the same standard and hiring procedures that staff coaches are held to. Sometimes a sport director is so happy to simply find a coach that he or she doesn't take the necessary steps to be sure this potential coach is right for the program. Before you recommend a walk-on coach, be sure the individual will adhere to your state and local requirements and follow the athletic department's written policies. Before a candidate begins coaching is a good time to sign the person up for a coaching principles workshop, even if the governing body does not require taking one. Make coaching education a requirement of coaching in your district.

## Publicizing the Need for Coaches

Many states require that certified on-staff personnel must be considered first when recruiting coaches, which is a wise policy (see chapter 6 for more suggestions on recruiting and selecting coaches). Especially with coaches you may want to call the sport director of a local college or university or some other sport programs in your community to obtain some referrals of potentially qualified students, athletes out of season, former athletes, or former college coaches (again, see chapter 6).

> When you hire a coach you must take care that the candidate meets special requirements *before* he or she begins coaching. Check with your state athletic and activity association and personnel director to determine the legal requirements for coaching. Some requirements are mandated locally; others are required by the state athletic and activities association. These coaching prerequisites may include
>
> - fingerprinting,
> - a background check by local or federal law enforcement agency,
> - a sports medicine or first-aid workshop,
> - coaching education from a college or qualified program or at least the willingness to take coaching education within a specified period of time after the coaching assignment begins, and
> - medical exams, tests, or vaccinations.

# EDUCATING COACHES

Successful athletic programs employ and train coaches who understand and practice the principles of effective coaching. Effective coaches possess a philosophy that puts athletes first and winning second (ASEP's philosophy). They understand sport psychology, pedagogy (planning), physiology (conditioning), and risk management (legal duties of coaches). They communicate well with players and parents.

But the reality is that many coaches do not come to us understanding all these principles. Our athletic programs now demand a tremendous number

of good coaches. Yet many coaches today were influenced by former coaches who practiced less effective methods and (most of whom) had little or no training in effective coaching principles. As sport director you therefore have an obligation to provide coaching education to all coaches to assure athletes get the best possible coaching.

## The Educating Imperative

Coaching is a profession. We must promote *lifelong* learning for it. Coaches in most athletic departments have varying levels of coaching knowledge. So sport directors have a responsibility to educate *all* coaches, regardless of their level of coaching knowledge, so make sure that each member of the staff continually strives to be his or her personal best. Remember your legal obligation to recommend and train competent coaches. The American Sport Education Program offers a comprehensive coaching education program to enable the sport director to meet the needs of every coach from grades 6–12.

> As an instructor for the ASEP Leader Level Course, I often lend coaches the videotapes that are used to present the workshop. The videotapes refresh the coaches' memory on important aspects of coaching, such as philosophy, psychology, physiology, planning, and management. The coach can review the text *Successful Coaching* by Rainer Martens and go back to coaching with greater confidence.

## Professional Organizations

As sport director you must create a professional atmosphere with your coaches. It is important to promote professionalism first with coaching education. You can strengthen professionalism still further by encouraging coaches to join professional organizations and associations. Professional organizations give them a medium and resource to improve themselves and others in their sport. These are the key organizations that you should encourage coaches to belong to: local coaches associations (sport-specific), state coaches associations (sport-specific), and the National Federation of Interscholastic Coaches Association (NFICA; all coaches are eligible).

These associations offer many benefits, including

- information on how to be a more effective coach, through both coaching principles and sport-specific knowledge;
- local, state, and national conferences that provide speakers and workshops to improve coaches;
- sport-specific information in association newsletters, magazines on coaching, and newsletters from allied organizations;
- the opportunity to nominate athletes for honors and recognition;
- the opportunity to be honored as a coach for years of service, contributions, or service to an organization; and
- the opportunity for coaches to speak at conferences and workshops to share knowledge with other coaches.

In addition it is worthwhile to recommend that coaches attend coaching workshops and clinics sponsored by coaching associations, colleges, or sporting goods manufacturers.

## Making It Happen

You may wonder how you can motivate coaches to make the time for coaching education or joining organizations or associations. Well, it's like most everything else in life: if it is important to the success of your program, then you must find a way to make it happen. As sport director you must find ways to motivate coaches to want to become the best they can be.

> I have been able to convince the local board of education and superintendent that coaching education is an insurance policy for the school district. If the school district loses a lawsuit someday because of a negligent coach, how much will it cost? I argue that it is much less costly to spend money on coaching education now than to lose a lawsuit in a negligence case.

Here are a few ideas that might encourage your coaches to join professional organizations or take a qualified coaching-education workshop or clinic—or they may stimulate you to develop other motivational ideas.

- As you mentor coaches, model your own appreciation of the benefits of professional organizations and lifelong learning.
- Have the athletic department, booster club, or board of education pay for all or part of the cost of coaching education.
- If it doesn't violate state ordinances or board policy, have the athletic department pay for the coaches' dues in professional organizations.
- Negotiate a one-time pay raise or step increase for coaches who complete a qualified coaching education workshop. (The workshop or clinic must be preapproved by your department.)
- Challenge your head coaches to set the tone for their lower-level coaches by having them join professional organizations and coaching education clinics.
- Ask your best coaches what it would take to convince other coaches of the value to them and their athletes in joining professional organizations and enrolling in coaching education clinics.
- Ask your fellow sport directors who have outstanding coaching staffs for some tips on ways that they create this professional atmosphere.
- Work to make coaching education and joining professional organizations part of the self-selection process when recommending new coaches. In other words, have the coaches promise to get involved in self-improvement as a prerequisite to coaching.
- Identify workshops and clinics that present pertinent issues for coaches (e.g., the steps in due process, conflict resolution, accommodating disadvantaged youth or those with special disabilities, gender and diversity issues). Budget money in your athletic department budget to send coaches to these types of educational programs.

Don't be discouraged if you have some coaches who still avoid these issues. You owe it to the athletes in your program to improve your staff by continually striving to create an atmosphere of self-improvement.

# RECOGNIZING COACHES

As sport director you must never forget that coaches are people too. In other words, they need to feel worthy, just as we know our athletes do. In this area you must look at yourself as the coaches' coach. Just as we expect coaches to satisfy athletes' needs for motivation and recognition, so we must satisfy that need in our coaches.

## Motivation

The best way you can help coaches feel worthy is to tell them they are doing a good job. In other words, catch them doing something correctly and tell them how good it was or drop them a personal note of appreciation. This is an example of an external motivator.

For coaches to truly feel worthy, however, they must feel good about themselves on the inside as well. So you must be aware of ways to motivate your coaching staff both externally and internally. Become familiar with these examples of external and internal motivators, and include them as you work with coaching personnel.

### Internal Motivators for Coaches

Let's look first at the kinds of actions that commonly motivate good coaches. Here are qualities and actions coaches are capable of that make them feel good about their professional work and personal worth. All of these internal motivators become self-motivating and last for a long time.

**Caring about young people.** When a student athlete is having problems in school, in sport, or at home he or she needs a caring person to act as a sounding board or someone to listen. Coaches are in the best position to fulfill that need. What a warm, wonderful feeling a coach can get by knowing that he or she makes a difference in a young person's life.

**Demonstrating knowledge of a sport.** Coaches work hard to learn more about their sports, and they want to know it has constructive outcomes. They attend clinics and workshops to improve knowledge and strategies. When a new offense works, it makes the coach feel proud and excited.

**Gaining public recognition or fame.** Everyone wants to feel worthwhile, and being known and recognized in your school and community gives a coach a strong feeling of acceptance.

**Having fun.** Most coaches played the sport they now coach when they were young. Coaching keeps alive that feeling of fun that they remember from having played the sport.

**Love of the sport.** Many coaches derived positive attributes and experiences from their own sport experiences, and they have a strong desire to pass along that love of sport to their athletes.

**Being in charge.** There are those who lead and those who follow. Leadership traits often develop at a young age, and many coaches have a need to be in charge to feel fulfilled.

**Traveling.** Coaching gives one the opportunity to travel, and with it the excitement of planning overnight trips, going to local or national workshops, and, especially during the summer, traveling across this country to play.

**Having social contacts.** Many coaches are people persons. They are gregarious and love to network and talk about their sport with other coaches, officials, or parents. The joy is in the relationships they have and the new ones they will develop.

### External Motivators

Let's look next at the kinds of external actions that may motivate many coaches. These, too, are qualities and actions that make coaches feel good about their professional work and personal worth.

**Working to increase salaries.** Coaches work long and hard. Many of today's coaches feel that if the money is there, it will give them the motivation to make the sacrifice to coach.

**Working to add assistant coaches when appropriate.** How many coaches have left the ranks because they didn't have enough help to operate their programs? Assistant coaches undertake a lot of administrative burdens and allow a head coach more time to coach.

**Gaining rewards for taking coaching education workshops or courses.** Getting a stipend or public recognition for developing their knowledge in coaching helps motivate many coaches to be the best they can be.

**Arranging schedules to not have a class in the last period of the day.** It is nice to have a free period anytime, but if it comes at the end of the day, the coach gains time to prepare just prior to practice. This is another way for a sport director to show outwardly that what coaches do is important and worth the effort to arrange free time when they need it the most.

**Getting coaches in the buildings where they coach.** This helps a head coach be more effective and efficient. If the person teaches in the middle school or a different high school in the district, the communication between you and the coach and between the coach and the players is greatly diminished. A coach does a better job by being in the building.

**Finding ways to legally fund coaches' shirts, warm-ups, and other clothing or gear.** Coaches appreciate any type of clothing that they don't have to pay for. One suggestion is get boosters to fund basic clothing for every coach as part of developing school pride. Another is to try to get suppliers to provide these small perks. Check your state's laws as to purchasing personal items for coaches. Is it legal or not? If you do purchase coaches clothing from board funds or fund-raising projects, find out whether they must be part of inventory at the end of the season.

**Having appreciation dinners, golf outings, or picnics.** One way to encourage positive thinking about coaching is to plan activities together. These don't have to occur often, although it is nice to make them a tradition, such as a golf outing in the spring. You can use booster-club funding, for example, and most coaches don't mind paying a bit for these things.

## Creating a Recognition System

Keep a file on every coach. You will find that over the years the file will expand to include a coaching history of that person. Track the individual's years of service and coaching victories. An athletic department should develop a policy to periodically recognize staff for years of coaching service in the school district. Form 8.1 is an example that you can adapt to fit the needs of your athletic department for giving recognition. The best (and probably the only) reason for keeping won-lost records is that

 **Form 8.1**

# HEAD COACH RECORD

Name of coach _____ Sport _____

Year named head coach _____

Record:

| 1980-81 _____ | 1986-87 _____ | 1992-93 _____ | 1998-99 _____ |
|---|---|---|---|
| 1981-82 _____ | 1987-88 _____ | 1993-94 _____ | 1999-00 _____ |
| 1982-83 _____ | 1988-89 _____ | 1994-95 _____ | 2000-01 _____ |
| 1983-84 _____ | 1989-90 _____ | 1995-96 _____ | 2001-02 _____ |
| 1984-85 _____ | 1990-91 _____ | 1996-97 _____ | 2002-03 _____ |
| 1985-86 _____ | 1991-92 _____ | 1997-98 _____ | 2003-04 _____ |
| Col. total _____ | Col. total _____ | Col. total _____ | Col. total _____ |

Grand total _____

Other accomplishments:

**Form 8.2**

# COACH'S FEEDBACK TO ADMINISTRATOR AND DEPARTMENT

**Directions:** To help us improve the effectiveness of the athletic department, please take a few moments to respond to the following statements. Circle the best response and write a brief description of specific observations that led you to that response.

1. The sport director understands the athletic department philosophy of the school district and promotes it with coaches, parents, and athletes.   Yes _____   No _____   Don't know _____
   Observations:

2. The sport director provides positive leadership in the athletic department by enforcing policies that support the program's philosophy.   Yes _____   No _____   Don't know _____
   Observations:

3. The sport director consistently enforces athletic department policies in all sports.
   Yes _____   No _____   Don't know _____
   Observations:

4. The sport director helps provide a safe environment for the athletes to participate.
   Yes _____   No _____   Don't know _____
   Observations:

5. The sport director communicates well with coaches, parents, support staff, and athletes.
   Yes _____   No _____   Don't know _____
   Observations:

6. The sport director makes every effort possible to secure qualified coaching staff and encourage them to pursue coaching education courses or clinics.   Yes _____   No _____   Don't know _____
   Observations:

7. The athletic department provides equipment and uniforms comparable to the schools that we compete with.
   Yes _____   No _____   Don't know _____
   Observations:

8. The sport director is knowledgeable in the field of athletic administration (selection of officials; preparation of schedules; providing qualified support staff; arranging transportation, budgeting, and finance; securing financial support for the program).   Yes _____   No _____   Don't know _____
   Observations:

9. The sport director models and promotes good sportsmanship.   Yes _____   No _____   Don't know _____
   Observations:

10. The sport director keeps the coaching staff current on meeting notices, rule changes, and other important matters.   Yes _____   No _____   Don't know _____
    Observations:

11. The strengths of our athletic department can be briefly described as _____
    Observations:

12. The weaknesses of the athletic department can be briefly described as _____
    Observations:

many coaching associations give certificates in recognition of attaining a certain number of victories. Give some thought to this record keeping, however, so that winning is not perceived as more important than your mission to help students. If you feel winning would become a priority with this type of recognition, then don't do it.

## Encouraging Feedback

Remember the old saw that what is good for the goose is good for the gander? If you are to evaluate your coaches and their programs, then you give them the opportunity to evaluate you and your ways of doing things. The benefit of this mutual evaluation is to enable you to better determine which procedures might be changed to improve the effectiveness of the athletic program. This evaluation process gives the program greater credibility with your coaching staff as well. Allowing coaches to evaluate you gives them more ownership in the overall program. Use form 8.2 as an example of a way to have the coach give you feedback about your administration of the program. This is not an appraisal of you as a person. If coaches are critical, don't take it personally (as difficult as that may be).

One coach found it very difficult to accept critical comments from his players on the feedback instrument he distributed at the end of the season. I showed him a number of critical comments that coaches had made about the athletic department and told him how I used those comments to improve my performance and the overall effectiveness of the department. It might help if coaches or anyone else giving feedback can remain anonymous; you should get more honest information if you don't ask for the responder's name. The more often you ask for feedback, fortunately, the easier it gets to look at the comments objectively.

# EVALUATING COACHES

The more effective you are in evaluating the coaches on your staff, the more influence you will have on the quality of coaching in the program. It is important that both you and the coaches understand the mission and purpose of evaluation as a tool to improve coaching in the school district. Review the discussion in chapter 6 on evaluating personnel in general before reading the more specific suggestions here that pertain to coaches.

Some of your coaches may resent being evaluated. They may feel uneasy because they cannot live up to the standards your department sets. Don't worry. You must convey to all coaches that coaching is an art and not a science, and that your goal is to improve coaching through the evaluation process. If coaches reach their own goals, then young athletes in the program will benefit.

Keep in mind several important points as you think about evaluating coaches:

• Design evaluation instruments with the help of successful coaches to appraise the coaching skills that are important to implement your athletic program's philosophy. Ask coaches for their input into the construction of checklists or goal-setting items to give them some ownership and diminish potential fear.

• Make checklists an important aspect of the evaluation system (see samples in chapter 6). Checklists enable the sport director to efficiently gain information on critical components of a coach's role, such as safety issues and coaching competence.

• Include setting goals as part of the process. Goals motivate coaches to work toward professional growth, and, moreover, they can be intrinsic motivators.

• Timelines for meetings, observations, and appraisals should be discussed and agreed upon at your preseason meeting with coaches.

• Be sure to satisfy the athletic department's goals and objectives for coaching in the process you set up.

• Consider having the coach receive feedback from athletes and parents (see sample in form 8.3) to help ensure that both the coach's and athletic department's objectives are being accomplished.

• When weaknesses are identified on checklists, you must implement a mutually agreed-on strategy to strengthen the area and set a reasonable time frame to improve.

 **Form 8.3**

# PLAYER FEEDBACK FORM

**Directions:** Please answer all questions honestly. Your input will help make our athletic program better. Answers are important, so if you must be critical please be constructive. These questionnaires are confidential, and no one (including those in the athletic department) will know of your identity.

Student athlete profile: Male _____ Female _____

Sport _____ Age _____ Grade _____

Coach's name _____ Years on the team _____

Place the appropriate letter on the line to best describe how you feel.

1. _____ Being involved in athletics at North Olmsted High School has made my high school experience
   a. Much more fulfilling      b. Somewhat more enjoyable
   c. Not made a difference one way or the other      d. Has had a negative effect

2. _____ The students in school support my team
   a. Very often      b. Sometimes      c. Never

3. _____ The facilities used for my sport, compared to others, are
   a. Above average      b. Very comparable      c. Not as good as others      d. Very poor

4. _____ The uniforms and equipment provided by the school for my sport are
   a. Above average      b. Very comparable      c. Not as good as others      d. Very poor

5. _____ Eagle Boosters (parent boosters) supports my team (compared to other sports)
   a. As well as others      b. Does not support our team often
   c. Does not support our team at all      d. Not aware of Eagle Boosters

6. _____ Team rules and regulations set forth by my Coach are
   a. Clearly communicated      b. Communicated irregularly
   c. Not communicated      d. Nonexistent

7. _____ Training rules with regard to alcohol and drug use during the season on our team are followed by
   a. All members      b. Most members      c. Some members      d. Few members      e. Do not know

8. _____ Training rules with regard to alcohol and drug use outside of the season on our team are followed by
   a. All members      b. Most members      c. Some members      d. Few members      e. Do not know

9. _____ My Coach is knowledgeable about his or her sport.
   a. Very knowledgeable      b. Average      c. Not knowledgeable      d. Other _____
   _____

10. _____ My Coach      a. Shows no favoritism      b. Sometimes shows favoritism
    c. Always shows favoritism      d. Does not apply to my coach

11. _____ Practice times are      a. Too late      b. Too early      c. Just fine      d. Other

12. _____ Practice is      a. Too long   b. Too short   c. Just right   d. Too often   e. Not often enough
    f. Other _____

13. _____ In dealing with players my Coach is      a. Consistent      b. Inconsistent

14. _____ My Coach is
    a. One of the best in the league      b. An adequate coach      c. A very good coach      d. Other _____
    _____

15. \_\_\_\_ The team chemistry is characterized by this phrase:
   a. Everyone works as a team.    b. Most everyone works as a team.
   c. Some work as a team.    d. Few work as a team.

16. \_\_\_\_ The team attitude is    a. Excellent    b. Good    c. All right    d. Not good    e. Very poor

17. \_\_\_\_ My Coach's strengths are: _____

18. \_\_\_\_ My Coach's weaknesses are: _____

19. \_\_\_\_ If I had the power to improve my team or my sport I would change the following things: _____

Checklists alone might result in some problems for the evaluator. Coaches might argue, for example, about receiving a score of 3 rather than a score of 4. They might wonder how an evaluator could give any rating at all based on a single observation or one visit. If checklists are used as the sole tool for evaluation, they might create an atmosphere of distrust. Once you lose trust, you've hampered growth and development. How effective any coaching evaluation system will be depends on how well you combine checklists with goal-setting tools to assess coaching skills and encourage professional growth.

## Components of Coaching Evaluation

Consider including these components in your evaluation system for coaches:

### 1. Preseason Meeting to Discuss Evaluation Process With the Coach

Before the season officially begins a sport director should hold a meeting with each head coach and any other coach who is going to be evaluated to discuss several very important topics. It would be wise to have a written agenda like the sample in figure 8.5. Plan to discuss what, where, and when observations and evaluations (checklists or summative tools) will take place. Identify goals and objectives for the season (formative tools). At this point it is important to stipulate the criteria on which coaches will be evaluated. The criteria for evaluation, or what the coach will be evaluated on, are as follows:

• Minimum competencies in planning, organizing, and motivating athletes; modeling appropriate behavior; knowledge of the sport; and communication. (These will be evaluated through informal and formal observations of the coach. Formal observations will be determined at the preseason meeting, informal observations can occur anytime. A summative tool or checklist will be used for this appraisal.)

• Attainment of specific goals for that sport. (The effectiveness of the action plans determined by the coach and sport director will be assessed at the end of the season using the formative tool filled out by the coach. The coach and sport director will evaluate the degree to which goals were reached and the effectiveness of the action plans.)

The overall evaluation will be based on what the athletic department expects (competencies or a

---

**Agenda for Evaluation Meeting**

---

To: Head coach in basketball

From: Sport director

Date: October 15

Re: Preseason meeting to discuss evaluation process

The following items will be discussed at our preseason meeting regarding your evaluation as head coach in basketball. Please bring this agenda with you to the meeting which will be held in my office at 3:00 P.M. on Friday, November 1.

   I. Purpose of evaluation process
      A. Improve coaching.
      B. Confirm that the athletic philosophy of the school district is being followed.

   II. Description of evaluation instruments (tools)
      A. Summative tool (checklist)
      B. Formative tool (goalsetting)
      C. Athletes' feedback
      D. Parents' feedback
      E. Summary evaluation

  III. Evaluation procedure
      A. Timelines for meetings
      B. When and where observations will be made
      C. Date for final evaluation

**Figure 8.5**   Agenda for preseason evaluation meeting.

summative tool) and what the coach and sport director expect (growth and development or a formative tool). Make it clear that the instruments are tools to help improve coaching in the district.

Be sure the coach and you discuss the coach's written goals (formative tools; see chapter 6, form 6.6, p. 73) for the season. You can help by being sure the goals are measurable, attainable, and within the coach's control. Remind the coach that these goals will be revisited at the end of the season.

## 2. Coaches' Self-Evaluation

Filling out a self-evaluation enables coaches to reflect on their roles and goals for the season. There is an example of such a form developed for general support staff members in chapter 10 (see form 10.2 on p. 148). You can adapt this form for coaches and give it (or some other evaluation form) to your coaches before the season begins, so that they have time to become familiar with its contents. After the last contest in the season, it should then be filled

out (prior to the final meeting) and included in the final evaluation. Encourage the coaches to step back in evaluating themselves. This is not a time for gamesmanship on their part. You will find that some coaches automatically give themselves high marks for fear of self-incrimination, whereas others are unduly harsh on themselves. As time goes on and they become more confident in their skills, they will become better self-evaluators.

## 3. Head Coach's Evaluation of Assistant Coaches and Lower-Level Coaches

Particularly in large athletic programs and in sports with more than one team, it is helpful to work closely with the head coach in evaluating assistant coaches and lower-level coaches. One of the goals of your athletic department should be to recruit and develop skilled coaches, and you and your head coach can use the evaluation process to help accomplish this goal. In some school districts, head coaches may not be able to evaluate other coaches because they do not possess an administrative certification from the state department of education. Regardless of the situation in your state, you still want your head coach to give feedback about other coaches in that sport.

Form 6.4 (in chapter 6, p. 70) is an example of an assistant or lower-level coach's evaluation form. Spend time with every coach to be sure they all are fulfilling their roles as they have been contracted to do. As sport directors we are committed to helping all coaches improve, not only the head coaches.

## 4. Players' Giving Feedback to Coaches

It used to be rare that player feedback was used by coaches to improve their coaching or help them determine if the goals for the season were being accomplished. Today's cooperative-style coaches do not hesitate to make this feedback an important part of the overall evaluation process. A sample that can be adapted to your needs can be found in form 8.3.

If you can step back and look at your program objectively, it makes sense to ask players for feedback about the coach and program. After all, if your philosophy is athletes first and winning second, it means you cannot know that you are meeting the needs of your athletes unless they can tell you what is happening, right or wrong. A word of caution is necessary, however, because athletes must feel they can be honest without fearing retribution by the coach. For that reason, the instruments must be anonymous, and all teams must be allowed to give feedback so that the procedure becomes the norm, something that is an expected part of the season. On the other hand, you also cannot allow the players' feedback to become the sole evalution tool as an attempt to improve coaching.

One of our football coaches, with more than a hundred players, received five critical comments. The golf coach also received five of them. I was able to help the football coach keep the critical comments in perspective; after all, he had fewer than 5 percent negative comments. The golf coach, in comparison, had 50 percent negative remarks, and we definitely had to see some changes to be responsive to what the players were telling us. A few negative feedback comments are not out of the ordinary.

## 5. Parents' Giving Feedback on the Program

Parents can help the athletic department accomplish its goals by being supportive of the coaches and program. One way to gain parental support is to give them the opportunity to give feedback about the program. As with other constituent groups, you are more likely to receive support from the parents if they feel ownership in the program. The feedback we get from parents is most helpful if it focuses on the goals of the program. If parents feel we met the majority of our goals and objectives, then it will be apparent to them, regardless of the team's record, that we enjoyed a successful season. Keep this thought in mind when developing your feedback instrument. You will find forms in chapter 9 that are examples of instruments used to solicit feedback from parents.

## 6. Conveying Feedback and Expectations to Returning Coaches

The checklists should enable you to later communicate how strong or weak a coach is in particular coaching skills and duties. The form you share with coaches should be to the point and easy to fill out. It should allow you to give written feedback on areas that need improvement, but also on the areas in which the coach is performing extremely well. If weaknesses are identified, then suggestions for improvement should be added.

If you are going to recommend this coach for the next season and have pointed out areas that need improvement, you must allow time for the coach to discuss the suggestions with you that are on the evaluation. The likelihood of improvement will be greatly increased if the coach agrees with your suggestions or is permitted to contribute his or her own suggestions. It would be appropriate, at this time, to indicate to the coach if the areas of weakness are major or minor. That is, if these weaknesses do not improve, will the coach be in jeopardy of being released next season?

## 7. Procedures for Releasing or Not Retaining Coaches

As hard as you try to improve coaching, as much as you practice mentoring skills, as much as you care about these coaches as individuals, there come times when you have to release, suspend, or not retain a coach. Usually these situations do not come as a surprise to you or the coach. They likely occur after serious attempts over time at helping the coach improve. Releasing a coach is different from not retaining the individual. Let's look at each situation separately and offer some suggestions for dealing with both.

We should consider *releasing or suspending* (or both) a coach during the season, or abruptly, when the following conditions exist:

- The coach is a physical danger to the athletes or him- or herself.

- Evidence of a felony is presented.

- The coach knowingly violates athletic or board policies after previous violations have occurred.

This kind of information should be in the policy manual that was discussed in chapter 2. If any of these conditions exist, you should consider suspending the coach with pay until an investigation can be conducted. Be sure to familiarize yourself with due process to demonstrate that you handled the situation with a sense of fairness.

You should consider the following course of action once you or your department is made aware of any serious violations made by a coach:

- When allegations are made, ask questions of those making the allegation to obtain as much information as possible. Write the information down so you don't lose any facts to your memory.

- Inform the building principal and superintendent. It will be their responsibility to inform the board of education.

- If the situation warrants (e.g., sexual imposition or abuse with athletes), solicit the help of the local police department.

- Determine if questions need to be asked of anyone else who might have knowledge about the allegations. You may consider asking questions of those who are directly involved in the situation or who may have special knowledge of the situation, such as the board of education's lawyers.

- Call a meeting as soon as possible after information is gathered with the coach, his or her counsel, the principal, the board of education counsel, and anyone else suggested by the lawyers.

- Follow due process steps with regard to informing the coach of the charges, allowing the coach to respond to the charges, and informing the coach of his or her right to appeal your decision if he or she disagrees.

- Be sure to take copious notes along the way, and save the notes and any written communications in case of future lawsuits.

Not retaining a coach for the next season is an altogether different situation than releasing a coach. If the evaluation process is working properly, the coach should realize long before your telling him or her that things are not working out. In fairness to the coach, prior to the next season you should complete a letter placing him or her on warning and give a verbal explanation expressing the concerns. The letter should state where changes need to be made and the suggestions you have to help the coach make those changes. Every coach has weaknesses, but in reality most coaches possess strengths that far outweigh their weaknesses. When a coach has a preponderance of weaknesses or doesn't seem able, after much help and support from the sport director, to improve in key coaching skills, then it is time to prepare the person for the inevitable. The truth is that not everyone possesses the skills to coach in an interscholastic athletic program.

You hope that the coaches you recruit and recommend understand and put into practice the philosophy that your athletic program subscribes to. Always keep in mind that the student athletes must come first. You cannot tolerate any coach who doesn't understand or practice the skills and philosophies that help athletes develop physically, psychologically, or socially.

You should consider *not retaining* a coach if the following conditions exist:

- A coach has not corrected the weaknesses that have been pointed out in the evaluation process. A strong effort must be put forth to suggest ways to improve on the weakness.

- A coach puts winning and selfish goals before the program's goals. Another way to state this is that the coach makes winning more important than the athletes' physical, psychological, and social development.

- A coach refuses to improve in significant coaching competencies or to follow the philosophy of the athletic program.

- A coach does not possess the knowledge to teach the skills necessary to compete at the interscholastic level. This assumes that efforts to increase the coach's technical knowledge have been made.

- A coach exhibits inappropriate behavior around athletes. In other words, the coach is not an appropriate role model.

- A coach does not perform legal duties and exposes him- or herself and the school district to lawsuits.

## Keeping Coaches' Employment Records

Typically there are two kinds of files that should be kept for coaches: a personnel file housed in the personnel director's office and a memory file that you should maintain.

The personnel file (maintained by the personnel director or school district superintendent) contains these kinds of items:

- Evaluations
- Citations
- Formal disciplinary documents
- Multiple year contracts
- Results of the background check
- Initial application and resume
- Tuberculin test results
- Fingerprinting results

The memory files (which you maintain) contain these kinds of items:

- Correspondence, both positive and negative
- Won-loss record (optional)
- Evaluations
- Meeting documentation (meetings with coach, parents, players, others)
- Yearly contract
- Coaching education transcripts
- CPR card (copy)
- Sports-medicine course documentation
- Copy of resume or application

### Summary

In this chapter you learned how to:

1. recruit competent coaches for your sport program and continue to educate them through meetings, checklists, and encouraging their professional growth;

2. establish a recognition system that helps motivate coaches intrinsically and extrinsically;

3. develop an evaluation system for the purpose of improving coaching;

4. encourage feedback from players, parents, and the coach; and

5. develop forms to assist you in giving the necessary information and feedback to recognize coaches and improve their effectiveness.

# Chapter 9
# Involving Parents

Working with sport parents is a relatively new area of leadership responsibility for sport directors. We now work more closely to educate parents about the athletic department's philosophy and the role they can play in the development of young people in our athletic programs. Parents can be a very positive support system for athletes and the athletic program.

In this chapter you will learn about these topics:

1. How you and the parents of athletes in your program can help one another support athletes, team, and school.

2. How to achieve productive parental involvement.

3. How to interact with parents to resolve conflict.

4. How to recognize parents' needs in the sport program.

5. How to develop an agenda for a parent orientation meeting.

# YOUR RESPONSIBILITIES TO PARENTS

The primary participants in your athletic program are the young athletes. Their parents play a major supporting role that can affect the success or failure of their children's sport experience. As a sport director you have a responsibility to recognize the importance of the parents' role and do your best to educate parents to support their athletes, the coaches, and the school.

> A boys' basketball coach in our school district was outstanding in the way he communicated with parents. He understood that most parents care only that their sons or daughters are happy and that the coach cares about them. Of course, we all know some parents exist who are not supportive, focusing solely on the benefits their child may derive from the sport experience. In our program one mom and dad fit that description all too well in their dealings with the coaches of their three older children. When their youngest boy entered the program, he had become a starter on the basketball team already as a sophomore. As a senior, however, he was not working hard or contributing to the team. The boy acted as if the position were guaranteed to him. The coach arranged a face-to-face meeting with the parents. He explained how important their son was to the success of the basketball team and told them he needed their support in a decision he had made to motivate the boy to work harder and become not only more productive but also a leader on the team. The parents agreed to support whatever the coach decided because they had been convinced that the coach was operating in the best interests of their son. They knew he was not out to "get" the boy.
>
> After that coach met with the parents, he met with the boy to tell him that he needed more effort and commitment and that a younger player deserved to get the starting position. At the same time he left it open to the senior, who was more talented: the position would be his when he decided to take a leadership role and set a better example for the rest of the team. After only two games the senior changed his attitude and became one of the best leaders we ever had. This would not have happened without the support of his parents. I applauded my coach for having the wisdom and courage to communicate so effectively with parents.

You, too, must provide the leadership to welcome and involve parents into the athletic program. Through you, the parents must see that the program is organized and well run, operating for the benefit of their children. Moreover, they must see that it is a safe activity existing to improve their children as well-rounded citizens. Then you will earn a support base that can help you and your staff accomplish those objectives.

You also have a responsibility to educate parents on the things they can do to fulfill their roles as sport parents. Most parents operate from an emotional base, without thinking how their words and actions can affect their athlete and the program. By informing parents of the dos and don'ts in being supportive sport parents, you can allow coaches to perform their appropriate functions without being questioned. Athletes can enjoy their own sport experiences without worrying about interfering parents who do not trust the coach.

Furthermore, you are responsible to inform parents of the content of the athletic program. Parents want to know the athletic department's philosophy, what the policies are, and what the consequences are for violations of policies. They also want to know how they can play a supportive role in the development of their youngsters. A preseason meeting is a forum to educate parents on what they want and need to know about the program, the coaching staff, and the team. The preseason meeting gives parents an opportunity to ask questions to clarify their understanding of policies, information, and expectations.

# PARENTS' RESPONSIBILITIES TO THE ATHLETIC PROGRAM

The success of an athletic program is greatest when those involved in the program cooperate and support one another. Parents have important roles and responsibilities to the athlete, school, and team. You must help parents understand how to be constructive and help their athletes develop psychologically, socially, and physically.

## Having Reasonable Expectations

Parents should understand that most young people participate in sport to have fun, develop skills, strive to win, and be with friends. Parents should allow their children to choose their own sport experiences—and not push them into sport or demand that they become a standout, more like mom or dad when they were athletes.

Setting realistic expectations is of paramount importance, and parents can help their children in this area. By and large, most young people know how good they are in relation to other athletes. Parents should be careful not to impose unrealistic expectations on their youngsters, which will come to frustrate both the athlete and parent. An athlete can't attain expectations that are set too high, and the youngster will soon stop trying or even quit the sport. Frustrated parents will end up blaming coaches or others for their athlete's inability to attain these unrealistic expectations.

## Being a Good Sport Parent

You can help stave off this situation by initiating good discussions with parents. Here are some key reminders to give parents when you meet with them or prepare a newsletter to distribute to them:

1. Encourage—and don't pressure—your athlete to play.

2. Provide a supportive atmosphere at home by accepting your athlete's performance goals and allowing your child to succeed or fail without your interference.

3. Keep winning in perspective, and help your athlete do the same. Focus on the lessons of life that can be learned from playing these games. Remember the sport is only a game and you should not portray it as more than that. Encourage your children by making positive comments and finding the good in every situation.

4. Help your athlete set realistic performance goals that are measurable (such as improving one's time in the 200-meter dash), controllable, and attainable.

5. Help your athlete meet team duties and responsibilities, such as caring for uniforms, filling out the necessary forms for participation, informing the coach of allergies or other medical problems, and informing the coach of a tardiness or absence.

6. Give up your athlete to the coach at practices and games. Don't interfere with coaching or team decisions. Attend preseason meetings with your athlete to learn more about the program.

7. Model good sportsmanlike behavior at contests.

8. Communicate with the coach when you have a question about rules, policy, or informational items. Involve the coach to help you when you are experiencing difficulties with the athlete at home or in the classroom.

9. If you have a concern about the coach's ability to develop the athletes psychologically, socially, or physically, make an appointment with the sport director to discuss these concerns.

## Contributing to the Team and School

Parents have a primary responsibility to support the team and school. This support will not only improve the team and the athletic program, but it will also keep parents busy in roles that are positive (not roles that lead to conflict). Being part of the booster club and volunteering to help the coach and team (as scorers, statisticians, videographers, and in other ways) are important contributions that parents can make to the team and school.

## BOOSTER CLUBS

What better way is there to put parents' energy and interest to good use than to involve them in an organization whose mission is to improve the quality of the program? Most booster clubs raise funds to buy the things that cannot be purchased by the normal athletic budget. In many communities, boosters' activities raise as much money as do gate receipts. Boosters are instrumental in providing teams with uniforms, equipment, meal money, transportation, and facilities. And boosters also provide resources for program operation through their volunteer work. Many parents get right in there to help at team functions.

One caveat is to be aware of self-serving individuals who want to run your program for you. Some parents might want to fire a coach, direct all funds to one sport, or criticize every decision you or your coaches make. As the sport director you must not allow these negative individuals to interfere with either your or the coaches' role. Rather, you must

> Sport directors and coaches may not take on particular extra tasks because of the time involved. Hosting a dinner for a visiting team would be a good example. To make this event happen takes a lot of time and energy. This is an excellent opportunity to get parents involved. The more you can direct parents' energies into such positive ventures, the more they will see the benefits of their being involved.

educate these parents on the philosophy and objectives of the program and encourage them to play a more positive role. If they do not fall in line, then they cannot be permitted to be involved—for the sake of the student athletes. As sport director be sure your booster club's constitution and by-laws support your athletic department's philosophy. They should contain language that prevents parents from being involved in the hiring or firing of coaches.

A supportive, positive booster club can be a program's greatest asset. It is important, however, that the role of the booster club be clearly defined. It must be clearly communicated to the parents in the booster club that operation of the athletic department is not a function of a booster club. These are issues, for example, that are *not* appropriate for a booster club to be involved in:

- Personnel decisions
- Distribution of funds
- Scheduling

With parameters for involvement clearly defined, a booster club becomes an essential part of a successful athletic program. Bear in mind, however, that a booster club is a voluntary fund-raising and service organization, not an adjunct administrative branch of the athletic department.

# ASSURING PRODUCTIVE PARENTAL INVOLVEMENT

You are responsible for providing a safe, beneficial, and enjoyable experience not only for the student athletes but also for their parents. And, in turn, parents expect professionalism from the sport director and program's coaches. This professionalism provides a planned, well-organized, well-run athletic program. If things do not run well, you can be assured that parents will raise complaints and concerns.

You cannot conduct a successful athletic program, on the other hand, without involving parents who are willing to support the athletic department's objectives. As the sport director you must do three key things to achieve productive parental involvement:

1. Develop and communicate your expectations.
2. Conduct a preseason meeting for parents.
3. Indicate to parents where the team needs volunteer help.

## Develop and Communicate Your Expectations

It is your responsibility to develop and communicate expectations to parents as they enter the athletic program. The expectations should center on their role as parent, booster-club member, and spectator. As sport director, one of your personal goals might be to help parents grow as good sport parents. You could write an article for parents in the boosters' newsletter or hand out information at the preseason meeting.

First, acknowledge that you have certain expectations of parents. You might reasonably ask them to do the following:

1. Understand and support the philosophy and objectives of the athletic program and the team.
2. Understand and support the expectations the coach has of the athletes and support the coach in achieving these expectations.
3. Attend all parent meetings called by the athletic department and coach.
4. Understand the role of a parent (explained earlier) and continue to develop their knowledge by reading literature and asking questions. You can give parents handouts, for example, to inform them about youth problems and enlist their help (see figure 9.1 about parents' fighting against drug use by their children).
5. Join the boosters' organization to show support for their child, the team, the program, and the school.

**Youth: Full of Life, Not Drugs**

**Educate Kids Early**

Attitudes toward alcohol and drugs are formed early in life. Most children have their first alcohol or drug experience between the ages of 12 and 14. The earlier you begin talking openly about alcohol and drugs to your children, the more likely they are to accept your views and information—rather than relying on other kids or the media.

Take advantage of situations when an alcohol or drug-related incident catches your child's interest. Use the opportunity to give them your views and accurate information.

**Take a Firm Stance**

When children are aware that their parents disapprove of alcohol and drug use, they will be less likely to indulge in this sort of activity. So take a stance and be firm. Tell your children exactly what you expect of them, and don't be afraid to hand out punishment if they don't honor those expectations.

We recommend **NO** use of illegal drugs ever, and **NO** use of alcohol until of legal age. Sit down with your children and tell them what you expect of them and why. Inform them of the consequences if they don't follow your expectations. Impose consequences that are important to your children. Follow through and be consistent rather than severe.

**Prepare Kids on How to Say "No"**

Give your children a head start by practicing what to say when someone puts pressure on them to use alcohol or drugs. Tell them that saying "**no**" is hard for everybody, including adults.

Ask them questions like, "What would you do if your best friend offers you some beer?" "What if some older kids came up to you and offered you some marijuana?"

Help them come up with responses to use, such as, "No thanks, I'm not into that" or "No thanks, I'm allergic." And of course there's nothing wrong with just plain "**NO**."

**Be Aware of What Your Kids Are Doing**

Be selective about TV shows, movies, and concerts that show drug and alcohol use as being normal and fun.

Check ahead of time to see if parties will be chaperoned, and make sure alcohol and other drugs will not be present. Don't be afraid to say no to your kids if you have any doubts.

Try and get to know your children's friends and their parents. Know where your kids will be, whom they'll be with, and what they will be doing. Set reasonable curfews for your children, and let them know they can call home for a ride at any time.

Putting limits on your kids only shows you care: They may not like it now, but they will thank you for it later.

**Figure 9.1** Sample drug pamphlet information.

6. Volunteer to help and support the booster club fund-raisers.

7. Encourage other parents and community members to join the booster club.

8. Insist that the booster club support the athletic program and coach through winning *and* losing seasons.

9. When concerns or complaints arise, allow the sport director and the coach—not the booster club—to first tackle the problem and determine its solution.

## Conduct a Preseason Meeting

The best method for the sport director to begin communicating expectations to parents is by conducting a preseason meeting. If the parents understand the expectations as set forward by the athletic department, they will develop a sense of ownership in them. This meeting should be scheduled at least one week before the first contest, and *notification should go out well in advance* of the meeting, so parents of athletes that make the team can plan to attend it. Many athletic departments make this a mandatory meeting for at least one parent. If a parent fails to attend, the athlete may be denied the privilege of participating until the information from the pre-season meeting can be covered with the parent(s). Some schools require either attending the meeting or a parent's signature acknowledging receipt of the team's rules and athletic department's policies.

## Before the Meeting

Be sure to give parents good advance notice of the meeting. You should send a letter to parents an-nouncing the meeting and the importance of hav-ing them attend it. Figure 9.2 shows you an example of such a letter.

Spending adequate time planning and organiz-ing the preseason meeting will pay many dividends. Some important reasons for holding the preseason meeting are having the chance to

1. explain to parents the objectives of the program,

2. acquaint parents with you and the coach(es) who will be spending so much time with their sons or daughters,

3. inform parents about the nature of sport,

4. tell parents about what is expected of their youngster and of them,

5. learn about the parents' concerns,

6. establish clear lines of communication, and

7. gain support from parents by explaining what they can do to help.

## Formulating an Agenda

Having a good agenda for the preseason meeting will enable you to cover all the expectations you have and convey all the information that is impor-tant for the athletes' participation. You should con-duct a meeting with coaches first (see chapter 8), to go over the agenda and their responsibilities at this

---

**Preseason Letter to Parent**

November 13, 1998

Dear Parents:

The Athletic Department cordially invites you to attend the annual preseason meeting for winter sports. This meeting will convene at 7:00 P.M. in the gymnasium on November 19th. This meeting is **manda-tory** for at least one parent. The purpose of this meeting is to update you on the philosophy, policies, and procedures of the sport your son or daughter is involved in.

Schedule

| | |
|---|---|
| 7:00 P.M. | Welcome – Kyle Zimmers |
| 7:00–7:15 P.M. | Eligibility rules, boosters, philosophy of athletics, sportsmanship, nutrition, announcements, athlete handbook |
| 7:15–8:00 P.M. | Coaches and parents meeting |

It is imperative that every athlete and his family be represented so we may begin the season on a correct note. If you cannot attend you must make arrangements with your coach to obtain this impor-tant information.

Sincerely,

Winter Head Coaches

P.S. The athletic department will have adult and student tickets to Varsity and J.V. home contests in all fall sports. You may purchase as many tickets as you would like. Unused tickets may be used for winter home events.

---

**Figure 9.2**   Sample preseason letter to parents.

important function with the parents of their athletes. Keep in mind this is the first impression the athletic department makes on many of the parents, and it is your best opportunity to develop good public relations and show the true professionalism of the athletic department and its coaches.

You can read a sample of a typical preseason meeting agenda in figure 9.3. In developing your agenda recall all the common questions you get from parents throughout the year. Try to answer the most frequently asked questions by making them an item.

---

**Preseason Agenda**

### Jefferson Athletic Department

To: All head coaches

From: Thomas Tobbins

Date: November 12, 1998

Re: Preseason meeting for parents and athletes

On Wednesday, November 19th, at 7:00 P.M. we will be having a meeting for the parents and athletes for all winter sports. Please notify your coaches and have them attend. Listed below is the schedule and agenda. We expect all parents to attend. Parents are to report to the gymnasium for a brief meeting and then go with you to the following rooms:

Eaglets - Room 361

Boys basketball - Gymnasium

Girls basketball - Media Center

Wrestling - Eagles Room

Swimming and diving - Cafeteria

Hockey - Room 457

Cheerleader - Room 831

Gymnastics - Room 162

Schedule and agenda

7:00 P.M.

Welcome - Kyle Zimmers

Explanation of pamphlets

Eligibility rules, boosters, philosophy of athletics, sportsmanship, nutrition, announcements, athlete handbook

7:15 P.M.

1. Meet the Coaches.
2. Philosophy of program; distribute handbooks and pamphlets; explain.
3. Expectations—handout for each program.
4. Team rules—attendance, letter requirements, training rules.
5. Forms— emergency medical, insurance, physicals.
6. Schedule and location of contests.
7. Uniform responsibilities
   a. Cleaning
   b. Return at the end of the season.
8. Request parents to help with videotaping, statistics, etc.
9. Directions to contests.
10. Questions and answers to the coaching staff.
11. Joining Boosters - if 75 percent join, it means greater benefits to team.
12. Other (whatever the coach wants to talk about).

---

**Figure 9.3** Sample preseason meeting agenda.

Parents of youngsters in soccer, tennis, baseball, softball, and other sports whose contests may not be played at the school site always call the office to find out where the contest is. Do your homework and give directions to all away-contests. Put the directions on the back of the season's schedule. This is the kind of information parents want. Don't wait for them to ask.

## Informing Parents of the Team's Operation

Most parents have a need to know specific kinds of information. By anticipating their questions, you can probably satisfy their need to know about the team's operation. Most of these kinds of information can be distributed at the preseason meeting:

- Athletic department philosophy, purpose, and objectives
- Athletic department rules and policies, including penalties for violations
- Schedules of contests with directions to away events; times of bus departures and schedules
- Communication guidelines for coaches and parents (see figure 5.1 in chapter 5, p. 51)
- Sportsmanship expectations for parents, athletes, coaches, and fans

- Requirements for participation, such as eligibility information, physical card, emergency medical form, hospitalization insurance, risk of participation warning, training rules
- Team philosophy and expectations as supplied by the coach
- Team rules
- Team's wish list for parent volunteers (see form 9.1)
- Ticket policies
- Booster club membership information
- Parents' responsibilities for uniforms and equipment supplied by the school
- Participation fees, uniform fees, or other financial obligations of parents
- NCAA Clearinghouse information
- Information about coaching staff, including qualifications of coaches

## Indicate to Parents Where the Team Needs Volunteer Help

The preseason meeting is also the best time to ask parents for help. You might hand dads a letter inviting them to join a team of fathers (see figure 9.4). It would be advisable to prepare your coaches to list the areas where they can use help. Send them a copy

---

**Volunteer Sign-up**

**Jefferson Athletic Department**
Kyle Zimmers, Athletic Director

August 20, 1997

To: Junior Varsity Football Dads

How would you like the best view of your son's game? We are looking for "A Few Good Men" to man the chain gang at the home J.V. football games. We need a commitment to all five home games. Volunteering gets you into the games free, a hot dog and coke at halftime, plus our eternal thanks for helping out.

   So if sitting by your wife or with the fan who cheers at the wrong time really bothers you, then get close to the action and join the Eagles chain gang. If interested contact Tim Flannery or Tom Humphrey in the Athletic Office at 779-8797.

**Figure 9.4**   Sample letter to fathers.

## Form 9.1

# POSITIONS COACHES NEED HELP IN

The Volleyball Team needs volunteer help in the areas indicated below. If you can help, please contact the head coach immediately.

| Position | No. of volunteers needed | When needed |
|---|---|---|
| Videographer | 1 | All games |
| Lines judges | 4 | 2 each, JV and V |
| Statisticians | 2 | 1 each, JV and V |
| Concessions | 2 | Home games |

Name _____ Telephone (home) _____

Position I can help _____ (business) _____

of form 9.1 to help them list the positions they may need help in. Once the areas are decided it helps to have a form that can be passed out at the preseason meeting to identify individuals who would volunteer to help. Form 9.2 can be easily duplicated and distributed to parents. Having your school principal address the parents is also a good idea. It sets the tone by establishing the overall importance of the athletic program in a child's education. Parents will help out more if they believe there is top-down support for the athletic program.

**Assisting the Coach—a Supporting Role**

Every team wants individuals to assist in its operation and contests. Coaches are always looking for competent individuals to assume some of these tasks. Many tasks demand specific knowledge or know-how, but many others can be performed with little or no skill.

These are some important areas in which parents might assist the coach and the team:

- Keeping the score book—this task involves

## Form 9.2

# SIGN-UP SHEET FOR VOLUNTEERS

Name _____ Address _____

Phone (home) _____ Phone (work) _____

Fax _____ E-mail _____

I can volunteer my time in the following area(s):

| | |
|---|---|
| ____ Refreshments after game | ____ Line-judging |
| ____ Keeping game statistics | ____ Selling |
| ____ Videotaping games | ____ Helping raise funds |
| ____ Acting as Booster representative | ____ Writing newsletter |
| ____ Selling tickets | ____ Concessions |
| ____ Taking equipment to games | ____ Other |

some knowledge of the sport and some specific knowledge of how to score.

- Operating the scoreboard—this task can be accomplished with a short lesson on the use of the scoreboard panel.

- Videographing events—many contests are videotaped to help players improve skills and tactics. Some knowledge of school-owned cameras might be necessary, but most cameras today are user-friendly.

- Keeping statistics—as with scoreboard operation, a 15-minute lesson on the specific statistics (e.g., offensive rebounds, defensive rebounds, turnovers) that are important to help the coach evaluate team performance and how to record them can develop a parent into a statistician.

- Helping transport equipment—this task always seems to beg for assistance.

- Announcing over the public address—be sure to give guidelines to the announcer on sportsmanship, being impartial, and maintaining decorum throughout the contest (see chapter 10 for expectations of public address announcers).

- Providing refreshments—this is a good task for generous moms and dads willing to help supply meals or light refreshments for pre- and post-game events.

- Acting as publicity director—this task might include supplying information to news media and to boosters' or school newsletters. Be sure the sport director and coach screen and approve all releases.

- Helping with a fund-raising project—coaches can use help in coordinating fund-raising for the team.

- Designing a telephone tree, assisting with team pictures, selling spirit items, working the concessions stand—these are a few of the many miscellaneous activities that parents can perform.

## Parents as Spectators

Parents play an important part in the athletic program as spectators at events. It is important that parents model sportsmanlike behavior and insist the same of other spectators. Remember that actions speak volumes. You might remind parents that the opposing team is not an enemy, just a group of competitors who are youngsters much like their own children. The opponents work as hard preparing for the contest as do their own kids, and they have the same emotional needs as have their own children. Coach parents on these keys to being helpful spectators at contests or events:

- Cheer in support of our team. Do not cheer against the opposing team.

- Be enthusiastic for your child and others on the team. Don't act as if your child is the only one on the team.

- Stay in control of your emotions. Do not yell at officials, coaches, or players. In other words, don't act like a young child who doesn't know better.

- Respect the coach by not giving instructions to your child, especially at a contest.

- Never leave a contest in anger or disgust. This kind of behavior is embarrassing to everyone who sees it.

- Never go to a contest or any school-sponsored event after having been drinking or doing drugs.

- Regardless of the outcome of the game, get in the habit of thanking the coaches and volunteers who helped conduct the event.

# RESOLVING CONFLICTS WITH PARENTS

More sport directors and coaches leave their jobs because of problems associated with poor communication and an inability to resolve conflicts than for any other single reason. Conflict is natural. Expect it. In any long-term relationship conflicts arise. This is true in sport programs also. How you deal with it will determine how smoothly your season goes. It is important that you handle conflicts in a consistent manner. You must decide how you want to be perceived as sport director and how you want people to respond to you. By mirroring this behavior to the person in conflict, chances increase for the behavior to be reflected back to you.

At the preseason meeting we present parents with our expectations of sportsmanship. We make it clear that as parents they are role models, and we expect parents to act in a sportsmanlike way to coaches, players, officials, or the visiting team. If parents violate this expectation, they will definitely hear about it and may be asked to leave. I recall a district volleyball game where a first-year parent vehemently complained about an official's very first call of the game. I happened to be sitting two rows behind this dad, and I called down to him, "Mr._____, remember you're a role model. Our student body is watching you." My intention was not to embarrass him, but to make the point loud and clear that parents should support the athletic department's philosophy.

The best leadership style to use in conflict is the cooperative style. Listen to all sides, be the calming force, and give proper direction when tempers settle down. If you seek *win-win* solutions to problems, you have a good chance of resolving conflict. If you look to win—or if the other party is trying to make you lose—the chance of resolution is slight.

A physician parent of one of my student athletes often talked with me about how other parents lost their cool at games, not trusting the coach and acting too hard on their children. He couldn't understand how parents allowed themselves to get so wrapped up in their children's sport experience. When the doctor's children reached high school age, I noticed that he stopped talking to me, a definite red flag to a sport director that something is wrong. I stopped him after practice one day and asked him if everything was all right, as he didn't seem to be his usual friendly self. The doctor began to tell me how his daughter was being benched because the coach didn't like her, how he couldn't understand why the coach played certain players, and how big a problem I had in my athletic program because of this coach. I asked him to see me so we could talk more about this. When we met, I reminded him of our conversations several years earlier. I asked him if this was his daughter's problem or *his* problem? I

asked whether he had talked to the coach? I empathized about how he felt, but also reminded him that having children involved in athletics can be like a roller coaster ride from one day to the next. And it is hard for parents to let go and allow their children to fend for themselves. The doctor admitted to me that his daughter was not having nearly as great a problem as he was; he promised that if things did not improve, he would make an appointment with the coach.

## Develop a Written Policy

It is helpful to the sport director, coaches, parents, and participants to have a written policy outlining the procedure for handling conflict (see chapter 5, page 51). If parents are to be allies, they need to know, understand, and support the expectations of the athletic department. These expectations must be communicated effectively—beginning at the preseason meeting and continuing throughout the year. The written procedure should contain the following:

- What parents should expect from their child's coach
- The coach's philosophy
- The chain of command
- What is appropriate to discuss with the coach
  a. The skill development of the participant
  b. Concern over the physical or emotional well-being of the participant
- What is *not* appropriate to discuss with the coach
  a. Playing time of the parent's son or daughter
  b. Participants other than the parent's son/daughter
- When it is appropriate to confront a coach
- Where it is appropriate to confront a coach

## When Does the Sport Director Get Involved?

Your parent-coach guide to communication should set parameters about when, how, and what to talk about together. The guides in figures 5.1 (chapter 5) and 9.5 set expectations that parents and coaches can count on. Discuss these communication guidelines fully at the preseason meeting. In addressing conflicts, attempt to resolve the problem *at the lowest possible level*. If a parent has a conflict with a coach, the problem should be resolved there and not with the sport director. If the conflict cannot be resolved at that level, then a predetermined "chain of command" should be followed.

---

We can't acknowledge it enough: sport is emotional. The sanest person can go off the deep end at a sporting event, especially when his or her "flesh and blood" relative is involved. Unfortunately, the most common time for parents to approach coaches is right after a game ends. The parent is upset, the coach doesn't want to hear it, and the sport director is suddenly facing crisis management. With a parent-coach communication guide distributed and in place already, you improve chances that

- the parent might not approach the coach just at the game's conclusion because that time would violate the guidelines.
- the coach would stop the parent and remind the individual that it was inappropriate to talk now but to call the coach later.
- the coach would walk away, remembering that it is better to give the parent time to cool off.

---

## Helping Parents in Their Efforts at Resolving Conflicts

Three keys for sport directors are to educate parents on the importance of (1) communicating to learn and improve, rather than to protect, defend, or destroy; (2) getting the child's perspective; and (3) understanding their role in discipline situations.

Parents need your leadership and guidance to develop good communication and to learn about procedures to handle their concerns and the conflicts that might arise in the athletic setting.

### Communicating to Learn and Improve

Humans have an unbelievable capacity to resolve conflict peacefully *if* they develop certain attitudes

that allow it to happen. Animals, on the other hand, rely on instinctive reactions to conflict. People possess the same instincts as animals do, but humans have the ability to reason and solve problems with their minds, a distinction brought out in figure 9.5.

It is easy to see from this chart that if we wish to resolve conflict, we must use our intelligence to solve problems. We must develop our skill and understanding as problem solvers. Many conflicts with parents stem from a lack of information or their having misinformation. Therefore we first should inform parents in order to resolve the conflict.

### How Animals and Humans Respond to Conflict

This chart indicates the range of reactions animals and humans have when confronted.

| Animals might | Humans might |
|---|---|
| Fight | Fight or contend by<br>• Insisting<br>• Blaming<br>• Accusing<br>• Criticizing<br>• Shouting<br>• Using force |
| Submit | Submit or yield by<br>• Giving in<br>• Giving up<br>• Agreeing to end it<br>• Surrendering |
| Flee | Withdraw by<br>• Not talking<br>• Leaving either physically or emotionally<br>• Changing topic |
| Freeze | Not act by<br>• Waiting<br>• Doing nothing<br>• Getting tongue-tied |
| (Not applicable) | Problem solve by<br>• Talking<br>• Listening<br>• Gathering information<br>• Thinking<br>• Resolving<br>• Generating options<br>• Negotiating |

**Figure 9.5** How animals and humans respond to conflict.

These steps can help you convince parents to seek to learn and solve many conflicts:

1. Eliminate misunderstandings first. Ask questions to clarify issues and find out if there is in fact a conflict or problem. If a problem does exist, go to the next step.

2. Discuss your issues and their issues. Find out what parents want and determine what you or the coaches want. Express your feelings and encourage parents to do the same. Remember to separate people from the problem; this will definitely help.

3. Brainstorm possible solutions with parents. Remember in brainstorming not to put down or eliminate any idea until you begin to prioritize solutions.

4. Look for solutions that satisfy the concerns of both parties. A good solution is many times a compromise for all involved.

5. Put everything in writing so there are no future misunderstandings or misinterpretations. Form 9.3 can help you stay on task and give both parties a document in writing.

Remember there are two sides to every story. The truth lies in the middle. It is the job of the sport director to be fair-minded and to arbitrate the conflict. A final decision cannot be based on emotion but must be supported by program policies, guidelines, and all the pertinent facts of the dispute. Remind those in conflict that adolescent students make mistakes. Do not formulate rules that have never-ending consequences. Although students must learn

 **Form 9.3**

# CONFLICT RESOLUTION WORKSHEET

**Directions:** When a conflict arises have the parties that disagree use this worksheet to help resolve the conflict.

1. Describe the conflict _____
_____
_____

   Is this a true conflict or is it a misunderstanding? _____

2. List your interests and the other party's interests (try to prioritize them).

| Yours | The other's |
|---|---|
|  |  |
|  |  |
|  |  |
|  |  |
|  |  |
|  |  |
|  |  |
|  |  |

3. List some possible solutions. (Think about compromising, bridging the gap, cutting your losses, or benefitting both parties.)

that there are consequences for breaking a rule, they do not have to be put in a jail with the key thrown away. Educate the student on what he did wrong and give him an opportunity to improve.

### Getting the Child's Perspective

Sport directors and coaches have jobs because of the participation of student athletes in interscholastic sports. When problems arise, we sport directors should make every attempt to obtain the athlete's perspective to help solve the problem. If we promise to keep the athlete's best interests in mind when making decisions, we rarely make mistakes.

Parents and coaches need to be reminded from time to time that decisions must be made to benefit the development of young people. When gathering information in the problem-solving process, we all should always include the athlete's perspective—before making a decision.

> A wise athletic director once told me to look at all conflicts from three perspectives before making a decision: your view, their view, and an objective third party's view.

### Understanding a Parent's Role in Discipline

When athletes violate athletic department, team, or school policies, the coach or sport director must invoke penalties or consequences as prescribed in the policy handbook. These situations become emotional for everyone involved in them, but particularly for the athlete and his or her parents. Effective athletic departments always involve parents in some way in the process of disciplining student athletes. Those programs that neglect involving parents will confront more problems than they can solve.

These are some key ways that you can use to involve parents when levying penalties for student violations of policy:

- When a violation of a rule or policy occurs, call the parents to inform them and ask for their support. If a penalty is invoked, you need for parents to agree with the coach and athletic department about the outcome.

- Involve parents in the discipline hearing with the coach and athlete so they feel part of the process.

- Inform parents at the preseason meeting that the athletic department and coach will solicit their support when disciplinary action is necessary for the benefit of a participant. The athlete will have a better chance of learning how to follow rules if both the coach and parents are in support of one another. Parents should understand that without their support a mixed message is sent to the child, and this only confuses the student athlete.

# RECOGNIZING PARENTS

Parents have specific cares as they enter the world of interscholastic sports, just as athletes have needs and coaches have needs. Parents' concerns usually focus on the well-being of their athlete, although they sometimes stem from a parent's selfish needs. It is important for the good of the athletes and the program that sport directors recognize and try to satisfy a parent's needs.

Let's look at some of the more common needs that many sport parents have when they become involved in our sport program. These are not negatives, and many of them are indeed positive wishes.

## Parents Have a Need to Know

They want to know all about the coach, what the coach stands for, how the team operates, what the rules of the team are, what the penalties are, how to get to games, and so on. The preseason meeting is the vehicle an athletic department uses to inform parents. Communicating with coaches is also an important factor in satisfying that parental need to know.

## Parents Have a Need to Be Involved

Make sure to involve the parents of your athletes. Parental involvement can take many forms, from driving athletes to and from practice to being an officer in the booster club. Sport directors must encourage and support parents who involve themselves in positive ways.

You are instrumental to the success of booster clubs, and you can support the parents of your athletes in ways that also recognize them:

- Support their projects.

# ◢◣ Form 9.4
# PARENT FEEDBACK TO ATHLETIC DEPARTMENT

As parents of students involved in interscholastic sports, please take a few moments to give our athletic department feedback. Your perceptions and opinions are important to us and will help improve our department for our student athletes.

**Directions:** Please circle one and use the space below the question to add your personal observations.

Strongly agree   5                    4                    3                    2                    1   Strongly disagree

1. My daughter's/son's sport experience has helped her/him develop into a better person emotionally, psychologically, and physically.
         5                    4                    3                    2                    1
   Observations: _____
   _____

2. My daughter's/son's uniforms and practice equipment make us proud to be a North Olmsted parent.
         5                    4                    3                    2                    1
   Observations: _____
   _____

3. My daughter's/son's equipment and facilities are adequate and ensure a safe experience.
         5                    4                    3                    2                    1
   Observations: _____
   _____

4. My daughter's/son's coach adheres to the rules and policies of the athletic department.
         5                    4                    3                    2                    1
   Observations: _____
   _____

5. The policies and rules of the athletic department are established in the best interests of the student athletes.
         5                    4                    3                    2                    1
   Observations: _____
   _____

6. The athletic department's awards and recognition program promotes and encourages student athletes to strive for excellence.
         5                    4                    3                    2                    1
   Observations: _____
   _____

7. Things we should continue to do in the athletic department are
   Observations: _____
   _____

8. Things we should stop doing in the athletic department are
   Observations: _____
   _____

9. We should consider changing the following things to improve our athletic program for the student athletes.
   Observations: _____
   _____

- Help them determine the needs of the athletic program.

- Direct booster volunteers to the tasks that need completing.

- Prevent the booster club from working against the philosophy and objectives of the program.

- Empower members to actively support coaches and athletes.

## Parents Have a Need to Give Feedback

Feedback from parents can be negative (their yelling at the coach from the stands) or positive (their sending a letter about an enriching experience the athlete has had). Effective programs supply parents a vehicle to give feedback about how the athletic program operates and the effectiveness of the coach. When feedback is encouraged in the spirit of making the sport experience more positive for athletes, it usually becomes nonthreatening.

For parents to feel ownership in the program, they must have an avenue to give constructive feedback to coaches and sport directors. Athletic programs do get feedback, but often it is neither constructive nor solicited by coaches or sport directors. Rather, it comes in the form of negative comments about the coach, emotional outbursts at contests, or just plain gossip about everyone in the program. Much of this negative-type feedback stems from the frustration parents feel at not having a formal way of expressing their opinions.

One way to gain parental support is to give them the opportunities for conveying their feedback about the program. Let's say it again: you will more likely receive support from the parents if they feel ownership in the program. The feedback from parents must center on the goals of the program. When parents feel we have met most of our goals and objectives, regardless of the team's record, they also recognize that we enjoyed a successful season.

Keep this thought in mind when developing a feedback instrument for parents. These instruments must indicate the things that you should continue to do for athletes, the things you should stop doing, and what changes you might consider in order to improve your program and coaches. Forms 9.4 and 9.5 are examples of tools that athletic departments can use to gain valuable feedback from parents.

 **Form 9.5**

# PARENT FEEDBACK TO COACHES

Sport _____ Level _____ Year _____

As a parent of a student athlete in our interscholastic athletic program your feedback is important to us. Our coaching staff feels that to make our program better for the student we must gain valuable feedback from our parents.

**Directions:** Circle the number that best describes the way you feel and use the space below each item to state your observations that would support your feelings.

Strongly agree  5          4          3          2          1 Strongly disagree

1. Our coach(es) operate the program in the best interests of all the participants.
      5          4          3          2          1
   Observations: _____
   _____

2. We understand the goals and objectives of the program represented by our coach.
      5          4          3          2          1
   Observations: _____
   _____

3. Our coach treats all participants fairly and consistently.
      5          4          3          2          1
   Observations: _____
   _____

# Form 9.5 *(continued)*

Strongly agree   5              4              3              2              1  Strongly disagree

4. We can approach our coach to discuss concerns about our son/daughter.

     5              4              3              2              1

Observations: _____

_____

5. Our coach is a good role model for our son/daughter.

     5              4              3              2              1

Observations: _____

_____

6. Our coach is knowledgeable about the rules and strategies of the sport.

     5              4              3              2              1

Observations: _____

_____

7. Our coach is a good communicator.

     5              4              3              2              1

Observations: _____

_____

8. Our coach is organized and plans ahead.

     5              4              3              2              1

Observations: _____

_____

9. Our coach takes an interest in our daughter/son academically and outside of the sport.

     5              4              3              2              1

Observations: _____

_____

10. Our coach has improved the skills in this sport for our daughter/son.

     5              4              3              2              1

Observations: _____

_____

11. Our coach understands how to motivate athletes.

     5              4              3              2              1

Observations: _____

_____

12. Our coach should continue to do the following things:

Observations: _____

_____

13. Our coach should stop doing the following things:

Observations: _____

_____

14. Our coach should change the following things:

Observations: _____

_____

*Summary*

In this chapter you learned to

1. involve parents in booster clubs as spectators and volunteers;

2. hold a preseason meeting to discuss their and your responsibilities;

3. update them on the department's schedule, regulations, and activities; and

4. recognize parents' needs to know, be involved, and give feedback.

# Chapter 10
## Supervising Officials and Support Staff

An athletic department staff includes athletic officials, secretaries, contest supervisors, maintenance and custodial personnel, security and crowd-control personnel, scorers, timers, announcers, transportation personnel, and any individual connected with the function of the athletic department. The overall mission of athletic programs is to develop good citizens for society by teaching young athletes to respect themselves and others and be responsible for their own behavior. Sport directors and coaches cannot accomplish this mission without the help and involvement of the myriad individuals who make up the support staff and supervisory officials of the athletic department.

In this chapter you will learn about these topics:

1. What responsibilities officials and support staff have and your role in supervising them.

2. How to recruit and retain officials and support staff.

3. How to give staff members recognition and make them feel a part of the athletic department family.

4. How to help staff members communicate and resolve conflicts.

5. How to develop procedures to evaluate officials and support staff.

# RESPONSIBILITIES OF OFFICIALS

Officials are active participants in all contests. If the officials are professional and conduct themselves so, they have the ability to avoid or minimize situations that might otherwise become volatile. On the other hand, officials can also be catalysts for inappropriate behavior by players, coaches, and spectators. It is important for everyone involved in the contest to understand the responsibilities of the official. The responsibilities are to

- fulfill officiating services as prescribed in a contract between school and official;
- inspect facilities and equipment prior to contest;
- be licensed in the state that they perform their services;
- enforce the rules of the game;
- maintain sportsmanship by coaches, athletes, and fans; and
- remain impartial.

A sport director can do several things to facilitate the smooth operation of the contest and to meet the needs of the officials, coaches, and players. It is important that everyone involved in the contest work as a team. The officials must understand their role as overseers of the contest, enforcing the rules and protocols of the contest. They must also understand that the game is for the players and not for them, the officials. The coaches, too, must understand the responsibility of the officials in this environment. It is critical that coaches respect the officials. Successful coaches do not use officials as excuses. Working as a team, with officials understanding the role of the coach and the coach understanding the role of the officials, creates the optimum environment for the student athletes to compete in.

Everyone expects officials to be objective during the contest. It is important that the officials be well trained and understand the rules of the contest. It is also necessary for them to stay alert to safety during the contest. An official should not permit play to reach a state that might put players at risk of injury or allow competition within an unsafe environment. If a safety question arises, the official should bring it to the attention of the coach and the sport director so the issue can be safely resolved. In the event of high-risk play, again, the official must communicate with the coaches and the sport director to express concerns and find appropriate resolution.

There are many risk situations that officials need to inform sport directors and coaches of. Some common risks that officials check for are inadequate or missing padding, damaged equipment, dangerous field conditions, and rough play. An area of great concern these days is playing outdoors when there is a threat of lightning. Officials have the authority to stop play if they feel the lightning might become a threat to the players, coaches, or fans. In many sports the official is responsible for checking that the playing surface and equipment meet established standards set by manufacturers and that the playing conditions satisfy the rules of the sport. If a playing surface is found inadequate, the official must notify the coach and the sport director to correct the situation.

A sprinkler head on a soccer field was exposed. During the official's pregame inspection he discovered the raised sprinkler head. The official contacted the sport director who arranged for the maintenance department to bring in additional soil to cover the sprinkler head.

## Your Responsibilities to the Officials

There are various things you should do as preparation for the arrival and departure of the officials. Prior to the arrival of an official, you should have a **contract** (see figure 10.1, p. 137) prepared with the following information, which should be signed and returned by the official:

- Date of contest
- Time of contest
- Location of contest

- Competition level of the participants (e.g., varsity, junior varsity)
- Directions to the contest
- Rate of pay
- Name of the opponent
- Names of other officials assigned to the contest

When the official arrives at the contest site, he or she should be greeted by personnel representing the sport director. The person greeting the official should provide the following:

- A voucher for the official to sign, if required by the school.
- An adequate place (one that is private and can be locked) for the official to dress and prepare for the contest. Don't forget that when you employ both female and male officials, they should have separate dressing rooms and shower facilities.
- Information that is specific to the contest site: how do the officials enter and exit the facility?
- Any league or conference rules that might be specific to the contest.
- Expectations concerning players, coaches, and officials for the contest.
- Game security, including information about the location of security officers, the sport director, or other pertinent school personnel during the contest.
- A feeling of welcome and hospitality, perhaps by having refreshments at half time and after the game. Some sport directors provide soap and towels for a shower after the game.

Once you have completed the pregame protocol, it is important to make sure that the official understands your expectations. If you have a checklist of responsibilities, you might discuss it with the contest official and ask if there are remaining questions.

# RECRUITING OFFICIALS

One of the generalizations heard most commonly in the athletic community is "There just don't seem to be any good officials." As we know, officiating requires fast-paced, subjective decision making that does not favor one team or the other. Because of this requirement, officiating can be as difficult as it is rewarding. As sport directors we should keep promoting officiating among young athletes and young coaches. Their involvement in officials' organizations is critical to maintaining the necessary supply of officials. We also must take the lead in maintaining the respect that the officials' position requires and demands. Without maintaining our integrity about and respect for officiating decisions, we will not be able to recruit the high quality of individual capable of officiating varsity-level contests. If we allow officials to be demeaned, we hinder their ability to do the type of job we expect—and we do not create an environment that new officials want to enter, thus failing to replenish our pool of officials.

## How Many Officials?

In preparing for an upcoming season, you must determine the number and quality of officials needed for each contest. For example, you consider if having five officials for varsity football mandates that it is necessary to have five officials as well for junior varsity or freshman contests. Determining the number of officials for a varsity contest is typically done at the league level; lower-level (such as middle school) contests are often left to the school to determine. As you determine the number of officials to use at the various levels, one additional consideration is how many available officials there are. And considering student safety is critical. It would not be wise to play any level of football with only one official, but one volleyball official may be adequate for a middle school game.

## What Level of Officials?

Once you establish how many officials are needed, you should then determine what skill level each official must possess. The experience and skill required to officiate at a varsity-level contest will be greater than that needed for a freshman contest. Many states have licensing or certification levels for officials. It is important for you to understand that within a licensing or certification level there are different degrees of expertise. A level-1 official has been determined to have the necessary knowledge and ability to officiate varsity-level contests. A level-2 official does not yet have the experience and skills necessary for varsity action. An official who may be adequate for a nonleague contest against a school that is not a traditional rival may still not be adequate for a contest against your school's primary rival.

Who is to officiate at a contest is a determination that you must make early on in the scheduling process. Using evaluations of officials can help you make this determination. When an officials' association secures the officials for your home contests, you must communicate clearly with that association the necessary skill level the official will need to have for the contests they are assigned.

## Securing Officials

In securing officials for contests it is often helpful for the sport director to use local, district, or state officials' associations. In many areas officials are assigned to contests by an outside individual or organization, which can eliminate the potential for bias that might occur if the school hires the officials. If the home school uses a third party to assign officials, there is little chance that an allegation of favoritism can be made toward the home team.

You should know what responsibilities you have in contracting officials, and if you are unclear about these responsibilities, it is important that you check with your state athletic association and its district legal counsel. State athletic associations often publish officials' directories as a service to member schools. Often these associations not only provide lists of officials but will also assign officials to contests. This is helpful when you have a large number of contests requiring officials. Some sport directors must find virtually hundreds of officials in a school year because of the many contests and wide variety of sports that their programs offer.

In soliciting officials for contests you should manage timelines and contracts. How early should you begin contracting for future contests? Timelines depend on the availability of officials. The fewer the officials, the sooner it is necessary to contract them for a contest. Second, the level of the sport can affect when you seek officials; varsity-level officials tend to be in higher demand than are lower-level officials. Past practice also influences timelines: some sports have a traditional method or timeline for assigning officials.

Typically, contracting officials more than two years in advance for varsity contests is excessive. The long duration between the contract and the contest allows for problems to arise that might require you to replace the official. Job transfers or retirement from officiating, for example, can leave you scrambling for a replacement for the official that was contracted three to five years earlier. A more appropriate time would be one to two years prior to the contest.

When you deal with an official at any level, it is prudent to have the official sign a **binding contract** (see a sample in figure 10.1). This protects both the school and official from any unforeseen event, and it communicates clearly to each party the necessary contest information.

# BUILDING A LASTING RELATIONSHIP

Competitive athletics can create strong emotions on the part of the coaches and officials. With most officials' associations, the official has the opportunity to turn down contests where a conflict may exist with a coach. In turn, schools have the opportunity to scratch an official, so the association knows not to hire them for that school's contests.

As a sport director you are aware that you will have a lasting need for officials. It is important to develop a good relationship with the officials. This is done by meeting the needs of both the official and the school and assuring that both parties are clear about their expectations of each other. Here is how you can foster a good working relationship:

- Communicate effectively with the official prior to the contest.

- Provide any necessary policy information that is pertinent from the school, league, or state association.

- Provide the official with a clear understanding of what is expected in the area of students', coaches', and officials' behavior during the contest.

- Provide the official with adequate facilities to change and discuss pregame strategies with other officials.

**Contract for Contest Official**

# Ohio High School Athletic Association
## Contract for Contest Official

| Day | Month | Date | Year | & Time | Site or Location | Fees & Expenses |
|---|---|---|---|---|---|---|
|  |  |  |  |  |  |  |

| Name and Address of Official | Position | Names of Other Officials |
|---|---|---|
|  |  |  |

The _____ High School and _____, a properly registered official enters into the following agreement: The said official agrees to be present and officiate the _____ contest to be played with _____ High School.

1. If either of the contracting parties fails to fulfill the terms of the contract, the party who fails to fulfill the contract will pay the other party a sum equal to the contest fee stated above unless the contracting parties both agree to waive the payment.

2. The official shall not be released from this contract in order to officiate another athletic contest - high school or college - without payment of the damage fee unless mutually agreed to in writing at the time the contract is signed.

3. The said school will pay the said official the amount stated above for services rendered provided that the obligation of the school ceases if and when the official ceases to be an OHSAA-registered official or if the contest is cancelled because of unfavorable weather, epidemics or other emergencies, and the official is notified of such cancellation prior to arrival at contest.

4. The obligation of an official ceases if both teams are not present within 30 minutes of the scheduled starting time unless notified that a team will be late. Officials will be paid as per contract.

5. This contract must be returned no later than _____

6. Other: _____

_____   _____   _____   _____
(School Administrator or Assigner)   (Phone–work)   (Phone–home)   (Date Signed)

## Official's Certificate

As a registered official of the Ohio High School Athletic Association, I acknowledge that when I am employed as an official that I am an independent contractor not an agent. I will administer in an unbiased and non-prejudicial manner all contests in accordance with contest rules and interpretation of rules as well as rules and regulations adopted by the OHSAA or its Board of Control. I further agree to be honest in my association with school administrators and the OHSAA and will not be a party to any attempt to establish officiating fees that other officials must follow. I further agree to honor each contract which I sign and will not request a school to void a contract except for illness, injury or a family emergency beyond my control. My conduct on or off the playing surface will be such as to bring credit to myself, the contestants, coaches and the OHSAA. I understand that failure to honor a contract without just cause or violation of the rules of the OHSAA could result in the suspension or termination of my officiating permit.

Official _____ OHSAA Permit No. _____ Date signed _____

Official's Phone: Home _____ Business _____ S.S. Number _____

**NOTE: SEND REMINDER NOTICE ONE WEEK PRIOR TO CONTEST**

**Figure 10.1**   Sample contract between a high school and an official. (Used courtesy of the Ohio High School Athletic Association.)

- Provide adequate security.
- Always treat officials professionally.

Local schools should do their part to honor officials during National Sport and Activities Week, sponsored by the National Federation of State High School Associations. Try to provide opportunities for officials to participate in recognition weeks or dedicate articles in the game program to officials.

# RESOLVING CONFLICTS

Once a conflict between an official and a coach or player occurs, it becomes necessary for the sport director to maintain open lines of communication with both parties. You must be sure you understand all parts of the conflict before you can begin to work toward its resolution. Often it is necessary to set up a meeting with the people in conflict to discuss the issue. This is resolving the conflict at its lowest level.

In addressing conflict with coaches and officials or with officials and players, it is important that each group understand its responsibilities. By having clearly established parameters and expectations, both parties have a greater chance to understand the appropriateness of their actions and behavior. It is good practice to discuss the value and difficulty of the task of officiating with coaches and players *before* the start of the season. It is also good practice to have officials discuss the necessary professional decorum they must demonstrate at contests in their association meetings. As the sport director, you can facilitate this by communicating your school's or league's expectations to officials' associations in a professional fashion before the season.

# EVALUATING OFFICIALS

To promote professional growth among the officials (and thereby provide student athletes with the highest quality of programs) you should have an evaluation process in place. Many sport directors evaluate officials with the assistance of coaches and offi-

cials' associations. Evaluation should be viewed as working with officials to improve their performance. In no way should you use evaluation to be punitive. The person doing the evaluation should be objective and knowledgeable about officiating the sport being observed. As discussed earlier, maintaining an adequate supply of quality officials is difficult, and it should be a priority for any sport director. In evaluating an official, therefore, it is especially important to identify not only the weaknesses but also the strengths the official has exhibited. In this way a balance is created, yielding a more accurate evaluation of the official. In completing an evaluation you might consider the following criteria:

- Knows the rules of the game.
- Understands the intent of the rules.
- Communicates appropriately with coaches and players.
- Arrives on time at contests.
- Wears appropriate uniform and uses appropriate equipment.
- Uses acceptable officiating mechanics.
- Handles difficult situations appropriately.

Finally, it can be advantageous to have officials complete a self-evaluation form identifying their specific areas of strengths and weaknesses.

## Releasing Officials

Once the decision is made to retain or release an official, you must communicate it to the individual. This can be done through the officials' association, the league commissioner, or directly by the school. When choosing to no longer contract with an official, there should be some clear basis. How much information you share with the official depends on the relationship you have. Ideally there should be open communication between the sport director and official. At times this is not possible, and a third party may be more effective in communicating with the official.

## Retaining and Promoting Officials

In communicating with the official to be retained, it is important to communicate *positive* traits and characteristics that the official has demonstrated, as well as areas that you feel need continued improvement.

This is especially important with young officials who are trying to move to a higher level of officiating. In providing information to officials, be as clear as you can, and cite specific examples where possible of the positive behavior. It is also important to indicate specific incidents of negative behavior. By providing a balanced evaluation to the official, you give the individual a greater opportunity to grow and develop into a fine official.

# YOUR RESPONSIBILITIES TO SUPPORT STAFF

Any individual who has responsibility in the athletic department or is responsible to participants and coaches in the athletic department is part of the support staff. In particular these people include assistant athletic directors, athletic department secretaries, equipment managers, game managers, athletic trainers, maintenance personnel, custodians, officials, scorers, timers, judges, bus drivers, and gate personnel. In your personnel management as sport director you want to help support staff understand their function and importance in accomplishing the department's goal of helping athletes develop psychologically, physically, and socially. Staff members may not feel they play an important part, and you must somehow communicate how important their roles are. Without support staff the games cannot go on. Each staff member plays an integral role in ensuring that the activities we provide are operated safely and efficiently.

You have the added responsibility to educate athletes, coaches, and parents about how important the support staff is to the success of the athletic program. Support staff members work better when they know how much we appreciate them, and we should recognize their involvement in the program. Do everything you can to assist support staff members in the performance of their jobs.

Set the tone at preseason meetings with head custodians, maintenance personnel, individuals responsible for game duties, transportation personnel, and, if you're lucky enough to have them, your secretary or assistants. At these meetings you can go over the philosophies and objectives of the program. Tell the staff verbally and in writing how important they are to the success of the program. Ask them to take the same pride in the program that coaches and athletes do. When possible, convene your support staff at a single meeting to ensure all personnel receive the same message. In any case, you should be consistent in what you tell staff members.

If a support staff member feels his or her role is insignificant, the individual may not go the extra mile that we are asking of everyone else in the program. Remember that every person in the athletic department influences your student athletes. If support staff are good role models, if they are enthusiastic about what they do, and if they enjoy young people, they can play an important part in helping develop the students.

# TRAINING SUPPORT STAFF

To communicate effectively with your support staff members, you must explain their function and encourage their giving feedback. Each support staff member should receive a sheet of paper with your expectations spelled out. In figures 10.2 through 10.5 you can see examples of expectations for a ticket taker, an announcer, a game manager, and a maintenance supervisor. The sport director should develop an expectation sheet for each person considered to be a support staff person. Solicit the input of others, such as the head of maintenance and grounds, the clerk treasurer, and head coaches, to assist you in creating these expectation sheets.

Often the education of support staff is overlooked because their impact on the overall program is not recognized. These staff members must have a working knowledge of the policies and procedures of the athletic department (just as coaches, athletes, and parents must) since they have an impact on our athletes' development. So the preseason meeting becomes an important opportunity to explain the role and function of each person connected with the program.

The support staff should also know and understand training rules and athletic department policies. Give copies of these relevant documents to the support staff and explain their significance to them. There are two reasons to do this: First it gives support people that feeling of ownership we have been

---

**Ticket Taker**

**Before the game**

____Make sure you have signs in place indicating home and visitors and the price of admission.

____Arrive at least one hour before the contest.

____Remain in designated area throughout the game. Never leave the money box unattended.

**During the game**

____Alert the contest supervisor or administrator on duty if there is an adult or student acting inappropriately.

____Tickets should be sold until the end of the game unless the administrator in charge decides otherwise. Be sure people that are waiting to gain free admittance know this.

**After the game**

____Assist maintenance by moving chairs and table out of the way of the fans leaving the contest.

____Assist contest supervisor in the counting of money and the completion of the ticket report.

____Remain on duty until the contest supervisor informs you that it is acceptable to leave.

---

**Figure 10.2**   Sample expectation sheet for support staff—a ticket taker.

---

**Announcers**

**Before the game**

____Arrive at least 30 minutes before the game.

____Obtain microphone from contest supervisor and check the PA system. If a problem exists, contact a custodian.

____Be sure you have home and visitor rosters, announcements, promotions, and sportsmanship statement.

**During the game**

____Be impartial, do not use slang, and don't become the entertainment.

____Announce facts after they have occurred. Don't anticipate. Be enthusiastic.

____Help out the contest supervisor by being aware of the mood of the fans. Help out in critical situations by helping calm things down.

____Read a sportsmanship statement and statements that will put the game in perspective for the fans.

**After the game**

____Please announce that fans should not go on the playing surface. Direct fans to the exits and parking lots.

____Remain on duty until the contest supervisor allows you to leave.

---

**Figure 10.3**   Sample expectation sheet for support staff—an announcer.

talking about (and they may be more effective than anyone else at giving athletes a positive direction). The second reason to include support staff in the training about the athletic policies and rules relates to the team concept. We foster greater likelihood of influencing young people positively when we add people to our team who know their roles and share a sense of duty to helping the youngsters develop psychologically, socially, and physically. Teams working together to accomplish a mission have a greater chance for success than individuals acting alone.

---

**Game Managers**

**Before the game**

____Arrive at least 1¹/₂ hours before the game.

____Set up gate with sign-in sheet, money box, admissions sign, rosters, tickets, game programs, and announcements.

____Inspect officials' locker room, visitors' locker and shower facilities to be sure they are clean and free of debris.

____Supervise the setup of the scoring panel, microphone, bleachers, and special equipment (volleyball nets, baskets, wrestling mats, etc.).

____Greet visiting team and cheerleaders. Direct them to dressing areas. Be sure they have chalk and erasers.

____Greet officials and direct them to the dressing area. Go over pregame checklist with each official. Let them know where you will be during contest; introduce them to coaches, scorer, and timer.

____Be sure announcer has rosters and announcements to be read for the game.

**During the game**

____Be near the contest at all times in the event the coaches or officials need you.

____Supervise the behavior of the fans and participants to be sure they are following athletic department expectations.

____Walk officials to dressing area at half time. Provide them with a beverage. Notify them three minutes before the second half is to start.

____Walk the officials to the dressing area immediately after the game to assure they are not approached by coaches or fans. Provide them with a beverage or water. Discuss any unusual incidents with officials and report them to the sport director.

**After the game**

____Assist the custodians in tearing down the gymnasium or field. Put microphone in sport director's office, along with the score panel.

____Supervise the fans as they exit the gym or field. Report any unusual or unsportsmanlike behavior to the sport director.

____Put money box and unused tickets in the safe in the sport director's office. Fill out box office report of tickets and receipts.

____Be sure visiting team and officials depart safely, and remain at the game until everyone has departed.

At all times be courteous and friendly to our visitors, their teams, and the officials. They are our guests.

---

**Figure 10.4**   Sample expectation sheet for support staff—game managers.

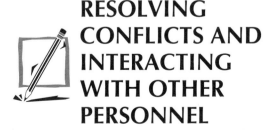

# RESOLVING CONFLICTS AND INTERACTING WITH OTHER PERSONNEL

The best ways to avoid personnel problems with support staff are to establish a chain of command, communicate effectively, and set guidelines for solving problems and resolving conflicts. These methods are especially important because support staff personnel are so numerous and perform such varied duties.

## Establishing the Chain of Command

Establishing a chain of command does not mean that you will operate your athletic department as a strict general might have during World War I.

---

**Maintenance Request**

---

To: Joe

From: Tim

Date: July 28,1997

Re: Fall maintenance requests

To prepare for the upcoming football and soccer seasons I have compiled a list of items that need your department's attention. If you would let me know if there are problems with any of these requests, I would appreciate it.

\_\_\_\_Inspect home and visiting bleachers for safety.

\_\_\_\_Test lights and replace as needed.

\_\_\_\_Inspect and test headphones, home and visitor.

\_\_\_\_Test sound system, wireless microphone, speakers, etc.

\_\_\_\_Line stadium fields per attached schedules for home contests.

\_\_\_\_Line practice fields per attached request.

\_\_\_\_Remove foliage overhanging walkway when entering from south end.

\_\_\_\_Fill any holes in the stadium, football practice field, middle school field, and practice soccer field.

On behalf of the coaches and players, we thank you in advance for the commitment your department makes to athletics. Many times you don't hear the positives that exist because of the conscientious work your maintenance staff performs.

**Figure 10.5** Sample maintenance request form.

Effective sport directors establish lines of communication to give support staff a clear picture of who is responsible to them and who they are responsible to. Think about it: don't you get frustrated when someone bypasses you to voice a concern? A clear line of communication can eliminate that frustration.

You must clearly state who is responsible for what. That will help ensure that support personnel don't overstep their bounds—and are not called upon to do so. The department doesn't want maintenance personnel deciding who may or may not use school-owned facilities. Nor do support staff want to be put into a situation where they become liable for their actions. A good example is a situation of crowd control. Supervisors who are not administrators should not decide who should be removed from a contest. The chain of command should indicate that the administrator in charge or security personnel who are trained in crowd control should be the only ones responsible for making those decisions.

Sport directors should train and enable support staff to direct people with questions or concerns to the appropriate person, the one who is responsible for that area. If a parent has a concern, for example, about which summer camp to send a child to, the support staff should refer that parent to the sport director or coach of the particular sport. Following a chain of command with stated responsibilities empowers support staff to work as a team with the administrators, coaches, and other staff members. You must establish guidelines for effective communication that are particular to your support staff. The purpose of creating guidelines is to set clear and realistic expectations that personnel can follow. The chart in figure 10.6 shows part of a typical chain of command for the athletic department.

## Communicating Effectively

Consider your own communication style. Do you believe in an open-door policy or want staff members to make an appointment? Figure 10.7 lists some keys to effective communication between a sport director and support staff. Distribute these guidelines or ones that you develop to all support staff and discuss them prior to the school year or season.

**Administrative Organization (1.4)**

**Chain of Command**

A. Board of education

B. Superintendent of schools
   1. Is ultimately responsible for all phases of the public school program
   2. Delegates his/her power of administration of the interscholastic athletic program through the high school Principal to the Athletic Director

C. High school principal
   1. Is responsible for all activities affecting students in his/her building
   2. Is closely involved with the operation of the athletic program
   3. Coordinates the athletic program with other school activities

D. Athletic director
   1. Directs the operation of the athletic program:
      a. Is responsible for all league schedules
      b. Is responsible for transportation
      c. Is responsible for obtaining officials for games
      d. Is responsible for all schedule changes
   2. Selects and in-services all coaches
   3. Evaluates the athletic program and the athletic staff
   4. Participates in budget preparation for the athletic program

**Figure 10.6**   Sample chain of command for athletic department.

**Keys to Communication**

Two-way communication among members of the athletic department team is important to help meet our goals. Below are some keys to effective communication.

1. Participate in a preseason or pre–school year meeting to discuss expectations of both the sport director and the support staff person.
2. When conflict occurs, make an appointment with the sport director to discuss possible solutions.
3. The sport director and support staff member should treat each other with respect and rely on each other (as would members of a team). In short, treat each other the way you would like to be treated.
4. Be clear on your roles and duties so as not to make decisions that are not yours to make.

**Figure 10.7**   Keys to effective communication for support staff.

I once worked with a night custodian who was responsible for cleaning the gymnasiums, locker rooms, and coaches' offices, as well as for raising or lowering the baskets, depending on how the gym would be used the next day. One morning he left me a nasty note accusing the basketball coach of locking up the winch machine, which was the device used to raise and lower the baskets. After talking to the basketball coach and the head custodian, I found out the machine had been taken to a shop to be repaired. So I called the night custodian in and asked him what he thought had happened. Then I asked him what he did to determine if he was right. He didn't try to find the truth because he had convinced himself that the basketball coach was out to make his life miserable. Without letting him know that I had already investigated the matter, I asked him if he would confront the coach in a positive way and see if he knew where the winch machine was. The lesson is that confrontation can sometimes be a good way to reach the truth. The custodian discovered that confronting the coach to learn the truth was better than going no further than an assumption.

## Setting Guidelines for Resolving Conflicts and Problems

Conflict is natural, especially in sport, where emotions sometimes run high. The key to minimizing conflict in the athletic department is to create an atmosphere in which support staff can discuss their concerns without getting their heads chewed off. As sport director you must set an example.

If you lose your cool or act defensively when someone asks a question and if you put people down to show your superiority, your support staff probably will not share their concerns with you. On the other hand, if you become a good listener, encourage feedback, treat staff with respect and dignity, and maintain a professional demeanor in all situa-

tions, you will begin to create a positive atmosphere in the athletic department. And you must provide in-service training for the staff on the keys to effective communication to help resolve conflict. Figure 10.8 gives some reminders to help you and staff members keep conflict in perspective and deal with it effectively.

# RECOGNIZING SUPPORT STAFF'S NEEDS

You are responsible for creating a team atmosphere, and as coach of that athletic department team you should treat team members alike. Support staff, just like athletes, coaches, and parents, stay better focused on performing their duties when their own basic needs have been met. To understand and meet those needs you must (1) meet regularly with your staff, (2) recognize individuals for outstanding work, and (3) reinforce the intrinsic things that motivate them to do their jobs.

## Meeting Regularly With Staff

It seems we spend half our busy days in meetings. One thing you may not want to read is how important it is to meet regularly with support staff. After all, how much time is left after you meet with par-

---

**Conflict Resolution**

Sports will be emotional at times. When that emotion becomes negative, it is up to members of the athletic department to show leadership in the resolution of that conflict or disagreement. Please become familiar with the reminders below and use these techniques when you find yourself in conflict.

1. Either talk or listen. These actions cannot both happen at the same time.
2. Make eye contact with the person.
3. Ask open-ended questions if you don't understand something.
4. Try putting yourself in the other person's place.
5. Focus your attention on the issues at hand, not on the person's behavior.
6. Use positive, open body language.
7. Remember that animals and humans respond instinctively to conflict but only humans can reason clearly if they choose to.
8. Set up a meeting if the conflict cannot be resolved immediately.

**Figure 10.8** Sample conflict resolution reminders.

ents, coaches, athletes, administrators, and others? Well, for your own sake as well as the team's, you must make the time to meet with support staff members regularly to discuss expectations, receive feedback, and evaluate performance.

This doesn't mean you have to meet every day. It does mean you should meet often enough to ensure that support staff understand their roles and feel good about being part of the athletic department. When you meet prior to the season with support staff, one expectation you should deal with is how often you will again meet during the season. Meeting regularly will help you reach your department's objectives, keep lines of communication open, and give support staff the feeling they are an integral part of the athletic department.

## Recognizing Support Staff for Outstanding Work

Support staff should be recognized, like anyone else on your athletic department team, for performing outstanding work and exemplifying attributes that are important for young athletes to see. These are some ideas about recognition to consider distributing to support staff to reinforce the ideals of your athletic department:

- Outstanding school employee award, given to the school employee who has made the greatest contribution or impact on the lives of young people

- Outstanding volunteer award, given to the volunteer who has made the greatest impact on the lives of young people

- Unsung hero award, given to the individual who doesn't receive the attention that others receive but performs duties above and beyond what is expected

- Most sportsmanlike staff award, given to the individual who exemplifies the true ideals of sportsmanship, ethics, and integrity

- Years of service award, given to loyal support staff after 5, 10, 15, 20, 25, and more years of service

- Greatest contribution to young people award, given to an individual who performed an act, donated time, or contributed something truly special to the young people involved in sport.

Support staff who receive these recognitions can be nominated by the various administrative heads whom you work with every day, parents, coaches, or athletes. It is important to identify support staff who really have *earned* the recognition, rather than simply giving out awards to everyone. Form 10.1 is a nomination form that could be adapted for your use to identify worthy recipients.

## Form 10.1

# NOMINATION FORM TO RECOGNIZE SUPPORT STAFF

Our athletic department operates as a team to help our student athletes become better citizens. To encourage members of our athletic department to model behavior that supports our department philosophy, we want to recognize support staff members who help make our student athletes and members of the athletic department family the best they can be.

Name of employee being nominated _____

Position _____

Name of person making the nomination _____

Position _____

Reason(s) for making the nomination _____
_____
_____
_____

The importance of the recognition will be directly related to the importance the athletic department puts on it. One way to place value on recognition is to present the award at an important event and follow it up with a press release. Consider some of these settings for making the presentations:

- Any home event that the support staff person is associated with
- Schoolwide assembly
- Preseason meeting of parents, coaches, and athletes
- Season-ending recognition night
- Board of education meeting
- A parent meeting, such as a PTA or boosters' meeting.

Figure 10.9 presents a sample press release that might be sent to local news media after the award presentation. The news release is important to let the community know that these individuals not only work in the school system but are also good role models for the youth.

## Reinforcing Intrinsic Motivation

You can help motivate someone extrinsically through praise, awards, and rewards for performances, but the long-term goal is to create an atmosphere in which support staff motivate themselves intrinsically. Recognizing outstanding support staff (which is an example of an extrinsic reward) is important for maintaining a positive atmosphere in the athletic department. To evoke their best effort and results, however, individuals must motivate themselves from within (intrinsic motivation).

Intrinsic motivation hinges on being self-satisfied. The support staff member who is intrinsically motivated enjoys working hard and going to work every day to help make things better for student athletes. Intrinsic motivators encourage us all to feel fulfilled, worthy, and happy when we are involved in a particular task or job. They tend to be long-term motivators and can be generated without the help of others.

For years I employed an official scorer for boys' basketball who loved what he did. He enjoyed being with coaches, athletes, and officials. He never played sport himself, but always liked to be where the action was. I would compliment him on the accuracy and neatness he showed in keeping the official score book for boys' basketball. I would praise him and say that he was the best scorekeeper in the area, hoping he would continue to stay on as our scorekeeper. One day he stopped me and said, "Tim, I appreciate the way you say nice things about how I keep the book, but that's not the reason I do it. I love being around the kids; they keep me young, and I enjoy doing a good job for them. They deserve the best." This man took pride in his work and that was a great intrinsic motivator for him.

As with our athletes and coaches, we want our support staff to enjoy the role they play because they do outstanding work and feel good about making

---

**Sample Press Release**

*For immediate release*

Last night the High School Athletic Department held its Fall Sports Recognition Assembly in the gymnasium. More than 400 athletes and 1,000 parents and community members were present to recognize team and individual accomplishments. Carl Hizer, a night-time custodian, was recognized by the athletic department for his outstanding contributions to helping young people become better citizens.

Carl received a plaque from the athletic director that stated, "Carl Hizer, a valued member of the Athletic Department, has helped make the school's athletes better citizens by his being a positive role model." Carl Hizer is one of many adults who care about the students at our high school.

**Figure 10.9** Sample press release.

the sport experience better for all participants. When we reinforce intrinsic motivators, such as doing a good job for the good of the kids, rather than only supplying the extrinsic rewards of money or praise, we are more likely to see support staff reach full potential.

# EVALUATING SUPPORT STAFF

One of the aims of your athletic department should be to encourage members of its team to put forth maximum effort and strive for improvement. Support staff who are achieving these aims will help assure the athletes an environment that will be conducive to develop. Here we focus on the evaluation of support staff and on giving and receiving feedback to improve performance. The goal is to create an environment that fosters support staff members feeling good about the evaluation process, taking ownership in it, and seeing it as nonthreatening. We explain their role and discuss procedures and timelines for giving and receiving feedback.

## Who Does What in Evaluation

The sport director is responsible for many support staff who perform duties in the athletic department. Usually that means having responsibility for evaluating the athletic department secretary, associates in the athletic department, and contest personnel. The sport director is not usually responsible for evaluating transportation, custodial, or maintenance personnel. These tasks are delegated to the supervisor of those departments. The sport director may help those supervisors by giving them feedback on the performance of individual staff members.

## Procedures and Timelines

Think in terms of how you would like to be evaluated. How would you like to be treated by the individual evaluating you? How do you know what criteria you will be evaluated on? What environment would best help you do your best? These are some of the questions you must answer as you begin to formulate your plan for evaluating support staff. Support staff will want to know the specific procedures for evaluation and have timelines for those procedures.

You should explain the evaluation process, the importance of self-evaluation, and the tools you'll use in the evaluation process. You also will need to discuss the timelines you will follow, set the date and time for the final evaluation, and determine when you would retain or release support staff. Let's look separately at these components.

1. *Preseason meeting.*   At the beginning of the school year or season, conduct a meeting of specific support staff that you are responsible for, as you do with your coaching staff. At this meeting you should hand out lists of expectations. Review the expectation sheets for support staff in figures 10.2–10.5 presented earlier. Spend time going over the expectations and encourage individuals to ask questions to clarify what you expect from them. This is an excellent time to explain department policies and philosophies and to explain how these people play important roles in supporting the program. Remember to reinforce the team approach. Explain that they will be evaluated on how well they perform in relation to the expectations. Your role is to *help people be the best they can be.* Your support staff needs to hear you say that and to see you back it up in the way you treat them. If the support staff trusts you, they will work hard to satisfy the expectations you have set for them.

2. *Self-evaluation.*   At the preseason meeting hand out a self-evaluation form (see form 10.2). This form should help individual staff members reflect on their roles in the athletic department. Tell them they will be filling out a copy of this form at the end of the season or school year before your final evaluation date. Be sure they understand that the feedback from this self-evaluation form is an important part of the total process. You care how they perceive themselves and encourage them to be self-motivated to be their best.

Ask them to take a step back when filling out the self-evaluation form. Keep in mind that support staff, like many other workers in our schools, may not be used to evaluating themselves as part of an overall evaluation process. Therefore, you must help them as they begin this process to be honest and objective.

3. *Other tools used in the process.*   You should also include a summative tool or checklist to help evaluate the many aspects of support staff responsibilities. Form 10.3 is an example of a summative tool or checklist that you can use.

## Form 10.2

# SELF-EVALUATION FORM FOR SUPPORT STAFF

Employee name _____ Date distributed _____

Please return to: _____ Please return by: _____

The athletic department requests that you take a few moments to provide feedback about your performance. To complete the form, circle the response that best describes your performance for each descriptor. If the answer is difficult to determine or cannot be determined at this time, circle the question mark. In the space below each descriptor labeled "Comments" write a brief description of the actions you took this season that led you to circle your response.

1.  I am on time in performing my duties.           Yes   No   ?
    Comments:

2.  I clearly communicate my questions and concerns with the sport director.   Yes   No   ?
    Comments:

3.  I demonstrate enthusiasm on the job.            Yes   No   ?
    Comments:

4.  I treat all students and adults as I would like to be treated.    Yes   No   ?
    Comments:

5.  I understand I am a role model to the students in my school.    Yes   No   ?
    Comments:

6.  I understand what is expected of me in my role in the athletic department.   Yes   No   ?
    Comments:

7.  I feel I am part of the athletic department team.    Yes   No   ?
    Comments:

8.  I am well organized.                            Yes   No   ?
    Comments:

9.  I maintain self-control.                        Yes   No   ?
    Comments:

10. I understand and believe in the policies of the athletic department.   Yes   No   ?
    Comments:

11. My greatest strength as a support staff member is _____.
    Comments:

12. My greatest weakness as a support staff member is _____.
    Comments:

Another useful tool available to have is a summary sheet, which combines the information you receive from the self-evaluation form, the summative or checklist tool, and general observations. Form 10.4 is an example you may use to summarize the performance of support staff.

4. *Timelines.* At the preseason meeting it is important to discuss timelines with the support staff members. They will want to know when they will be observed, when their self-evaluation form needs to be completed, and when the final evaluation will take place. Discussing these timelines will relieve

**Form 10.3**

# SUMMATIVE EVALUATION TOOL

Name of support staff _____ Position _____

Observer _____ Location and activity_____

Goals:  Duty proficiency
        Competence with students and adults

To complete the form, circle the response that best describes the support staff's performance for each descriptor. If the answer is difficult to determine or cannot be determined at this time, circle the question mark. In the space below each descriptor labeled "Observations" write a brief description of the specific performance that led you to circle your response.

1. Arrives on time.                                              Yes    No    ?
    Observations:

2. Attends required meetings.                          Yes    No    ?
    Observations:

3. Puts forth maximum effort.                          Yes    No    ?
    Observations:

4. Understands athletic department's philosophy.       Yes    No    ?
    Observations:

5. Understands expectations of duty assignment.       Yes    No    ?
    Observations:

6. Communicates problems to proper supervisor.       Yes    No    ?
    Observations:

7. Treats student athletes with respect.                  Yes    No    ?
    Observations:

8. Is concerned about the safety of the athletes and fans.     Yes    No    ?
    Observations:

9. Is a good role model for student athletes.           Yes    No    ?
    Observations:

10. Suggests ways to improve the duty or assignment.      Yes    No    ?
    Observations:

11. Displays enthusiasm while on duty.                  Yes    No    ?
    Observations:

12. Provides feedback to sport director when appropriate.     Yes    No    ?
    Observations:

13. Follows school district's policy.                     Yes    No    ?
    Observations:

14. Uses appropriate language while on duty.          Yes    No    ?
    Observations:

15. Interacts with student athletes and adults in a professional manner.   Yes    No    ?
    Observations:

*(continued)*

## ◢◤ Form 10.3 *(continued)*

# SUMMATIVE EVALUATION TOOL

16.  Interacts with colleagues in a professional manner.          Yes     No     ?
     Observations:

17.  Follows through with promises.                               Yes     No     ?
     Observations:

18.  Maintains poise in unexpected situations.                    Yes     No     ?
     Observations:

19.  Promotes good citizenship with student athletes.            Yes     No     ?
     Observations:

20.  Performs other duties (list).                                Yes     No     ?
     Observations:

## ◢◤ Form 10.4

# SUMMARY EVALUATION FOR SUPPORT STAFF

This form is designed to assist you in assembling the results from the other forms for each of your support staff. As you complete this form, you will review the results of the other forms and obtain a summary of your staff's strengths and weaknesses, which you can use in enhancing your program next year. Use this form at the final evaluation meeting with the support staff member.

Name of support staff _____

I.  Summative evaluation

    Enter the dates that observations were made.

    Observation dates: _____   _____   _____   _____   _____

    Concerns: _____

    _____

    _____

    Recommendations: _____

    _____

    _____

II. Self-evaluation

    Write the date on the line below to indicate when you received this form from the support staff person. Look over the results and make comments about how the self-evaluation compared to the results of the summative tool.

    Date collected: _____

    Comments: _____

    _____

    _____

| Timeline for Evaluation of Support Staff | |
| --- | --- |
| August | Preseason meeting with fall support staff.<br>Preseason meeting with annual support staff. |
| September–October | Observations for fall and annual support staff. |
| November | Final evaluation of fall support staff.<br>Preseason meeting with winter support staff. |
| December–February | Observations for winter and annual support staff. |
| March | Final evaluation of winter support staff.<br>Preseason meeting with spring support staff. |
| April–May | Observations of spring and annual support staff. |
| June | Final evaluation of spring and annual support staff. |

**Figure 10.10**   Sample timeline for evaluation of support staff.

some stress associated with the evaluation process. It helps deliver the message "no surprises," and many employees fear surprise. A timeline (see figure 10.10 for a sample) for evaluation of support staff should be completed and distributed before the school year begins.

5. *Setting the time and date for the final evaluation.* All dates and times should be mutually agreed to by the sport director and the support staff members. Seasonal support staff should set a final evaluation date soon after the sport season ends, and annual staff should complete evaluation procedures near the end of the school year. Do not delay the final evaluation meeting after the support staff's duties are completed. The feedback you give to the employee will have much greater impact and importance if it is received immediately.

6. *Retaining and releasing support staff.* Fortunately, many individuals enjoy working in the school environment. Many support staff have wonderful memories of their own school experiences and want to give something back by helping today's student athletes. Individuals who bring a smile to the job and are good role models for our young people are the kind of people we want to retain. If these individuals display weaknesses in the performance of their duties, it will show up in the evaluation process, and then action steps should be taken to help improve their performance. A good evaluation helps good employees become better. It is doubtful, however, if any evaluation system can improve all weaknesses.

Periodically, we encounter individuals who are not good for our program. Our evaluation tools may not help them improve, and we must consider releasing these individuals for the good of the students and the athletic program. The following types of individuals should not be retained. Your summative evaluation and final evaluation, along with any other written documentation, should confirm or verify that this particular person should be released:

- A poor role model; this might be an individual who uses vulgar language or exhibits behavior that sends the wrong message to young people.

- An individual who puts personal goals ahead of the goals of the athletic department; an example might be an announcer who uses the position to fulfill his need to gain attention and says things that detract from the athletes and the game.

- An individual who fraternizes with the students inappropriately; an example might be a support staff person who goes to student gatherings without the approval of parents.

- An individual who refuses to improve; although weaknesses are pointed out in the evaluation process along with suggestions on how to improve, the individual will not put forth the effort to improve.

When evaluating any individuals in the athletic program, you should keep in mind the goals and objectives of your program. If the staff member puts forth the effort to follow the department's guidelines, you should try to retain the individual. If the support staff person is the kind of individual you are concerned about having near student athletes, give serious consideration to releasing him or her for the good of the athletes. If you spend time evaluating your support staff, giving feedback to them and receiving it from them, they will know that you care how they perform their tasks. Take the time to evaluate support staff; it will pay big dividends to the athletes and coaches in your program.

*Summary*

In this chapter you learned about

1. the importance of officials and support staff and how to build lasting relationships and a feeling of teamwork with them;

2. the keys to effective communication with support staff and ways to resolve conflict; and

3. the importance of training support staff about philosophies, goals, policies, procedures, and expectations, and how to plan an effective evaluation procedure to help them improve.

# Appendix A
## Directory of National Sport Organizations and National Governing Bodies

## Sport-Specific Organizations

The following groups are active in providing information to develop their sports. The names of national governing bodies of Olympic sports are printed in bold letters.

### Archery
**National Archery Association**
One Olympic Plaza
Colorado Springs, CO 80909
719-578-4576

### Badminton
**USA Badminton**
One Olympic Plaza
Colorado Springs, CO 80909
719-578-4808

### Baseball
American Amateur Baseball
   Congress
118–119 Redfield Plaza
Marshall, MI 49068
616-781-2002

American Legion Baseball
P.O. Box 1055
Indianapolis, IN 46206
317-630-1213

Babe Ruth Baseball
P.O. Box 5000
1770 Brunswick Pike
Trenton, NJ 08638
609-695-1434

Dixie Boys Baseball
P.O. Box 193
Montgomery, AL 36101-0193
334-263-7529

The George Khoury Association of
   Baseball Leagues
5400 Meramec Bottom Rd.
St. Louis, MO 63128
314-849-8900

Little League Baseball
P.O. Box 3485
Williamsport, PA 17701
717-326-1921

National Amateur Baseball
   Federation
P.O. Box 705
Bowie, MD 20718
301-262-5005

National Baseball Congress
300 S. Sycamore
Wichita, KS 67213
316-267-3372

Pony Baseball
300 Clare Dr.
Washington, PA 15301
724-225-1060

**USA Baseball**
Hi Corbett Field
3400 East Camino Campestre
Tucson, AZ 85716
520-327-9700

## Basketball

**USA Basketball**
5465 Mark Dabling Blvd.
Colorado Springs, CO 80918-3842
719-590-4800

Youth Basketball of America
P.O. Box 3067
Orlando, FL 32802-3067
407-363-9262

## Diving

**United States Diving, Inc.**
Pan American Plaza
201 S. Capital Ave., Ste. 430
Indianapolis, IN 46225
317-237-5252

## Field Hockey

**U.S. Field Hockey Association, Inc.**
One Olympic Plaza
Colorado Springs, CO 80909
719-578-4567

## Football

Pop Warner Football
586 Middletown Blvd., Ste. C-100
Langhorne, PA 19047
215-752-2691

U.S. Flag and Touch Football League
7709 Ohio St.
Mentor, OH 44060
440-974-8735

## Golf

**American Junior Golf
    Association**
2415 Steeplechase Ln.
Roswell, GA 30076
770-998-4653

National Golf Foundation
1150 South U.S. Hwy. 1
Jupiter, FL 33477
561-744-6006

## Gymnastics

**USA Gymnastics**
Pan American Plaza
201 S. Capital Ave., Ste. 300
Indianapolis, IN 46225
317-237-5050

## Ice Hockey

**USA Hockey**
4965 N. 30th St.
Colorado Springs, CO 80919
719-576-8724

## Ice Skating

**U.S. Figure Skating Association**
20 First St.
Colorado Springs, CO 80906
719-635-5200

## Soccer

American Youth Soccer Organization
5403 W. 138th St.
Hawthorne, CA 90250-6496
310-643-6455

Soccer Association for Youth
4903 Vine St.
Cincinnati, OH 45217
513-242-4263

**United States Soccer Federation**
1801-1811 S. Prairie Ave.
Chicago, IL 60616
312-808-1300

U.S. Youth Soccer Association
899 Presidential Drive, Ste. 117
Richardson, TX 75081
972-235-4499

## Softball

**Amateur Softball Association**
2801 NE 50th St.
Oklahoma City, OK 73111-7203
405-424-5266

Bobby Sox Softball
P.O. Box 5880
Buena Park, CA 90622
714-522-1234

Cinderella Softball League, Inc.
P.O. Box 1411
Corning, NY 14830
607-937-5469

National Softball Association
P.O. Box 7
Nicholasville, KY 40340
606-887-4114

## Swimming

**United States Swimming, Inc.**
One Olympic Plaza
Colorado Springs, CO 80909
719-578-4578

## Tennis

**United States Tennis Association**
70 West Red Oak Ln.
White Plains, NY 10604
914-696-7000

## Track and Field

**USA Track and Field**
One RCA Dome, Ste. 140
Indianapolis, IN 46225
317-261-0500

## Volleyball

**USA Volleyball**
3595 E. Fountain Blvd., Ste. I-2
Colorado Springs, CO 80910-1740
719-637-8300

## Water Polo

U.S. Water Polo
1685 W. Uintah
Colorado Springs, CO 80904
719-634-0699

## Weightlifting

**U.S. Weightlifting Federation**
One Olympic Plaza
Colorado Springs, CO 80909-5764
719-578-4508

## Wrestling

**USA Wrestling**
6155 Lehman Dr.
Colorado Springs, CO 80918
719-598-8181

# Multisport Organizations

Amateur Athletic Union (AAU)
The Walt Disney World Resort
P.O. Box 10000
Lake Buena Vista, FL 32830-1000
407-363-6170

American Alliance for Health,
Physical Education, Recreation
and Dance (AAHPERD)
1900 Association Dr.
Reston, VA 22091
703-476-3400

Boys and Girls Clubs of America
1230 W. Peachtree St., NW
Atlanta, GA 30309
404-815-5700

Catholic Youth Organization (CYO)
1011 First Ave.
New York, NY 10022
212-371-1000

Jewish Community Centers
Association
15 East 26th St.
New York, NY 10010
212-532-4949

National Association of
Intercollegiate Athletics (NAIA)
6120 South Yale, Ste. 1450
Tulsa, OK 74136
918-494-8828

National Collegiate Athletic
Association (NCAA)
6201 College Blvd.
Overland Park, KS 66211-2422
913-339-1906

National Exploring Division, Boy
Scouts of America
1325 W. Walnut Hill Ln.
Irving, TX 75038
972-580-2433

National Federation of State High
School Associations
11724 N.W. Plaza Circle
Kansas City, MO 64195-0626
816-464-5400

National Junior College Athletic
Association (NJCAA)
1825 Austin Bluffs Pkwy., Ste. 100
Colorado Springs, CO 80918
719-590-9788

National Association of Police
Athletic Leagues
618 N. U.S. Hwy 1, Ste. 201
North Palm Beach, FL 33408
561-844-1823

National Recreation and Park
Association
22377 Belmont Ridge
Ashburn, VA 20148
703-858-0784

United States Armed Forces Sports
Hoffman Bldg. #1, Rm. 1456
2461 Eisenhower Ave.
Alexandria, VA 22331-0522
703-325-8871

United States Olympic Committee
One Olympic Plaza
Colorado Springs, CO 80909
719-632-5551

Women's Sport Foundation
Lannin House, Eisenhower Park
East Meadow, NY 11554
516-542-4700

YMCA of the USA
101 N. Wacker Dr.
Chicago, IL 60606
312-977-0031

YWCA of the USA
726 Broadway
New York, NY 10003
212-614-2700

# Sport Organizations for Special Populations

Disabled Sports USA
451 Hungerford Dr., Ste. 100
Rockville, MD 20850
301-217-0960

Special Olympics International, Inc.
1325 G St. N.W., Ste. 500
Washington, DC 20005-4709
202-824-0300

USA Deaf Sports Federation
3607 Washington Blvd., Ste. 4
Ogden, UT 84403
801-393-8710
TTY: 801-393-7916

United States Association of
Blind Athletes
33 North Institute
Colorado Springs, CO 80903
719-630-0422

United States Cerebral Palsy
Athletic Association
3810 West NW Highway, Ste. 205
Dallas, TX 75220
214-351-1510

Wheelchair Sports, USA
3595 E. Fountain Blvd., Ste. L-1
Colorado Springs, CO 80910
719-574-1150

# Appendix B
## Resources for Sport Directors

American Sport Education Program. *Event Management for SportDirectors*. Human Kinetics, 1996.

———. *SportParent Survival Guide*. Human Kinetics, 1994.

Clement, Annie. *Law in Sport and Physical Activity*. Benchmark Press, Inc., 1988.

Johnson, John R. *Promotion for SportDirectors*. Human Kinetics, 1996.

Kestner, James L. *Program Evaluation for SportDirectors*. Human Kinetics, 1996.

Koehler, Mike and Nancy Giebel. *Athletic Director's Survival Guide*. Prentice Hall, 1997.

Mamchak, P. Susan and Steven R. Mamchak. *Complete Communications Manual for Coaches and Athletic Directors*. Parker Publishing, 1989.

Martens, Rainer. *Successful Coaching*. Human Kinetics, 1997.

———. *Youth SportDirector Guide*. Human Kinetics, 1995.

Moore, Deborah. *Gender Equity in Interscholastic Athletics*. Ohio High School Athletic Association, 1997.

National Federation of State High School Associations. *Best of Interscholastic Athletic Administration*. Kansas City, MO: National Federation of State High School Associations and NIAAA, 1997.

National Interscholastic Athletic Administrators Association. *Comprehensive Guide to Athletic Administration*. NIAAA, P.O. Box 20626, Kansas City, MO 64195-0626, 1998.

———. *A Guide for College-Bound Student Athletes and Their Parents*. NIAAA, updated annually.

———. *Athletic Administration*. Leadership Training Course 502. NIAAA, 1998.

———. *Citizenship*. Leadership Training Course 503. NIAAA, 1998.

———. *Legal Strategies and Issues*. Leadership Training Course 504. NIAAA, 1998.

———. *Mentoring*. Leadership Training Course 505. NIAAA, 1998.

Office for Civil Rights. *Clarification of Intercollegiate Athletics Policy Guidance: The Three-Part Test*. On the Title IX Education Amendment of 1972. Washington, DC: U.S. Department of Education (400 Maryland Ave., S.W., Washington, DC 20202-1100), 1995.

Olson, John R. *Facility and Equipment Management for SportDirectors*. Human Kinetics, 1997.

Shea, Gordon F. *Mentoring: A Practical Guide*. Crisp Publishing, 1994.

———. *Mentoring: Helping Employees Reach Their Full Potential*. American Management Association Membership Publications, 1994.

# *Appendix C*
# *Coach's Guidelines*

## Mission Statement

The coach represents the most critical factor in a program. He/she is the motivating force in (1) an athlete's development, (2) the success of a program, and (3) the overall sportsmanship displayed by the athletes. Parents entrust their student to the coach expecting him/her to improve the whole person, not just the athletic skills. We expect coaches to take ownership of their programs and show the athletes (1) that hard work and patience pay off, (2) that all things are possible when the dream is shared by enough people, and (3) that in winning or losing you must maintain your poise and class.

## Goals and Objectives

1. Improve the skill level of players.
2. Improve the physical fitness of players.
3. Help each player develop an appreciation for the sport.
4. Demand the players learn and abide by the rules of the game.
5. Insist players practice good sportsmanship.
6. Encourage the development of patience, cooperation, and teamwork.
7. Develop mental toughness for competition in the players.
8. Encourage players to enjoy playing the sport.

## Coach's Responsibilities Before Coaching Begins

1. Interview with head coach.
2. Interview with principal/athletic director.
3. Submit to a criminal check by police department (fingerprinting).
4. Sign contract at Board Office.
5. Sign tax forms at Board Office.
6. Become certified in CPR and sports medicine.
7. Take ASEP–Coaching Educational Workshop when offered.

## Preseason

1. Meet with prospective team members (high school and middle school).
2. Attend rules interpretation meeting.
3. Hand out and collect physical cards, emergency medical cards, rules and regulations.
4. Schedule preseason physical conditioning.
5. Check with weight room supervisor on use of weight room.
6. Conduct parents' preseason meeting.
7. Inventory equipment.
8. Hand out equipment-use form for recording.

9. Complete bus transportation for away contests two weeks before first contest.

10. Submit eligibility information to athletic office.

11. Submit roster to athletic office as soon as team is chosen.

12. Schedule any scrimmages.

13. Inform athletic office of your event support people (scorers, managers, timers).

14. Pick up medical supplies from trainer.

## During Season

1. Check on transportation.

2. Check on officials.

3. Coordinate practice schedule.

4. Check on players' eligibility.

5. Update athletic office of all deletions and additions immediately.

6. Retrieve uniforms of athletes who quit or leave the team.

7. Keep medical kit supplied.

8. Maintain emergency authorization cards in medical kit.

9. Call parents of injured or ill athletes—keep head trainer informed.

10. Communicate frequently with athletic office.

11. Personal service contracts available in athletic office.

12. No "surprises."

13. Work with boosters.

## Postseason

1. Submit awards and year-end report to athletic office.

2. Collect, inventory, and store equipment. Coaches will not be paid until all uniforms and equipment are collected.

3. Return stopwatches, VHS equipment, and other items to the athletic office.

4. Charge players for lost equipment.

5. Meet with and evaluate all players; discuss next year with returning players.

6. Give suggestions for schedule to athletic director.

7. Give suggestions for repair and maintenance to athletic director.

8. Plan to attend at least one clinic or workshop.

9. Talk to prospective athletes at middle school.

## Expectations

1. Keep priorities in focus.

2. Remind athletes of importance of grades.

3. Always do what is in the best interest of the athlete.

4. Be positive with your players.

5. Treat them with respect.

6. Demonstrate enthusiasm—be animated.

7. No bantering or verbal abuse; no derogatory remarks or names.

8. When criticizing, focus on the act and not the actor.

9. Insist on integrity from all players.

10. Always supervise your athletes.

11. Document any unusual event: injury, vandalism, angry parent, suspension, etc.

12. Keep bus, practice area, and locker room clean.

13. Be knowledgeable about due process.

14. Don't give up on any athlete.

15. Dress appropriately.

16. Meet with athletic director to be evaluated.

17. All school awards must be presented at Recognition Night. Outside banquets or parties conducted to present awards are not permitted unless the varsity team has won a championship. Prior approval must be obtained from the athletic director.

## Parent-Coach Meeting

It is *mandatory* to meet with the parents of your squad after any cuts have been made but before the scheduled contests begin. The coach will include the following items in his/her agenda:

1. Coach's philosophy.

2. Team rules, training rules.

3. Expectations for players—commitment.

4. Health, safety, and welfare of athletes.

5. Risks inherent in the sport.

6. Injuries and emergencies—how we handle them.

7. Importance of following coach's directives.

8. Season goals and objectives.

9. Training and practice sessions.

10. Attending all practices; promptness.

11. Player selection ("cuts").

12. Playing time consideration.

13. Season scrimmages and contests.

14. Contingency plan for bad weather.

15. Any team social functions.

16. Fund-raisers, boosters.

17. Requirements for earning a letter.

18. Availability of school insurance.

19. OHSAA catastrophic insurance.

20. NCAA regulations on scholarships.

21. Monitoring grades of athletes.

22. Game protocol, sportsmanship.

## THE REWARD OF A THING WELL DONE
## IS TO HAVE DONE IT

# *I*ndex

**Bold** entries indicate forms.

**A**

Academic process, monitoring of, 85
Academics, balancing athletics with, 85
Advice, mentoring, avoidance of giving, 44
Affinity diagrams, group decision making and, 53
Agendas
  guidelines for setting, 52–53
  **for preseason meetings, sample agenda,** 121
American Sport Education Program (ASEP), philosophy of, 14, 20
Americans with Disabilities Act (ADA)
  job description guidelines, 34
  legal issues, 35
Amiable communication style, 50
Analytic communication style, 52
Applications
  **sample form for,** 62
  screening procedures for, 61–66
Arguments, resolution of, tips for, 53
Assistant athletic director, sport directors' teamwork with, 10
Assistant coaches
  coaches evaluation of, 110–111
  **sample evaluation form for,** 70
Athletes, needs assessment for, 29
**Athletic department, parent feedback to,** 129–130
*Athletic Department Personnel Policy Manual*
  coaches and student trainers, guidelines for, 30
  principles and objectives in, 21
  staff and parent behavior guidelines in, 23
Athletic program
  goals and objectives of, 82–83
  parents' responsibilities to, 116–117
  policies for, 21–22
  sport directors' teamwork with, 10
Availability, mentoring and, 43
Awards programs, 89–90

**B**

Background checks, staff selection and, 66

Barriers, mentoring, avoidance of, 45
*Board of Education Policy Manual,* personnel management philosophy in, 14–15
Booster clubs, 117–118
Brainstorming, conflict resolution with, 55

## C

Cardiopulmonary resuscitation (CPR), as requirement for coaches, 101
**Chain of command, for support staff, 141–142,** 143
Clerical staff, needs assessment for, 29
Coaches
  advertising for, 101–102
  **code of ethics, sample of,** 98
  communication guidelines for, 51
  conflict resolution with, 54
  education of, legal issues, 35
  education requirements for, 102–103
  employment records of, 113
  evaluation of, 107, 109–113
  evaluation of assistant and lower-level coaches, 110–111
  feedback by, 106–107
  **head coach record, sample form,** 105
  motivation of, 103–105
  needs assessment of, 27
  organizational structure and, 36–37
  orientation for, 93, 95
  **parent feedback to,** 130–131
  parents as assistants for, 123–124
  personnel procedures for hiring of, 4
  policy development and, 93
  professional organizations for, 102–103
  quality assessment of, 88
  recruiting of, 100–101
  responsibilities of, 95–97
  responsibilities of sport director to, 92–95
  retention or release of, 111–113
  safety checklist for, 94–95
  **sample evaluation form for,** 68–72
  sport director, responsibilities to, 97–99
  sports officials and, 136, 138
  student feedback on, 108–109, 111
  walk-on coaches, 101
Code of Conduct, guidelines for preparing, 85–88
Code of ethics, for coaches, 98
Collaborative negotiations, group decision making and, 53–54
Collegiate athletics, preparation for, 85
Communication
  components of, 50
  conflict resolution and, 54–56
  credibility and, 52
  fairness issues, 56–58
  guidelines for, 49–52
  informal *vs.* formal meetings, 56
  lines and opportunities for, 50

parent and coach guidelines on, 51
  with parents, 126–127
  problem-solving through, 52–54
  sending and receiving skills, 52
  styles of, 50, 52
  with support staff, 142–143
Community service opportunities, mentoring through, 88
Conferences, education through, 46
Conflict resolution
  guidelines for, 54–56
  with parents, 124–128
  **sample worksheet for,** 127
  sports officials and, 138
  **support staff and, 141–144,** 144
  written policy for, 125
Confrontation, mentoring and, 43
Consensus, on program principles, 20
Coordination, by sport directors, 6
Credentials, evaluation of, 61
Credibility, communication and, 52
Criticism, mentoring, avoidance of, 44

## D

Decision making
  characteristics of good decisions, 55–56
  by teams or groups, tips for, 53–54
Delegation of duties, by sport directors, 6
Department meetings, education through, 46
Disciplinary process
  parents' role in, 128
  personnel management and, 57–58
Discouragement, mentoring, avoidance of, 45
District personnel director, sport directors' teamwork with, 9
Diversity, on interview committees, 61
**Drug information pamphlet, sample pamphlet,** 119
Due process
  personnel management and, 57–58
  sport directors' familiarity with, 35
Duties, in job descriptions, 34

## E

Education
  conferences and workshops as, 46
  department meetings, 46
  individual meetings and, 46
  in-service training, 45
  *vs.* mentoring, 46–47
  orientation meetings, 46
  of personnel, 45–46
  requirements for coaches, 101–103
Educators, sport directors as, 8
Eligibility guidelines, coaches, 22
Emergency medical services, coaches' responsibility for, 99

Employment records, of coaches, 113
Environment
    coaches' responsibility for, 99
    coaching quality and, 88
    safety in, 88–89
Equipment manager, needs assessment for, 29
Equity issues, job description guidelines, 34
Evaluations
    of coaches, 107, 109–113
    coaching improvement through, 98
    components of, 67
    of credentials, 61
    **end-of-season evaluation form,** 89
    of injured athletes, 99
    mentoring and, 45
    personal and professional references, 63–64
    of personnel, 66–75
    planning for, 37–38
    preparatory questions, 37–38
    **sample forms,** 68–73
    of sports officials, 138–139
    **summary evaluation for support staff,** 150
    **summative evaluation tool,** 149–150
    of support staff, 147–152
    timelines for, 38
    tools for, 67–73
Evaluators, sport directors as, 7
Expectations
    of coaches, 111
    of parents, by sports directors, 118–119
    of student participants, 81, 84
    **of support staff, sample sheets for,** 140–141
Expressive communication style, 50
External motivators for coaches, 104–105

**F**

Facilities and grounds director, sport directors' team-
    work with, 9–10
Facility constraints, needs assessment of coaches
    and, 27
Fairness, in personnel management, 56–58
Feedback
    by coaches to administrators, 106–107
    communication of, in personnel evaluations, 67
    communication of, to coaches, 111–113
    from parents, 129–131
    of parents on coaches, 111
    by students on coaches, 108, 111
Fingerprinting, staff selection and, 66
First aid, coaches' responsibility for, 99
Formal meetings, guidelines for, 56
Formative tools, personnel evaluation, 67, 73
Fourteenth Amendment, fairness in personnel man-
    agement and, 56–57

**G**

Game managers, needs assessment of, 27

Goals
    **of Athletic Department (sample),** 82–83
    defining of, 18–20
    **identification form, sample of,** 73
    of sport directors, 81–84
    writing of, in personnel evaluations, 67, 73
Groups, decision making methods of, 53–54
*Guide for College-Bound Students,* 85

**H**

Head coaches, sport directors' teamwork with, 10–
    11
Human resources director, sport directors' teamwork
    with, 9

**I**

Impasses, resolution of, tips for, 53
Individual meetings, education through, 46
Individuals, conflict resolution with, 54–55
Informal meetings, guidelines for, 56
Information
    coaches' reporting of, 97–98
    communication of, to parents, 122, 128
    mentoring and, 43
In-service training, of personnel, 45
Interactive diagraphs, group decision making and,
    53
Interactive matrices, group decision making and, 53
Internal motivation, for coaches, 104
Interview committee, formation of, 61, 63
Interviews
    of candidates, 61
    preparation for, 61–66

**J**

Job descriptions
    Americans with Disabilities Act (ADA) guide-
        lines, 34
    annual review of, 31
    **for coaches, sample of,** 110
    development of, 30–34
    duties and responsibilities in, 34
    job title in, 31
    position description, 33
    qualifications, 33
    **sample forms,** 32–33
    supervisors, 33–34
    Title IX and equity provisions, 34
Job requirements, staff selection process and, 64, 66
Job title, in job descriptions, 31

**L**

Leadership skills
    communication, 49–52
    meetings, duties in, 52
    problem solving and, 52–54
    of sport directors, 6

League standards, needs assessment of coaches and, 27

Legal issues
  for coaches, 99
  personnel management planning and, 34–35

Levels of teams, needs assessment of coaches and, 27

Lifelong learning, importance of, for coaches, 102

Listening skills
  conflict resolution and, 55
  mentoring and, 43
  sport directors to coaches, 92–95

Local resources, for personnel management, 35

Long-term objectives, procedures for setting, 19–20

**M**

Maintenance personnel, needs assessment for, 29

Management skills, of sport directors, 6

Mandatory mentoring, avoidance of, 45

Meetings
  with coaches, for evaluation process, 109–110
  formal *vs.* informal meetings, 56
  leadership duties for, 52
  preseason meetings with parents, 119–122
  preseason meeting with support staff, 147
  with support staff, 144–145
  tips for conducting, 52–53

Mentoring
  behavior and skills needed for, 42–43
  behavior to avoid in, 43–45
  characteristics of, 41–45
  by coaches, of student participants, 100
  of coaches, 91–113
  community service opportunities through, 88
  evaluating and, 45
  historical background of, 42
  by sport directors, 6–7
  as voluntary contribution, 42
  *vs.* educating, 46–47

Mission, defining of, procedures for, 14–18

Motivation
  of coaches, 103–105
  of student participants, 84–85
  of support staff, 146–147

**N**

National Interscholastic Athletic Administrators Association, 35

NCAA Clearinghouse, 85

Needs assessment
  personnel management planning and, 26–30
  of student participants, 88–90

Negligence issues, sport directors' familiarity with, 35

News media, coaches and, 100

**O**

Objectives
  achieving consensus on, 20
  **of Athletic Department (sample),** 82–83
  defining of, 18–20
  prioritization of, 19
  short-term *vs.* long-term objectives, 19–20
  of sport directors, 81–84

Organization
  key members of, 36–37
  needs assessment of, 26
  personnel policy development in, 22–23
  by sport directors, 6

Orientation meetings
  education through, 46
  for new coaches, 93, 95

**P**

Parents
  booster clubs and, 117–118
  coaches' responsibilities for, 99–100
  communication guidelines for, 51
  conflict resolution with, 54, 124–128
  contributions to team and school by, 117
  disciplinary process and, 128
  feedback on coaches from, 111
  **feedback to athletic department,** 129–130
  **feedback to coaches,** 130–131
  involvement of, 115–132
  policy guidelines for, 23
  **preseason letter to, sample of,** 120
  productive involvement by, 118–124
  recognition of, 128–130
  responsibilities to athletic program, 116–117
  as spectators, 124
  sports director's guidelines for, 117
  sports director's responsibilities to, 115–116
  suspension or retention of participants and, 87
  as volunteers, 122–124

Personal philosophy
  development of, 15–16
  **form for,** 18

**Personnel attributes form,** 16

Personnel management planning
  development of, 25–38
  evaluation planning, 37–38
  needs assessment and, 26–30
  organizational structure and, 36–37
  personnel management plan development, 25–38
  recordkeeping and, 35–36
  by sport directors, 6

Personnel manager
  qualities of, 4
  role of, 3
  tasks of, 3
  teammates for, 8

Personnel needs
  assessment of, 26–30
  **form for determination of,** 28
  resource utilization for meeting, 30–32
Personnel records, management of, 35–36
Philosophy
  defining of, procedures for, 14–18
  **sample cheerleader philosophy,** 83–84
Policy development
  assisting coaches in, 93
  coaches' eligibility in, 23
  contest officials, 23
  principles and, 20–23
  responsibilities to students and, 80–81
  staff and parent behavior guidelines, 23
  written policy for conflict resolution, 125
Policy manuals
  philosophy stated in, 14–15
  principles behind, 20–23
Position description, in job descriptions, 33
Practice schedules, coaches' responsibilities for, 99
**Press release sample,** 146
Principles
  policy development and, 20–23
  **sample form for statement of,** 21
Priorities, prioritization of objectives, 19
Problem solving
  by coaches, 98
  leadership duties for meetings, 52
Procedural due process, personnel management and, 57
Professional organizations
  for coaches, 102–103
  for personnel management, 35
Promotion activities
  of coaches, 100
  mentoring and avoidance of, 44–45
Promotion of personnel, sports officials, 138–139
Protection, mentoring, avoidance of, 44–45

**Q**

Qualifications, in job descriptions, 33

**R**

Recognition
  **sample nomination form for support staff,** 145
  of support staff, 144–147
Recognition system for coaches, 105–107
Recordkeeping
  coaches' employment records, 113
  personnel management planning and, 35–36
  on student participants, 87–88
Recruiting
  coaches' responsibility for, 100–101
  guidelines for, 81, 84
  of sports officials, 135–136

References
  by coaches, 98–99
  evaluation of, 63–64
**Rejection letters, sample of,** 64
Rescuing, mentoring, avoidance of, 44
Reserved communication style, 50
Resources, utilization of, personnel needs and, 30–31
*Respondeat superior* principle, 99
Responsibilities, in job descriptions, 34
Resume, review checklist for, 63
Retention or release of personnel
  coaches, 111–113
  sports officials, 138–139
  staff selection, 67, 74–75
  supervisors, 138–139
  support staff, 151–152
Risk management
  coaches' responsibility for, 99
  sport directors' familiarity with, 34
Role models, coaches as, 100

**S**

Safety issues
  coaches safety checklist, 94–95
  needs assessment of coaches and, 27
  safe environment, tips for creating, 88–89
Scheduling
  coaches' responsibilities for, 99
  needs assessment of coaches and, 27
  personnel needs assessment and, 29–30
  by sport directors, 6
School, coaches' responsibility to, 100
School district
  personnel line and staff chart for, 4–5
  personnel management philosophy of, 14–17
School principals, sport directors' teamwork with, 8–9
Screening personnel applications, guidelines for, 61–66
Secretaries, sport directors' teamwork with, 10
Self-evaluation
  by coaches, 110
  **by support staff, 147,** 148
Self-selection, job prerequisites and, 66
Short-term objectives, procedures for setting, 19–20
Socratic method, mentoring and, 43
Sports director
  coaches' responsibilities to, 97–99
  conflict resolution between parents and coaches, 125–126
  as educator, 8
  as evaluator, 7
  leadership role of, 6
  managerial role of, 6

mentorship role of, 6–7
parents, responsibilities to, 115–116
personnel evaluation by, 66–67
personnel management by, 5–8
responsibilities to coaches, 92–95
in school district, role of, 4–5
sports officials, responsibilities of, 134–135
students, responsibilities to, 80–81
as supervisor, 7–8
support staff and, 139
teammates in personnel management with, 8–11
Sports officials
    conflict resolution with, 138
    evaluation of, 138–139
    in job descriptions, 33–34
    needs assessment of, 27–29
    policy guidelines for, 23
    recruitment of, 135–136
    responsibilities of, 134–135
    retention, release, or promotion of, 138–139
    **sample contract for,** 137
    sport directors and, 136, 138
Sports participants, suspension or retention of, 85–88
Staff behavior, policy development for, 23
Staff selection
    final recommendations and, 66
    guidelines for, 59–75
    retention and release of staff, 67, 74–75
    **sample personnel letters,** 65
    screening applications and interview preparation, 61, 63–66
    vacancies, announcement of, 60
**Student activity code, sample form,** 86–87
Student participants
    active participation, guidelines for achieving, 81, 84
    coaches' responsibilities for, 99
    evaluation of coaches by, 108–109
    needs assessment of, 88–90
    number of, needs assessment based on, 27
    perspective on parent conflicts from, 128
    responsibilities of, 81
    sport directors' responsibilities to, 80–81
Student records, management of, 36
Substantive due process, personnel management and, 57
Summative tools, personnel evaluation, 67–72
Supervision, by sport directors, 6
Supervisors
    conflict resolution with, 138
    evaluation of, 138–139
    in job descriptions, 33–34
    needs assessment of, 27

organizational structure and, 36
recruitment of, 135–136
responsibilities of, 134–135
retention, release, or promotion of, 138–139
sport directors and, 136, 138
sport directors as, 7–8
Support staff
    coaches' responsibilities for, 100
    conflict resolution with, 141–145
    evaluation of, 147–153
    motivation of, 146–147
    needs assessment for, 29
    needs assessment of, 144–145
    organizational structure and, 37
    recognition of, 145–146
    retention and release of, 151
    **sample expectation sheet,** 140
    sport directors and, 139
    training of, 139–140
Suspension with pay, guidelines for considering, 74

**T**

Teams in personnel management
    decision making methods of, 53–54
    sport director, teammates with, 8–11
Timelines
    availability of sports officials and, 136
    for evaluations, 38, 67
    **for support staff evaluation, 147–148,** 151
Title IX of the Education Amendment of 1972
    job description guidelines, 34
    legal issues surrounding, 35
    needs assessment of coaches and, 27
    provisions of, 56–57
Trainers, needs assessment for, 29–30
Training
    legal issues with, 35
    of support staff, 139–140
Transportation director, sport directors' teamwork with, 9–10

**V**

Vacancies, announcement of, 60
Values, mission and philosophy and, 14
Violence, conflict resolution and avoidance of, 54
Volunteering
    mentoring as, 42
    by parents, 122–123
    **sample letter to parents on,** 122
    **sample sign-up sheets,** 123

**W**

Walk-on coaches, 101
Workshops, education through, 46

# $A$bout the Authors

**Tim Flannery**　　　　　　　　**Mike Swank**

A former president of the National Interscholastic Athletic Administrators Association (NIAAA), **Tim Flannery** has spoken at local, state, and national conferences on topics such as leadership training, mentoring, recognition programs for student athletes, communicating with parents, and evaluating coaches. He developed the NIAAA's Mentoring Course as a part of their Leadership Training Program for athletic administrators, and he has conducted and assisted Leader Level workshops for the American Sport Education Program (ASEP) for over 200 coaches since 1989.

Flannery's hands-on experience comes from 15 years administering the athletics program of a large suburban school district. During this time he served as tournament manager for Division I and II soccer and basketball tournaments; coached boys basketball and football; and planned, promoted, and conducted a drug awareness seminar. His numerous awards include the Distinguished Service Award for Northeast Ohio (1998), a National Federation Citation (1996), and recognition as the National Council of Secondary School Administrators' (NCSSA) National Athletic Director of the Year (1996).

As assistant principal of Bay High School in Bay Village, Ohio, **Mike Swank** has 11 years' experience as an activities/athletic director. He has developed programs and spoken at the local, state, and national level on the topics of sportsmanship, staff development, communication, and coaching education. He also served on the committee that developed the Mentoring Course for NIAAA's Leadership Training Program.

Swank was formerly a member of the NIAAA publication committee and an editor for the Ohio Interscholastic Athletic Administrators Association's newsletter. In addition, he has been published at the local, state, and national level on topics covering sportsmanship, technology, media relations, staff development, and student leadership training.

# OTHER RESOURCES IN THE SPORTDIRECTOR SERIES

1996 • Spiral • 144 pp • Item ACEP0320
ISBN 0-87322-968-1 • $20.00

*Event Management for SportDirectors* is a handy tool for planning and managing practically any type or size of athletic event. It provides a comprehensive checklist of 18 categories (along with tasks to be completed for each category), allowing you to conduct even the most complicated functions in a systematic and organized manner.

Whether you're planning a major tournament, managing a fund-raiser, or hosting a small intramural competition, *Event Management for SportDirectors* will guide you each step of the way. This time-saving resource shows you how to plan and manage all of the critical aspects of an event.

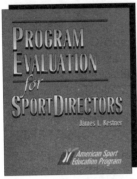

1996 • Paperback • 128 pp • Item PKES0505
ISBN 0-88011-505-X • $20.00

*Program Evaluation for SportDirectors* is a practical, hands-on resource that you can use to evaluate your personnel, facilities and equipment, and program offerings. It contains an easy-to-follow blueprint for conducting evaluations and 20 field-tested forms that can be used or modified to fit your specific evaluation needs.

First, the book explains how to reflect on personal and organizational philosophies, identify who will help in the evaluation process, assess which programs and individuals need to be evaluated, develop an evaluation plan, implement the plan, and review and revise the plan. The heart of the book shows you how to conduct effective personnel evaluations and how to evaluate facilities, equipment, and athletic programs.

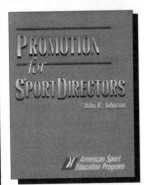

1996 • Paperback • 152 pp • Item PJOH0722
ISBN 0-87322-722-0 • $20.00

*Promotion for SportDirectors* is a cookbook of effective promotional ideas that will get your school lots of attention for very little money. The book gets you started by showing you how to plan for an effective promotional program. You'll discover how your school's philosophy about promotion meshes with your own, how to assess your promotional needs and limitations, and how to develop a comprehensive promotional plan.

This easy-to-use reference also explains each facet of a total promotion plan. You'll learn how to implement a positive public relations program, develop and distribute printed promotions such as programs and schedules, take advantage of radio and television promotion, boost attendance using special promotions, and obtain program sponsorships.

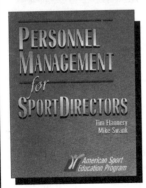

1999 • Paperback • 176 pp • Item PFLA0757
ISBN 0-88011-757-5 • $22.00

*Personnel Management for Sport Directors* is written for sport directors nationwide who deal in any aspect of hiring, maintaining, and managing staff and other personnel issues.
This resource offers general overviews and specific day-by-day instructions for handling the many responsibilities, large and small, of the personnel manager.

The book begins with global recommendations and ends with ways to directly apply these suggestions to suit the needs of personnel directors in a variety of settings and situations.

**HUMAN KINETICS**
*The Premier Publisher for Sports & Fitness*
www.humankinetics.com

Prices are subject to change.